# Lotus Notes at

*LOTUS BOOKS* Business Solutions Series

## Who Should Read This Book:

For managers and professionals who want to implement a strategic Notes system, this book shows how to make Notes a unique forum for information exchange and team collaboration. For users of Notes, this book takes you in and around the product, so that you can get the most out of Notes—quickly.

## What's Inside

- an overview of Notes that explores its potential and clearly explains how and why it works

- key tips for using Notes effectively—a look at Notes from the driver's seat

- guidelines for developing customized Notes databases that promote group productivity and the fluid exchange of information

- checklists to ensure the successful deployment of Notes in your organization. Topics include: how to pave the way, working with the corporate culture, plus security, administration, and training issues

## About *LOTUS BOOKS*

*LOTUS BOOKS*, written in collaboration with Lotus Development Corporation, help you derive the most from Lotus software. There are four series within Lotus Books:

**Start Here** books introduce beginning users to Lotus software with simple step-by-step instructions.

**Pathways to Mastery** titles provide the authoritative perspective and expertise from Lotus. Each book is a fast-paced, clear, and concise guide that helps you build on what you know and teaches new product features quickly.

**Business Solutions** books concentrate on using software to meet your specific business and professional needs; they provide essential tools for working faster and smarter.

**Technical Reference** provide advanced information for experts, programmers, and application developers.

# Lotus Notes at Work

## Sally Blanning DeJean
## David DeJean

**BRADY**

## *LOTUS BOOKS*

New York   London   Toronto   Sydney   Tokyo   Singapore

*LOTUS BOOKS*

Published by Brady
A division of Simon & Schuster, Inc.
in association with Lotus Publishing

Manufactured in the United States of America

10  9  8  7  6  5  4  3  2  1

ISBN: 0-13-540394-4

# Dedication

To all the English teachers who were sure one day we would write a book. And to all the science teachers who never suspected it would be on a technical subject.

SBD and DD

# Acknowledgments

Writing a book about Lotus Notes has been an adventure on the frontier of PC technology and practice. We are very grateful to the companies who helped equip us for the expedition and the experts who guided us on the way.

Several companies graciously lent hardware and software to the project: Arche Technologies, whose Rival 386-25 ran Notes night and day for much longer than we intended; Intel Personal Computer Enhancement Operation, maker of the estimable AboveBoard; Canon USA, whose laser printers poured out chapter after revised chapter; Halcyon Software, whose DoDot proved the best thing for screen captures, and Zenographics' SuperPrint, the best thing for showing us what we'd captured.

Among our guides we are particularly grateful to Susanna Opper, whose enthusiasm and support took many forms, and to Irene Grief at Lotus Development Corp. Looming behind everything else is the work of Douglas Engelbart, whose generosity with his time and ideas in interviews kindled our interest in workgroup computing.

Our thanks to the many people in organizations using Notes who shared their time and their knowledge in interviews. Many of those names appear in the text, but many more, for a variety of reasons, do not. Our appreciation, also, to the people who have thought deeply about Notes and workgroup computing, and shared their insights with us.

This book began as a review of Notes in *PC/Computing* magazine which benefited from the contributions of staff members Todd Bannar, Paul Bonner, Carol Ellison, Don Steinberg, and Peggy Wallace, and the guidance of editor-in-chief Michael Edelhart.

The manuscript owes much of its present shape to our editor at Brady Publishing, Susan Hunt, and its readability to the sharp pencil of Deborah Asbrand.

Most of all, this book is a tribute to the people who made Notes: To Ray Ozzie and his staff at Iris Associates, especially Tim Halvorsen, who was endlessly patient with questions; to the Notes Group at Lotus, who freely shared their knowledge and plans for Notes, their beta software and even their desks—notably Brownell Chalstrom, Bruce Hitchcock, Linda Hutchinson, Francois Koutchouk, Peter Orbeton, and Bill Lott. Larry Moore, Vice-President of Lotus' Communication Products Group, buoyed our enthusiasm for the project with his excitement over his product, and with Susan Jensen he opened many doors at Lotus and at Notes customer sites. Cheryl Pierson was always helpful. Special thanks to Eric Sall, who was supportive above and beyond the call of duty.

*Sally Blanning DeJean and David DeJean*
*Newton, Massachusetts*

# Contents

# Section 3:  CREATING AN APPLICATION  /  103

## Chapter 5   The Development Environment  /  105

## Chapter 6   Building An Application  /  139

## Chapter 9   Expanding Notes with Additional Programs  /  217

# Section 5:   NOTES AND THE ORGANIZATION  /  235

## Chapter 10   Deploying Notes in the Organization  /  237

# Introduction

In the 1970s, I attended the University of Illinois as a student of computer science. The curriculum included numerical analysis, data structures and algorithms, graphics, operating systems, assembly language programming, and so on. At the Digital Computer Laboratory, aspiring young programmers like myself spent hours laboring over a keypunch, preparing our card decks for submission to the department's IBM 360.

The programs that we worked on, mostly class assignments, were decidedly data processing in nature. After all, we were being trained to be the corporate programmers of the world. We would design and write programs for the storage and processing of corporate data, for transaction processing, for trend analysis and scientific data visualization, for statistical analysis and reporting.

Across the street from the 360, at the Computer-Based Education Research Laboratory, something else was going on. Something completely different. Dozens of people in darkened rooms were staring, glassy-eyed, into the orange glow of graphics terminals. The computer system that they were using was known as PLATO—Programmed Logic for Automated Teaching Operations. Few of these people were programmers. Most of them were students learning chemistry, physics, languages, and business.

But late at night, few of them were learning anything. They were banging away at their keyboards at a furious pace, playing Airfight, Empire, or Dogfight with other people at terminals halfway around the world. A number of them were chatting in Talk-o-Matic, a real-time conferencing program. Most were conversing with their friends and colleagues using either the Personal Notes or Group Notes communication functions of Plato, forerunners of what we now think of as electronic mail and bulletin boards.

For me, there was no contest. I wanted to graduate, so I kept punching cards. But my heart was across the street. PLATO wasn't used for data processing or analysis. It was used for education, entertainment, communications. It was exciting! Through the system, I developed friendships with people across the country I had never met face-to-face. The environment was so compelling that many of my friends dropped out of school because they were addicted to the "infotainment" that PLATO offered. They would take any job that granted them continued access to the system.

Cut to several years later: 1981. For the previous three years I'd worked at Data General in their Commercial Systems division, developing a new operating system to run COBOL applications. Now I was working at Software Arts, developer of VisiCalc. Things were really hopping. We were at the center of the burgeoning PC industry. I began to get that feeling again. I saw people using these little computers who had never used computers before. They were acting compulsive about them, using them for new and different things that couldn't be done on the minicomputers and mainframes of the time.

But these personal computers were completely isolated; they had no connection to each other. There was no way for people to use them to talk to one another, no way to communicate. Even the mundane minicomputers that I had been using offered electronic mail facilities — why couldn't PCs? I decided that something had to be done!

Two friends of mine from the PLATO days, Tim Halvorsen and Len Kawell, had made similar observations about PCs while working at Digital Equipment Corporation on the development of the VAX/VMS operating system. With the tremendous vision and support of Mitchell Kapor at Lotus as brainstormer, financier, and facilitator, the three of us set out on our mission: to recreate the information/communication environment that was so successful on PLATO, but to do it using PCs in a business setting.

Why was the PLATO communication environment so compelling to us? Because it dealt with interactions between people, not analysis of numbers. It dealt with information as opposed to data. Data is just facts. You fill out a form, you press a key, the data is stored. Later, if you fill out a query, you get your answer or report. Plain and simple.

Information, on the other hand, is recorded knowledge. It's a subjective opinion. It's a judgment call. It's a hot tip. It contains sarcasm or subtle innuendo. It's the stuff that makes up interpersonal communications! When dealing with knowledge, the techniques for finding answers to questions are better understood by librarians than by computer scientists. It requires a rich body of recorded information, good indexing techniques, a lot of reading, and the intuition gained by experience and exposure to information.

We began the project because we believed that the tools needed to manipulate data (forms packages, query tools, report writers) were not the same as the tools needed to deal with information. We wanted to create a compelling interpersonal communication system — a computer-assisted collaboration system that would enable companies to build customized information-sharing applications.

After six years of development, three of them spent in close contact with customers, we feel that we've accomplished what we set out to do. Lotus Notes has already begun to change the nature of the organizations that have committed to it. Information flows more freely, problems are resolved, and questions are answered more readily. The PC is being used in these companies as a communications appliance—often by people who never felt they needed a PC before.

We know we've done well when we talk to users. They enjoy using Notes! We're proud parents, and we're smiling as we watch our 6-year-old grow up to be everything we've always known that it could be.

Ray Ozzie

# Section 1
# Introducing Notes

The personal computer has been well named. In its first decade of widespread use, it has become a central piece of business equipment at the same time that the nature of the work done in businesses has been undergoing profound change.

PCs have appeared on office desks by the millions because they boosted the productivity of their users. This personal productivity increase hasn't been easy to quantify, and there's been much argument over justifying investment in PCs. But the proof of the pudding is in the eating: PCs have become ubiquitous in business, giving real meaning to office automation just as office workers have found themselves metamorphosing into "knowledge workers" (in Peter Drucker's felicitous phrase) and wrestling with ever-larger volumes of information. The PC has made it possible for these workers at least to maintain their productivity, providing programs to do word-processing, spreadsheets, database management, and desktop publishing (and a range of more specialized functions that seem limited only by the imagination).

Still, the use of PCs has been fundamentally *personal.* And as PCs have become a standard feature of the office landscape, it has become obvious that one reason they haven't had a more dramatic impact on productivity is that knowledge workers spend a large portion of their time working in groups away from their PCs. The team is becoming the basic unit of tactical business practice. Yet PCs have not supported the activities of business teams well. Increasing both the velocity and volume of information flows between and within groups in the modern business has become crucial to success, yet few PC programs address the need for helping groups communicate and manage information.

Computer technology is moving in the right direction. Local area networks provide the necessary physical links among PCs, and graphics and control devices like the mouse have expanded the vocabulary of user interfaces. To these hardware and software improvements, add the increasingly sophisticated understandings of the interactions of groups and how to support them with computers being forged by researchers.

The result is a new discipline called computer-supported group work or workgroup computing, among other names, and a class of programs called groupware. What these programs do varies widely, from project managers to group authoring tools to electronic messaging to workflow management. What they have in common is their use of personal computers to provide more or less rudimentary support for the activities of workgroups.

The most advanced of these programs is Notes, from Lotus Development Corp. Notes is a group communications product that allows people using PCs connected on local-area networks to create and access shared information. This book takes a close look at Notes, its role in supporting the productivity of groups, and its benefits for business. The focus is on Notes and organizations, rather than Notes and individuals: unlike most books about PC software, this is not a user manual. The five sections that follow examine various aspects of Notes and the issues that surround its adoption by organizations:

- Section 1 looks at what Notes is, and what it is not. Chapter 1 briefly introduces Notes and its major functions, then describes what four pioneering organizations did with the program. Chapter 2 looks at the three major functional areas of Notes (text management, workgroup communications, and security) and discusses the program's similarities to and distinct differences from several familiar types of PC software, including group calendaring programs, project managers, database managers, and transaction processing systems.

- Section 2 is a view of Notes from the driver's seat. Chapter 3 covers the basics of using the program: working with Notes applications, sending electronic mail, and creating and retrieving documents by using forms and views. Chapter 4 reviews the example databases and application templates provided with Notes, working applications that cover a variety of functions.

- Section 3 goes beyond merely customizing a template to examine the development of a Notes application from the ground up. Chapter 5 looks at the process of developing a computer program, and the organizational issues developers must be especially aware of in designing Notes applications. Chapter 6 follows step-by-step the creation of an application. Chapter 7 discusses advanced capabilities and application structures.

- Section 4 examines the issues of administering a Notes installation. Chapter 8 examines the need for dedicated personnel and the role those people play, system installation and management, the extensive security features and requirements of Notes, and issues of network compatibility and utilization. Chapter 9 discusses other network applications that can be integrated with Notes through gateways (such as facsimile servers and other electronic mail systems) and through Notes' application programming interface (such as custom software to provide access to corporate databases from inside Notes).

- Section 5 deals with deploying Notes in the organization. It covers such issues as how a corporation can evaluate Notes and its own need for the program, and what resources the organization must provide for introducing Notes, equipping and training its personnel, and sustaining the growth of Notes.

# Notes at Work

**B**usiness organizations have invested heavily in personal computers, and they have struggled to demonstrate a return on that investment. The anticipation was that computerization would do for the white-collar workforce what automation had done for the factory worker, that capital investment would make dramatic improvements in worker productivity.

But early results were not positive. The reason was that the methods of the assembly line don't translate to the tasks performed by knowledge workers. Personal computers, like factory automation, amplify the labor of individual workers. But what businesses are only coming to realize is how much of the work of dealing with information in an organization is a group activity—and how little of this group activity is supported by computers.

Groups meet to exchange information, hatch strategies, debate issues, reach decisions. But computers are best at analyzing figures, drafting reports, retrieving data—all activities of individuals, not of groups. If PCs are going to measurably improve productivity in the office, what's needed are new ways of using personal computers to support groups in their activities of information management and communication.

Notes provides this support for groups by building usable functions on the platform of PCs and networks in business offices, automatically structuring information for retrieval, speeding information flows, and reducing the learning curve for new technologies.

Notes provides an integrated working environment—integration that happens on two levels. Members of groups individually can do real work in Notes —writing and filing sales contact reports, drafting evaluations and documentation, recording customer service contacts—using a set of productivity tools that offer the same benefits as other integrated programs such as Microsoft Works and Lotus Symphony: the various tools (the applications for working with text, numbers, and communications) share a common command set and consistent interface that make them easier to learn and use.

Then Notes adds another level of integration that is especially important to groups: integration of those productivity tools with the functions for communicating that work. Notes' document-management functions automatically fit the documents into a structure and give them identifiable types so they can be retrieved: electronic mail, discussion topics or responses, and the specialized forms used within applications that can be identified by name—Client Information, Product Evaluation, Monthly Activity Report.

Software that supports this kind of communication among the members of a group and adds value to the information by ordering it for access is something new for PCs. Notes is a pioneer program, one of a relatively limited number of programs that have made forays into the unexplored territory of group-oriented software. And among these, Notes displays a unique understanding of the information-centered work people long to do on PCs. In the past, people had no choice but to approach their business work in groups—staff meetings, committees, teams, departments—and their PC tasks as individuals. Nor did local area networks alone change this reality: LANs linked the machines, but not the people, who remained locked into largely stand-alone applications. Even electronic mail has not been especially helpful for this sort of work-centered communication: leaving a word processor and starting up an E-mail program reinforces the separation between the work and the communication, rather than reduces it. In most companies the systems used to support work and communications are still separate—writing and numerical analysis may have moved to the PC, but communication is still handled by phone calls, face-to-face meetings, and interoffice mail.

The productivity tools in Notes can be divided into three major functional groups: wide-area electronic communications, text editing, and document management. Notes delivers these capabilities to all the members of a group through the standard graphical user interface of Microsoft Windows or OS/2 Presentation Manager in a high-security environment across a standard PC local area network.

- **Electronic mail** is built into Notes, not just as a stand-alone application, but as a set of functions that can be combined with other capabilities: Copies of new documents can be automatically transmitted to other group members; an expense-account database can automatically route completed forms for approval. Notes' easy modem-based wide-area connectivity is well suited to providing electronic messaging to a geographically dispersed group, as well as to duplicating the database applications of Notes across multiple servers.

- **Text editing and formatting** support the creation of documents that include multiple typefaces and sizes. Text, tables, spreadsheet data, and graphics can be imported from other programs and formatted using a tool set that, while not as complete as stand-alone word-processors, is capable of comfortably producing multi-page documents, and powerful enough to do straightforward charts and lists for presentations.

- **Document management**, the core of Notes' functionality, provides the tools for creating and managing databases of documents. The documents can take any shape, from conventional database records containing brief data fields to lengthy reports that include graphics and text in a variety of typesizes and fonts. Notes structures and summarizes these bodies of documents, categorizing them, delineating relationships, and providing access to individual documents for quick, easy retrieval.

On a function-by-function basis, there's little that is dazzlingly original about Notes. Its electronic mail, for example, isn't that different from other packages on the market. Similar comparisons can be made to database managers, word processors, presentation graphics packages, executive information systems, newswire and data-retrieval services, and a variety of more specialized packages to do things like client tracking and document management.

The genius of Notes lies in the length of this list of programs it compares to. These programs all do what they do as well as or better than Notes does. But none of them handles as many functional areas as Notes. The integration of previously disparate tasks in Notes means that no E-mail package can match its message-formatting capabilities, and no word processor can equal its document management. What database manager can turn a data-entry form into an E-mail message just by adding a field named SendTo? Notes is a brilliantly programmed exemplar of the art of the possible, a whole much greater than the sum of its parts.

Notes makes its capabilities available in a completely customizable way, so that databases can be designed to meet the needs of particular projects or purposes: The documents in one database may be reports on the group members' contacts with customers. Another database may contain requests for purchase orders, which Notes can route to persons who must authorize them. Another may be an ongoing computer-based conference among the group members in which topics are introduced and responses are indexed accordingly. In all of these, the flexibility of Notes means that the database applications can be adapted to meet the information needs and working patterns of the group, rather than forcing the group to change the way it works in order to use Notes.

This flexibility (and Notes' potential) are indicated by how difficult it is to describe Notes in a few words. Before Notes was introduced, Lotus stressed "document management," but dropped that in favor of "group communications" as the product was brought to market.

Notes' refreshingly simple approach to tying together scattered local area networks across a company provides the technological underpinning for communication and information management that transcends the boundaries of the individual workplace or local area network. In doing this, it broadens the concept of the workgroup as well. No longer is a workgroup just those people who sit in adjacent offices, or near each other on the organization chart. Workgroups can be *ad hoc,* interdepartmental, or special-purpose. In this, Notes promises to provide much-needed support for some of the most advanced ideas in management, from inter-company task forces to flatter organizational structures to Japanese-style "Quality First" programs.

Several companies have experience with these capabilities of Notes. The development cycle for Notes has been a long and extremely open one. Lotus and the programmers of Iris Associates, the development team behind Notes, have worked closely with companies testing Notes to determine the strengths and limitations of Notes, and shape it to meet the needs of the test sites. The results — after as much as two years of work in some cases — point up areas where the companies, developing their own applications for Notes, have found particular benefit.

# Client Tracking at Manufacturers Hanover

Manufacturers Hanover Trust in New York City was one of the earliest test sites for Notes. MHT is one of the biggest commercial banks in a very competitive market: It looks for advantage over its rivals wherever it can find it, and has long been sensitive to the potential of computers as a competitive tool. In fact, Manufacturers Hanover had just completed a yearlong study of computer technology and its relationship to the bank's services when Lotus asked MHT to participate in the beta test program for Notes.

Notes looked like a promising solution for some problems identified in the study — particularly for sharing specialized business information among the members of a product-related sales team or development group — or even across workgroups.

MHT decided to try Notes out on a client tracking application. A score of account managers in Credit Services, a division that represents the bank to its business clients, was selected as a pilot group. According to Christine Thompson, the managers needed to help in tracking information about client companies and their contacts within them. Thompson is a vice president in MHT's Infonet division, a service organization which functions as a liaison between the bank's PC users and its data-processing departments. The people in Thompson's division do systems analysis, developing specifications and prototyping software systems, so that it was natural that they should become the application designers for Notes.

Their first effort was a Notes database titled Company Profiles, which centralized background information on Credit Services clients—addresses, histories, financial reports on the companies, even information on contacts' personal interests. This information had not previously been managed in any formal way. Thompson's department developed the Notes application and the Credit Services staff keyed in their data to build the initial database.

The account managers, who at first grumbled over the labor of keying in the data, quickly grew to appreciate having it accessible in one place, according to Thompson. It doesn't wander off the way the paper files too often did—and because it never goes missing, it's always there to be consulted or updated. When a manager is away or on vacation and her client calls with a question, another manager can check Notes to see the client's status. For accounts with more than one officer assigned to them, Notes is a help in coordinating their efforts and avoiding duplication.

The Company Profiles database also contains the lengthy planning documents the account managers use in order to lay out a marketing strategy for each client. These documents are created using a different form from the one used to enter vital statistics on the clients (see box, Forms and Views on page 10).

While the forms allowed the Credit Services staff to enter text-oriented data, the real value Notes added to the Credit Services data was in the views designed by the Infonet staff. In the Company Profiles application, the Location view sorts clients by city. Account managers use this view to leverage their investment of time and expense in travel: When they plan to visit clients out of town they check the Location view to see if other client calls can be scheduled in the same vicinity.The Special Interests view lists the hobbies and personal interests of client contacts, from scout troops to golf to modern art. It has proven to be surprisingly useful. MHT sponsors civic events and periodically plans special gatherings for its customers. The Special Interests view is useful in the planning and issuing of invitations to such events. It provides MHT with guidance as to which customers would like which events, and what kinds of events the bank should plan.

The account managers in Credit Services use the Customer Contacts view to keep track of their day-to-day contacts with the clients. The most frequently used form in this application is a call report, with fields for recording the call's subject, products that were discussed, and comments or information relevant to the contact and the client.

From this call report form, several views were created to help the managers. One serves the purpose of a tickler file. It lists actions to be taken,

## Forms and Views

The information structures of Notes are based on two fundamental data-management tools: *forms,* used to capture information, and *views,* organized presentations of information from the forms.

Notes' forms provide templates for entering information and saving it as documents in the application. Forms can be as simple as a quick electronic-mail note, with fields for To, From, Subject, and Text. Or they can be as elaborate as the finished version of a lengthy report, with headlines, charts, graphs, and chapters of text. To accommodate this flexibility, a field in a Notes document is very different from a field in a typical PC database program. It can be of virtually any length (the actual limit is four gigabytes of data —which provides plenty of room even for large graphics files), and its formatting options allow for text in a variety of type faces and sizes and colors. Text can be imported and exporting with this formatting intact.

A view in Notes is essentially a database report—it displays information from selected document fields in tabular form, with each row in the view representing a document. But it also serves as a menu of the underlying documents. Click with the mouse on a row in a view and the document it represents is opened up.

A view provides a way of looking at the relationships among the documents in an application, and there can be many views created for an application. The MHT Company Profiles database, for example, includes one view that sorts all the documents by client, and another view that lists only the account managers' planning documents.

responses owed to the client. Another view lists the products discussed. (This view has turned out to be especially useful to junior product managers, who use it to see what account managers consider important.)

While the initial test of Notes involved only account managers, MHT is moving to add supervisors and senior account managers to Notes to eliminate a paperwork bottleneck. Currently, when a senior account manager visits a client, the account managers print out or photocopy all the documents pertaining to the client. These status reports put more paper on the desks of the senior account managers than they could possibly wade through. And the reports take the account managers away from more productive work. The Company Profiles and Customer Contacts databases will allow the senior account managers to stay current without disrupting the work of their subordinates.

Eventually, Manufacturers Hanover will use Notes databases across department lines, says Thompson. The bank offers a variety of services to Credit Services' customers. Coordination of MHT's contacts with those clients would benefit the bank—and the customers. The information collected and organized by Notes promises to be a valuable tool for planning, from the small scale (would more clients prefer a golf tourney or a theater party?) to the long range (what does the accumulated information in the "Customer Contacts" database reveal about a particular product's potential customers?).

## Bringing Structure to Full Text

The bank's client-tracking and status-reporting applications draw on a couple of Notes' strengths: its full-text orientation and its ability to categorize and sort information according to predesigned schemes. Traditional database managers are oriented toward small pieces of information, such as a zip code, or a part number. They do not deal well with longer text documents such as the call reports, sales plans, meeting minutes, contract drafts. Yet this information is the lifeblood of an organization. Notes forms are especially good at handling long text fields. Users can create and format text in Notes, or import it from files created by other word processors. Tables and spreadsheet files, charts and graphs, even scanned images can be imported into text fields as well.

Other fields in the form can provide standard categories for the indexing of the finished document. This standardization of input is the key to sharing information among the members of a group, and the reason for the emphasis on designing a database application in Notes. Notes is not "personal information manager" software—it doesn't order information that has been entered randomly. Such an approach wouldn't serve the needs of a group. Common access to information depends on common understanding of how the information is structured, down to such details as the spelling of client names so that they index properly. Notes provides ways of easily ordering the information as it is created. The graphical interfaces that Notes runs under are a help in this, because they provide a vocabulary of checkboxes and selection buttons that make it easy to select categories or company divisions or product names that then index correctly in the database's views.

## Status Reporting at Lotus Development

Lotus Development Corp. took advantage of Notes' categorizing and sorting capabilities in its own sales activity reporting database. The application was one of the most ambitious early implementations of Notes: It was used by nearly 300 sales and marketing personnel in the field, and some 80 executives in Lotus' Cambridge, Massachusetts, headquarters. It is a model that many companies have shown an interest in duplicating.

The building blocks of Lotus's sales activity database are the field personnel's monthly reports that detail customer contacts and pass along sales and product ideas, marketplace information, and intelligence about competitors' sales activities.

The Notes application replaced a paper-based system that yielded up a two-inch-thick report once a quarter—a process that had problems, according to Ron Turcotte, who created and administers the sales activity application. For one thing, the quarterly production schedule was too long. After three months, every problem had grown into a crisis. And the formidable, yet essential, report would all too often lie in an in-basket unread until it was thrown out to make room for a new copy. The paper report was indexed only by sales contacts and market intelligence. It was difficult to look at its contents any other way—by priority, for example, or by Lotus product.

When the sales activity reporting application was put into use, the field people did not have access to Notes. Instead, Turcotte developed an application in Agenda, Lotus's personal information manager package, which all the field personnel use. Agenda is a freeform database with a macro language and the ability to take data typed almost randomly and parse it into a structured presentation. The field representatives entered their region and group, set a priority for the information, keyed in the text of their reports and forwarded them to their regional supervisors. The supervisors then edited the reports into a single document and added their own reports, covering not only marketing but administrative and personnel matters. These reports were then sent to Cambridge, where Agenda macros categorized the data and prepared it to be imported into Notes.

The field reports were imported into Notes, which became a distribution medium for the information to its executive readership, and provided access through a set of views. (One of the example databases shipped with Notes, called Sales Activity Reports, is a fictionalized version of this Lotus application.)

The great value of the Notes application has been in time saved, according to Jim Manzi, the chief executive officer of Lotus. The salespeople and management in the field can now do in hours what once took days, and the report's production cycle has been shortened by three weeks. "The work is more valuable because it's more current and more accessible," says Manzi. "It's a win on time and quality, for sure, and on capacity to respond."

Another major plus for the system is the variety of views it produces. Executives can see what is happening in a particular region, how a certain product group is doing, or what topics have high priority. "Even if this system took longer to use than the old paper system it would be worth it," maintains Turcotte, "because of the value of the data: People have information they didn't have access to before."

One mark of the system's early success was the field reps' attitude toward it. Even though the field reps did not have access to Notes themselves, they felt they were getting better and faster responses to their needs from the home office because their reports were being distributed in a more timely fashion.

This success did not come easily. A first attempt at a sales reporting application went down in flames, says Turcotte. As a result, this second effort was treated as a new product within the company, with formal training sessions and support services. The experience taught Turcotte a lesson that other managers of Notes systems also stress: Training is a key to building a successful system in Notes.

## Security for Sensitive Documents

The sales activity reporting database takes advantage of the security and access control features of Notes to provide individuals with access to information based on their roles in the group. Access to the database itself was limited to the executives. Some views were created with privileges that allowed only senior management to view them. Views which include reports on personnel matters from the regional supervisors are available only to sales department managers. Evaluations and other sensitive documents are hidden from users in other departments.

Another interesting aspect of the Lotus application is its integration of a pre-existing information-management system with Notes. The field people were using Agenda before the status reporting application was developed. Turcotte's Agenda templates and macros let the field people continue to work with a program they knew, while providing an output file that was easily imported into Notes. This model will doubtless be followed often: An existing application, anything from a spreadsheet template on a laptop to a corporate database on a mainframe, used as a front end to gather information, and Notes used as the back end to distribute and display the information—with all the flexibility that its views provide.

# Project Management at Corporate Software

Corporate Software looked at Notes in the light of its own communication needs and saw something very different in Notes—a project-management system.

The company, based in a Boston suburb, sells PC and Macintosh software and hardware add-ins. Its strategy in establishing a customer base among Fortune 1000 companies has been to provide customers with extensive support before and after the sale—product evaluations, purchasing assistance with timely delivery and purchase activity reports, management of upgrades, and a variety of publications.It was in its role as a software evaluator that Corporate Software first recognized a need for Notes. Twice a year, the company publishes a thick paperback book called *The Corporate Software Guide* which it sends to its customers. The *Guide* is 1,100 pages of evaluations of the 700 or so software and hardware products Corporate carries. Each time Corporate Software adds a new product to its list, a review must be added to the *Guide*. As software versions change those changes must be noted in the *Guide*.

Corporate Software wanted to ease the cumbersome task of updating the *Guide*. The company wanted software to manage the quantity of text and to track the people and task assignments involved. Two departments shared the work of doing the product evaluations—the technical support group and the marketing staff. Coordinating the two workgroups was hard, and it was difficult to find out a project's status. Because the text of the evaluations was not centrally stored and available to all involved in the project, people working on an evaluation sometimes had to track down others who had worked on it to compile needed information.

To complicate matters further, Corporate Software wanted to involve its offices in London and in France and Germany (only London actually took part in the Notes beta test). These offices needed to communicate regularly with headquarters. They had much material to share—and an unfortunate tendency to duplicate each others' work for lack of communication.

Mary Stark was Product Manager for Spreadsheets at the time of the test, and one of the people central to the evaluation process. Stark had used the evaluation system before Notes, and she reports that Notes helped her keep track of the stages in the evaluation process much more efficiently than had previously been possible. She liked being able to open a view and check the status of an evaluation. She also felt that by keeping all the data together and in a central location accessible to the users, the marketing and technical staffs were able to coordinate their work better and in a more timely fashion.

The evaluation process at Corporate Software begins when anyone within the company suggests to a product manager a new product the company might carry. The company designed its Notes application to track all the activities pertaining to an evaluation from this initial step.

The application's structure matched a form to each major milestone in the process. The multiple forms actually meant less work, not more, because of Notes' inheritance capabilities (see box, Inheriting Data in Forms).

---

## Inheriting Data in Forms

Notes can pass the contents of fields in one document to fields with the same names in another document. A name and address, for instance, once entered in a form that contains a client profile, doesn't have to be retyped into a form that reports on a phone call to the client.

The Windows interface makes inheritance easy for the user because multiple documents can be active at once. When a master document is open (or highlighted in a view) and a form that inherits data from it is opened, Notes will fill in the fields that inherit data.

Inheritance not only saves work for Notes users, it insures consistency in the spelling of data like company names, so that when a view sorts a database by the contents of a field such as Company Name all the documents will be grouped together correctly.

---

Corporate Software used the following forms in its *Guide* application:

- **The Product Recommendation form** could be filled in by anyone to alert the product manager to an interesting product. The form includes the vendor's name and contact information, the category of software or hardware, and a brief description of the product. On the basis of these recommendations, the product managers would contact vendors and consider whether the product fit Corporate Software's marketing goals.

- **The Vendor Information form** would be used by a product manager to record dealings with interesting possibilities — contact names, costs, and an assessment of the company's interest in working with Corporate Software.

- **The Market Analysis form** inherits some of the information entered in the Vendor Information form. In addition, it gathers information used by Corporate Software's marketers to analyze competing products and resellers.

- **The Product Analysis form** is a counterpart of the Market Analysis form. It, too, inherits some of its information on the vendor and the product, and gathers product specifics that provide the basis for the review.

- **The Discussion on Product form** proved to be a great way to share the expertise of analysts and product managers. It creates an open forum for both departments to share information. Each new document adds a topic to the discussion—mention of an article in the trade press, perhaps, or a report on a user's experience with the product. Discussion Response forms let readers respond, and keep the topics and responses grouped for easy reading (see box, Response Forms). The marketing department used this information, along with Market Analysis and Vendor Information documents, to discuss whether the product warranted a technical evaluation.

- **The Evaluation form** is started by a technical staff member when a product manager orders an evaluation. Corporate Software developed a different evaluation form for each software category—spreadsheets, databases, word processors, and communications. Each form was very detailed and ran for several pages.

---

## Response Forms

Response forms work something like inheritance, but in addition to any data that is inherited, a document that is created using a response form also inherits a relationship to the "master" document (in Notes, it's called an original topic document). In views, response documents are always grouped with the original topic document they respond to. This original/response structure is presented visually in the views.

Like the Corporate Software application, most applications include a response form as a way of promoting discussion on a topic. But even in databases that aren't intended to take advantage of this "computer conferencing" benefit of Notes, a response form is usually included as an easy way to add a correction or amplify a statement or offer an idea.

---

When the evaluation was over, if Corporate Software decided to carry the product, the evaluation and some of the vendor information was exported to a desktop publishing program, edited by a technical writer, and formatted for inclusion in the *Guide*. The evaluation documents were also available to support personnel who used the information to answer clients' questions.

# Infrequent Connection of Servers

Corporate Software replicated Notes databases once a day between the Boston headquarters and the London office (see box, Replicating Databases). This infrequent connection of remote servers to maintain multiple copies of a database is contrary to conventional methods of providing access to databases, but it rests securely on some basic assumptions about the contents of Notes applications and the uses they will be put to.

---

## Replicating Databases

Notes runs on a local area network, but sometimes Notes applications must be shared beyond the bounds of a single network—the workgroup using the application may be so big it reaches across several LANs, or the members of the group may be scattered across several departments, or even several cities. When the application is replicated, the Notes servers on the various networks connect (usually across dial-up telephone lines) to harmonize their copies of a database: Documents new or updated in one copy are added to the other, and deletions are processed in similar fashion.

Replication is an extremely flexible process controlled by the Notes' administrator to meet the needs of the organization. Some companies replicate their E-mail databases every 15 minutes and less active applications only once a day. Because there is no single master copy of an application in Notes, replication schedules can be set up to balance communications efficiency against cost. One company set up a central Notes server to replicate with remote Notes sites in a "hub-and-spokes" fashion to maximize the propagation of changes. Corporate Software, on the other hand, set up its replication in a "daisy-chain" model to minimize communication costs across the Atlantic.

---

Because the data in conventional database systems is expected to change rapidly (as bill payments are entered or airline seats are sold, for instance), these systems maintain just one copy of the data, and provide access to it from remote LANs via full-time leased-line connections. But the creators of Notes assumed that the contents of a Notes database would change relatively slowly compared to these fast-moving transactional systems, so that Notes could avoid the expense of full-time connections by maintaining multiple copies of the data where it would be used and updating them infrequently. This method worked for Corporate Software. The relative infrequency of replication and mail routing in Notes was still more communication than the London office had with headquarters previously, Stark notes: The London office liked participating in Notes; the people there felt less isolated and in closer contact with the home office.

## Discussions: What Notes Is Good For

The discussion forms in Corporate Software's database reveal one of Notes' most important capabilities.

Discussion applications in Notes work much like other computer conferencing software: Separate forms for documents that introduce new topics and documents that respond to existing topics allow Notes to index topics and their responses. Other views can provide access to the documents by date and time (which is all most E-mail systems can manage), by author, or by category, for example. (A basic discussion application with this set of views is one of the example databases included with Notes.)

Many workgroups using Notes create a new discussion application as the first step in helping define a new project or as the final step in winding down a completed project, to gather comments and critiques. Corporate Software's evaluation database took a more sophisticated approach by integrating the discussion documents as responses to the Evaluation form. The results were worth the effort. Stark reports that her work on spreadsheet products drew comments from London about similar European products she was unaware of as well as comments from people who had actually used the product under evaluation and who added valuable insights.

# A Vision of the Future at Price Waterhouse

The day Lotus announced Notes, Sheldon Laube announced that Price Waterhouse was buying 10,000 copies. It was a bold move that gave an instant legitimacy to Notes and to the idea of workgroup computing. The move put Laube, PW's Chief Information Officer, at some professional risk. Not only was Notes a new, unknown product, workgroup computing is still so new a concept that few models exist. A lot was riding on Laube's ability to sell Notes within Price Waterhouse, one of the Big Six accounting firms.Laube looked like the right man for the job. He is the first person PW has hired to oversee technology on the "practice side" (the revenue-generating end of the business) as well as the administrative side. His job is to be an integrator in a firm —and an industry—that has historically been decentralized.

Price Waterhouse has offices in most of the major cities of the United States and the world. The practice side of the business focuses on audit, tax, and management consulting for a client base that runs to large multinational companies.

Communication and collaboration among PW's divisions has been a problem. Some of these groups, such as audit, necessarily act as independent entities. Yet the audit staff, and its collective knowledge, needed to be accessible not only to each other, but to the rest of the organization.

Laube tells a story to illustrate why PW needed Notes: A colleague had come to him from a division of PW that consults with clients on employee benefits. A large part of this group's work is tracking changes in the maze of federal and state laws and regulations regarding employee benefits. About half the workgroup is in New York and the other half in Washington, DC; smaller regional offices are scattered in other major cities.

To share information, the offices sent faxes or paper copies. The result was too many paper documents, many of which arrived late. Some information missed the regional offices entirely. Because Washington was the hub of the operation, the staff there knew what was coming in from Los Angeles and Boston, but Los Angeles and Boston had no idea what was happening in each other's offices. The were missing much important, timely information.

PW had to find a way to help these people collaborate across geography and time zones. One demonstration of Notes was all it took to convince Laube's colleagues that there was a solution. Nor was that an uncommon reaction, according to Laube: "Notes is difficult to describe, but when we show it to people they react viscerally and intuitively. They understand what it is all about and they can almost always think of practical ways to apply it to their needs."

Part of this success is surely due to Laube himself. When he talks, he exudes the kind of solid confidence in his own decisions that makes him the perfect champion for change within an organization. But he casts PW's decision as a clear-cut business case: "We are absolutely convinced that Notes can dramatically impact our ability to serve our clients."

In addition, Laube sees Notes as an integral part of how Price Waterhouse wants to do business—in a collaborative style, with information centrally located and readily available to people wherever they are working. Along with installations of hardware and networks, Laube and his department are developing four types of Notes applications to foster that transformation:

## Newsletter Replacement

One of the first Notes applications at PW was a practical solution to the kind of internal communications problem that plagues most companies. Laube's department is responsible for developing and publishing technology standards. It issues guides to the software and hardware it recommends and supports, and publishes lists of vendors to consult for pricing. Such information changes frequently at PW, as it does everywhere. To accommodate the guide's changing nature, a newsletter application in Notes was developed to replace the print newsletter and make the changes available as quickly as easily—and universally—as possible.

Another publication that Laube's staff has converted to electronic form is a directory of the partners in the firm, with a photograph and curriculum vitae of each person. A copy of the directory had been regularly distributed to each partner, but it was inevitably out of date by the time it was printed and constantly needed updating. Put into Notes, complete with scanned pictures of the partners, the information can easily be kept current and readily available to anyone who needs it.

## Historical Knowledge

PW wants to capture, organize, and retrieve the knowledge of their people in what Laube calls an "expertise bank." Because PW is such a large company, employees have discovered, sometimes too late, that work was being duplicated because one person or group did not know that another had previously done it. If this information could be captured and stored in a central location and then retrieved easily, it could improve the performance of the firm and save a great deal of time.

A prototype for such a system came from the tax division, which maintains a database of references to changes in the tax law and to articles and government documents of interest to the partners. The database entries were keyed in on a timeshared computer, and the documents they cited were put on microfiche—and, after a delay of some six months, were distributed to the firm's offices. Such a long lag became unacceptable: Tax law changes too rapidly. The Notes database lists the references in many different views designed with partner's needs in mind, and provides direct access to the full text of the indexed documents—no microfiche, no waiting.

George John, Laube's chief lieutenant, tells the story of an experiment his group had run with wire services, bringing articles on selected topics such as tax law changes into Notes. One such article caught the eye of a PW tax consultant in Los Angeles. Browsing through the test database, he read of a change in the law that had occurred only the day before. He immediately called one of his clients who would be affected by the change. That, says John, is the kind of quick response PW prides itself on.

## Hot Topics

Unlike the newsletter replacement applications, which are one-way distributions of information, the Hot Topics database is designed to encourage input from PW employees. The database has two views: Hot Topics lists anything that has happened in the last two weeks, and Research lists older topics. Hot Topics is actually a series of databases related to the different divisions of the organization. While these databases can be read almost like newswire services, they are actually structured as discussions, and include forms that readers within the division can use to respond to a topical item with additional references and comments. The Hot Topics databases serve not only to keep people informed of what is happening in the world but also within PW.

## Project Management

Like Lotus, Price Waterhouse quickly discovered the value of Notes for status reporting and project management. Laube, himself, manages a geographically dispersed group. His office is in New York, and most of the people who work for him are in Tampa, Florida; a handful are scattered across the country. He uses a Notes status reporting application to help him manage this staff. Each week, they file status reports on their activities and plans, including schedules and travel itineraries, and observations and comments. The system works so well, according to Laube, that he receives a flow of minireports throughout the week.

# The Audits Application

One of the most interesting and difficult Notes applications undertaken by PW tracked the status of an audit of a large corporation. Laube's group developed pilot programs in Notes for 10 of PW's major audit projects. From the results of these pilot programs, they would develop an application in Notes to track a corporate audit.

Tracking the audit process takes advantage of Notes' strengths in coordinating the work of geographically remote offices. Audits are massive administrative problems because they involve a tremendous amount of correspondence. For audits of multinational companies, information must be gathered from offices all over the world. The home office of PW usually initiates the work by deciding what needs to be done, where it needs to be done, and what documents must be collected so that PW can ultimately issue its opinion. For larger audits, the home office corresponds regularly with 50 to 100 PW offices throughout the world, issuing detailed instructions and receiving detailed answers.

This communication, historically conducted by FAX and mail, generates huge volumes of paper that must be tracked. PW wanted an overview of the audit process and a forum where the audit staff could summarize the work, discuss it, and reach a consensus about it. In the short term, according to George John, the audits benefit because Notes provides the information more quickly and, as a result, they can come to a consensus more quickly. Notes shortens the information lags that occurred while information was transported, collected, sorted, and categorized. The audit application is a prototype of the broader use for Notes foreseen by Laube, John, and their coworkers as Notes becomes the firm's standard forum for communication and management.

Price Waterhouse has made other interesting uses of Notes. A sales activity database helps coordinate the efforts of salespeople from different divisions dealing with the same large clients. A Notes database tracks customer service for a mainframe tax software package PW sells. Laube's people turned a training course into a Notes database—the course, on strategic selling and sales planning, is very highly regarded within PW. In Notes, it is more readily available as training for new sales people and as a refresher for others.

## Implementing Notes

Sheldon Laube obviously achieved a great deal when he convinced Price Waterhouse that Notes was what it needed. He had persuaded PW to invest a great deal of money in an untried product which, in that very large organization, would also require large investments in new or upgraded workstation and server hardware and the networking of three-quarters of the firm. The cost was impressive, but getting an organization to spend money can often be easier than actually implementing change, and Laube's goal in committing PW to Notes was nothing less than reshaping the way the firm did business.

Characteristically, Laube had a plan. His deployment strategy had two forks, a "high road" and a "low road."

The high road was strategic. The first to travel it would be opinion leaders, who would set the tone for Notes' later wider distribution. Laube carefully chose his first workgroups to take this high road. He looked around the firm for groups aligned with the strategic goals of the organization; and, within those groups, he targeted key areas and key workgroups. They were highly visible, geographically distributed, and led by well-respected members of PW. Most of these people were nontechnical and some hadn't even used a computer. They were the people who did the business that made PW profitable. (Laube cautions against showing Notes to technical types who dislike its E-mail, think the database should be relational, and may not even like graphical user interfaces.) The targeted workgroups got demonstrations of Notes. They were receptive, even enthusiastic. Laube gives the credit to Notes, saying the users easily grasped it, and quickly understood which of their needs it could appropriately meet.

Once a group was introduced to Notes, they began working with George John to design their application. (John, with experience in both the practice side of the business—he used to work in audit—and the technical side, was a natural for this sort of internal marketing for Notes.) When a workgroup designed its first databases, Laube encouraged the group to include among its users a partner or high-ranking executive and a staff-level person who became a training and support resource for the group. The partner's involvement attached value to the work. The resource person helped the group to become self-sufficient. They both helped the group assume "ownership" of Notes. This self-sufficiency quickly extended to designing and building their own databases, after help with the first two or three from Laube's technical staff in Tampa.

The low road was a set of temporary solutions such as dial-up connections and electronic-mail gateways for those offices not yet networked, or still using old equipment on which Notes would not run. Networks were the biggest stumbling block: When Price Waterhouse bought Notes, only about a quarter of its employees had access to LANs. PW committed to a three-year plan to install LANs and Notes in all of the more than 100 PW offices.

Eventually, all PW offices will be on Sheldon Laube's high road and Notes will have served the purpose he foresaw for it as a second wave of PC-based transformational technology: "Notes will transform our business and how we do it," he told the audience at Notes' introduction. "The first wave was spreadsheets. Notes is the second wave. In three years, at Price Waterhouse, we will spend more hours in Notes than in 1-2-3."

# Summary

While PCs have had a major impact on the productivity of individuals in organizations, they have provided little support for the work done by groups —the exchanges of information, the discussions that generate ideas. Notes is a pioneering product in a new class of PC software, called groupware. Notes is flexible, allowing groups to create applications that integrate technology into the enterprise without destroying the character of that enterprise. Notes achieves its impact by integrating a set of productivity tools used by individuals for doing work with the capabilities of the network for communicating that work among the members of the group. The functions Notes provides can be compared to more traditional PC software—electronic mail, database managers, word processors, presentation graphics packages, and more. But the integration of these functions has made it possible for companies, including Manufacturers Hanover, Corporate Software, Price Waterhouse, and Lotus Development itself to develop PC-based applications in Notes that support the work of groups.

# 2

······
······
······

# What Notes Is
# ... And Isn't

**T**raditional software packages maintain a rigid conceptual division between the "program" and the "data." Notes breaks down this distinction. It provides a working environment that eliminates the separation between the information and the tools that create it. It opens the program, allowing its users to mold and shape it to meet their needs, to customize it to meet the working methods of a group. To emphasize this self-containment, Notes refers to the tasks that users perform with Notes as "applications." An investment bank, for example, might develop an application that tracks merger prospects. The staff of a magazine might build an application that tracks production schedules.

Applications come in all shapes and sizes. An application may be a permanent piece of the way a company does business, or it may be something put together for a weeklong project. Groups that use an application may be as large as an entire company or as small as one person. An individual Notes user may work with dozens of applications, or just a couple of them (see box, A System View of Notes on page 26).

But while applications, or databases (Notes uses the two terms interchangeably), can meet an infinite range of needs, each one uses the same interface and comprises the same basic elements. Notes runs under graphical user interfaces (either Windows 3.0 or OS/2 Presentation Manager) that provide a consistent and complete environment. That means that the process of learning to use Notes builds on users' experience with a mouse and with menu-based command selection. Notes' display screens use the same menu bars and pull-down menus as other Windows and Presentation Manager (PM) programs. The graphical interface also provides for integration of Notes and other applications. Users running Notes under Windows can share information with other Windows programs through the clipboard, Windows' Dynamic Data Exchange (DDE), or Object Linking and Embedding (OLE).

---

# A System View of Notes

---

Notes is not a computer program in the same sense as a spreadsheet or a word processor, with a specific and limited set of functions. Notes is a software system with many parts, and many roles to play. It provides a user interface and, in individual applications, sets of functions for manipulating data. But Notes also provides a development environment, and system-management functions. Each of these roles is matched by a role for a Notes user:

- The end user sees Notes as a collection of applications or databases, each one customized to be used for a particular job.

- The application developer sees Notes as a toolkit for building and maintaining the individual applications. The complexity of Notes applications ranges from very simple discussion databases to complex programming projects with links to electronic information services or mainframe databases.

- The system administrator sees Notes as the software that maintains the database files on the Notes server on the local-area network and manages communications with other Notes servers at other sites.

---

Whatever the application, it has three major dimensions:

- **Information management**. Notes applications collect data—with a focus on free-form textual information—and structure it so it can be used by a group. Because every application uses the same set of tools, users can quickly and easily adopt new applications and move among applications as their work requires.

- **Workgroup communications**. Notes reaches well beyond the one-to-one message transfers of typical electronic mail packages to support the more complex communications structures (one-to-many, many-to-many) used by groups.

- **Security**. Notes' password protection, ID verification, and data encryption encourage users to entrust even the most sensitive communications to Notes' electronic transmission.

This chapter examines each of those three components and what it contributes to make Notes what it is. Then, a final section looks at what Notes is not: While the program has functions similar to those of familiar PC programs and systems, that doesn't mean Notes can replace them. Notes documents, like database records, are divided into fields, for example, but Notes is not a database manager like dBASE or Paradox.

# Information Management

Managing information so that it can be shared effectively is one of the most basic problems confronting groups. When several people work on a project, the documents they produce often are stored on several different PCs. Even in a networked office related documents may all be stored on the same file server, but in different directories with different access rights. In such environments, information is retrievable in bits and pieces, but access to all of the group's communications and responses and research papers and reports doesn't exist.

Notes provides that missing central place to store information, a coherent organizational scheme for ready access to the material, and assistance in searching for what is wanted.

# Forms and Views

The basic building blocks for Notes applications are forms and views: *forms* are canvases for capturing and displaying information, and *views* are the indexes to the collection. The developer of the application creates both.

A form has two functions: It provides a standard format for information being entered into the application and it serves as a frame for reviewing completed documents. (A form, once completed and saved, becomes a *document*.)

The form contains the fields that hold information. That information may be processed, or used in calculations, or formatted according to instructions provided by the field definition (see Figure 2.1). Complex field formulas can manipulate both text and numbers. A form can contain many different types of fields, from buttons and checkboxes for choosing preset keywords, to blank spaces which will accept thousands of words of text that can be formatted in different typestyles and colors. Forms can be created in endless variety to fit the demands of the workgroup.

Views resemble database reports or spreadsheets. They are divided into rows (for the documents) and columns (for the categories and fields see Figure 2.2). Like a database report, they take the information from the documents and display it in many ways.

Views, like forms, can be designed in infinite variety. To look at information in new ways, users can revise a view or create a new one. Views also provide access to the documents. They serve as indexes, to help users find particular

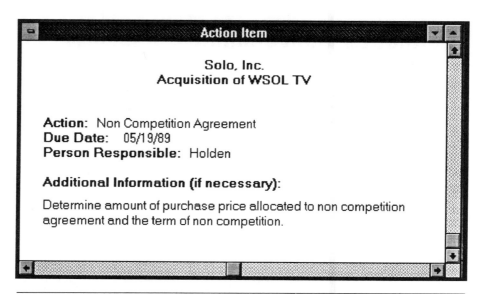

**FIGURE 2.1** A form provides structure for the documents created in Notes. Items of data within the document can be as short as a name or as long as an entire memo or report.

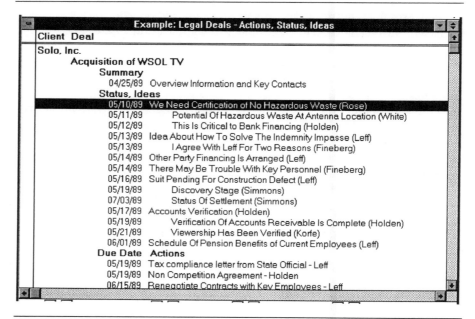

**FIGURE 2.2** Views display all or part of a document in a tabular form, with each row representing a separate document and each column a field within that document.

documents easily and quickly. And because the views show pieces of information in relation to each other, they serve as important tools for analyzing and tracking information.

## Importing and Exporting

Information from other programs can be imported into Notes documents or views. And conversely, Notes data can be exported to other programs. These import and export functions are probably used most frequently to exchange text between word processor files and Notes forms. In addition, data from 1-2-3 worksheets can be imported into Notes forms as tables (only the values are transferred—Notes can't save or execute the cell formulas). Graphs created in charting packages like Freelance Plus can be brought into Notes documents, as can graphics images. Database reports can be imported into properly prepared views.

Notes provides translations to and from a number of file formats for various types of applications: It translates word-processing documents, for example, to and from the file formats used by DisplayWrite, Manuscript, Microsoft Word, and several versions of MultiMate, WordPerfect, and WordStar.

Notes even extends the benefits of its document management to files it cannot actually open or manipulate. Lotus 1-2-3 worksheets, for instance, can be attached to a Notes document for filing and distribution, then exported again to be modified in 1-2-3. This lets you gather all the files for a project in one place, regardless of what program created them—and use Notes as a convenient indexing medium. (The evolving improvements in Windows DDE and OLE will eventually resolve some of the limitations of importing and exporting. DDE [for Dynamic Data Exchange] and OLE [Object Linking and Embedding] are mechanisms used by programs running under Windows to share data among applications, or to invoke applications which operate on the data. See Chapter 3 for more on these technologies.)

## Workgroup Communications

Much of our daily communication with others is done on a one-to-one basis—in telephone calls or conversations in hallways. We also communicate one-to-many—we speak in meetings and write memos and reports that are circulated to distribution lists. In the realm of the PC, conventional electronic mail is useful for both these communications models.

But much of business communication is in a many-to-many structure: A group of salespeople, for instance, collect information from their contacts with clients, and then share it among themselves. Many business meetings are accommodations of the need for many-to-many communications within the organization. The classical example is the Monday morning staff meeting where no decisions are made, but each staff member in turn reports on his activities to all the others. Such meetings are spectacularly inefficient, but often they are held despite protests because there has been no better way to communicate the information.

Even PCs and electronic mail systems haven't been able to support this many-to-many communication. But a Notes database provides the necessary formal structure for organizing the contributions of many people (linking responses to topic documents, sorting by category and date) to make many-to-many communications work on PCs.

## Notes' Electronic Mail

Notes' electronic mail system has a dual nature: First, it works much like other E-mail packages for sending one-to-one and one-to-many messages. You can send to individuals and to groups, attach files like spreadsheets, and insert text from word-processing files or Notes documents. Yet Notes E-mail is also structured as a standard Notes application. Mail is one of the choices on the main menu bar. Users do not have to exit from Notes or the application they already have open in order to work with E-mail. There are no new keystrokes or commands to learn. And you can build personalized views of your E-mail database to sort your mail the way you want to see it—by the name of the sender and then by date, for example. Notes' E-mail also takes advantage of Notes' security features for signing, encrypting, and secure routing of messages.

## Communicating Through Applications

Most E-mail systems provide only the simplest possible view of your messages —a list of messages arranged chronologically. But simple chronology is not an organizational scheme that can provide meaningful access to many-to-many communications. These communications, such as salespersons' call reports or analysts' discussions, must be categorized and grouped to have value. Notes applications provide this structure.

Notes' discussion applications organize the comments of a group, as we saw in the Corporate Software example in Chapter 1. The messages in a discussion application are usually no different in substance from typical traffic on an E-mail system—quick thoughts, ideas caught on the fly, and occasionally a long, carefully prepared document. Notes automatically groups such a jumble of messages into an ordered, accessible structure.

The Product Discussion, one of the example applications shipped with Notes, provides a blueprint for this many-to-many structure. It uses Notes' hierarchy of document types—main documents, which introduce new topics; response documents, which comment on or amplify main documents; and response to response, which provides yet another level of categorization (see Figure 2.3).

Combined with E-mail for side conversations and DocLinks—a function explained in Chapter 3—to serve as pointers for calling attention to other documents, the Discussion template provides Notes users with a robust computer conferencing tool. The Discussion and other template applications are discussed more thoroughly in Chapter 4.

| | # | Date | Rsp | Topic |
|---|---|------|-----|-------|
| * | 1 | 08/22/86 | | Introduction (Marc Kline) |
| | 2 | 09/14/88 | 1 | Dragging multiple icons (Ellen Byron) |
| | 2.1 | 09/15/88 | | No problem with a mouse... (Jim Menlo) |
| | 3 | 09/20/88 | 2 | New user (Rob Moran) |
| | 3.1 | 09/20/88 | | I can answer some. (Brian Law) |
| * | 3.2 | 09/20/88 | | The Answer to Question 3 (Barbara Mann) |
| | 4 | 09/30/88 | 2 | Some more questions about Notes and Notes culture (Rob Moran) |
| * | 4.1 | 09/30/88 | | The Tutorial Is In The Doc (John Vogal) |
| * | 4.2 | 10/04/88 | | Yes, there is a wish list... (Barbara Mann) |
| * | 5 | 10/03/88 | 1 | Are a lot of people lacking documentation? (Beth Jillford) |
| * | 5.1 | 10/04/88 | | Request for new doc (Judy Sanfillipo) |
| * | 6 | 12/20/88 | | Neat Iconizer for PM (Rob Wallas) |
| * | 7 | 01/31/89 | 4 | I need a scheduling application in Notes... (Rob Moran) |
| * | 7.1 | 02/07/89 | | I'm fooling around with that now (Ed Sands) |
| * | 7.2 | 02/08/89 | | Terrific! Thanks a lot. (Rob Moran) |
| * | 7.3 | 02/17/89 | | Is the application ready yet? (Beth Jillford) |
| * | 7.4 | 02/22/89 | | Not yet (Ed Sands) |
| * | 8 | 02/11/89 | 2 | OS/2 Users (Frank Bobson) |
| * | 8.1 | 03/14/89 | | Newswire Application Available? (Martin Roth) |
| * | 8.2 | 03/15/89 | | Industry Newswire is great (Steve Wright) |
| * | 9 | 02/24/89 | 4 | Problem in detecting @Doclevel in formula (Sam Grahm) |
| * | 9.1 | 03/06/89 | | Same problem with @DocChildren (Dave Turkot) |
| * | 9.2 | 03/08/89 | | It's a feature, not a bug? (Dave Turkot) |

Example: Product Discussion - Main View

**FIGURE 2.3** A Discussion database provides views (like this one from Notes' Product Discussion example) that group topic documents and responses in a way that visually indicates structure and provides information such as the number of responses.

## Support Beyond the LAN

Notes reaches beyond the confines of a single server or local area network. To share applications and information across many servers and networks, Notes replicates applications from one server to another across telephone lines or wide-area network connections. (For a fuller discussion of replication, see Chapter 7 on administering the Notes server.)

The Notes replication architecture is very different from wide-area networks, which typically use leased lines to keep multiple local area networks and mainframe computers in constant communication. Notes servers communicate only occasionally to update databases, on schedules set up by the Notes administrators, across communications links that are much less expensive than dedicated wide-area links. While this "seldom connected" communication scheme wouldn't work for traditional transactional database applications, it is well suited to the nature of the information and communication managed by Notes, which doesn't need to be updated on a minute-by-minute basis.

Notes also reaches beyond the LAN through electronic-mail gateways that transfer Notes E-mail to messaging systems such as PROFS, and systems based on the MHS and X.400 protocols, and customized programs that use the Notes application programming interface (API) to connect to external data sources such as newswires and financial data feeds. (For more on gateways and the API, see Chapter 9.)

# Security Features Of Notes

In business, access to sensitive information must be protected. Notes meets the needs of business for confidentiality and security by incorporating security provisions unparalleled in a networked PC program.

As a new user, you will receive an ID file created by the system administrator. This ID is entered into the Notes server's Name and Address Book, and it provides the basis for several of Notes' security measures.

You must provide your ID file to Notes when you log on to the Notes server —you may keep your ID on a floppy disk, or hard disk, or store it on the server protected by a password. Your possession of the ID is proof that you are who the ID says you are. Notes uses the ID to enforce security in several ways.

For example, when you create an E-mail message, Notes writes the name in your ID file into the "Author" field—it won't let you pretend you're someone else. E-mail can also be "signed" with an electronic signature that is part of the ID. The signature is used in a complex calculation that turns the number and placement of elements in the message into a numerical value—a value that changes if a single character is changed in the message. When the message is opened by its recipient, Notes recalculates the signature value and compares the result to the original sent with the message. If they differ, Notes informs the reader that the message has been tampered with.

Using encryption keys included in the user ID, messages can be encrypted so that only the intended recipient of the message can decode and read it. Even Notes servers have IDs, and data transmissions between servers may be encrypted, too, to guarantee that messages being replicated between servers aren't intercepted and read.

The ID file also plays a role in Notes' control of access to applications. The group lists that the administrator builds in the Name and Address Book have several functions. For example, all the individuals in a personnel department might be included in a group called "Personnel." Notes uses group lists to address electronic mail—the name "Personnel" can be used as the address for a message; every individual included in the group will receive a copy.

Notes uses the same group lists to control user access to applications. Every application includes a user access control list created by the application's designer. The designer can assign one of a range of access levels to each user or group list, to specify who may use the application and what they may do within it. One level allows users to read documents. Another level allows editing, and so forth.

In addition, the designer can assign privileges which selectively control who sees what even within an application. One user might be assigned privileges to see certain views and the documents that are indexed on them. Another user without the privilege would not even know the view existed—it wouldn't appear in her View menu. It's something like holding theater tickets: Some are given front-row seats; others without tickets can't get in. A few may even get backstage passes.

The ID file is such an important part of Notes security that it can be password-protected. When it is stored on the Notes server or a computer's hard disk, it can't be invoked without the authorization of its proper owner. (The ultimate security for an ID file, of course, is to put it on a floppy disk and keep it under lock and key.)

In addition to these security provisions based on the ID file and Name and Address book, Notes offers application-level security options as well. Documents and even individual fields within documents may be encrypted and the encryption keys distributed to a selected group. Then even users with access to the application and a privilege level sufficient to allow them to use the document won't be able to read it unless they have received the key. (For more on the role of access control and encryption see Chapter 7.)

# What Notes Is Not

Notes is obviously not traditional PC software. It does things traditional productivity software doesn't do. And it doesn't do things traditional PC packages do—many of them things we associate with database management, project management, or programs that wear the label of groupware. Many of these differences grow out of the "rarely connected" wide-area networking strategy invented by the developers of Notes.

Notes works best for collecting and providing access to information that doesn't change much once it is put into the database. The replication process in Notes that maintains multiple copies of databases is a marvelous solution for easily and inexpensively making large amounts of information available across long distances—so long as the information is relatively static. Where applications fit this model, Notes, with its very flexible application design tools, is a program with unprecedented power. But there are needs for data manipulation for which Notes is not well suited. The rest of this chapter examines these tasks and indicates why Notes is unsuited to them.

## Database Manager

Notes manages databases and stores information in field-oriented records, but it has little in common with familiar database managers, whether flat-file or relational.

The documents that hold data in Notes are roughly comparable to database records, and they capture data in fields. But Notes documents are expected to contain lengthy text—memos, reports, drafts of documents—rather than finely subdivided data, such as part numbers and inventory counts. There is a variety of field types in Notes, but data of the most commonly used type—the "rich text" fields that hold full text—cannot be indexed in views.

Notes is limited in its ability to manipulate data in reports. There is no provision for creating reports in Notes in the usual sense—no report writer, no *ad hoc* query capabilities. Notes views serve the function of reports, but users of a Notes database do not automatically have the capability to create a view—that's one of the privileges controlled by the database access control list, administered by the database manager. The limits on reporting are particularly obvious when it comes to manipulating numerical data: Views offer only the most basic summing functions within categories.

One of the most frequently heard criticisms of the first version of Notes concerned its lack of any protection against simultaneous changes to the data overwriting each other: Two users could open the same document and make changes to it without either being aware of the other. Even when User A saved her edited version, overwriting the original, she was left blissfully unaware of User B's existence. And when User B saved his version, it overwrote User A's changes, which were lost forever.

Protecting data against such overwrites has long been the basic requirement of any networked database manager—the data exists in only one version, and the program protects it with some form of file- or record- or field-locking to prevent two users from altering the same data at the same time, with the last change wiping out the prior.

But Notes databases can exist on multiple Notes servers that are not always connected to one another. And the program's replication algorithm treats all the copies equally—there is no one master copy, and changes made in any copy will eventually find their way into all the others. The "seldom connected" networking architecture of Notes and its replication of databases are central elements of the program. Adding record or field locking would completely change the nature of the program and the economy of its use.

The current version of Notes, Version 2.0, provides some safeguards against overwriting without making radical changes in the program's structure.

As a part of every document, Notes tracks the dates it was revised and the extent of the changes. The replication process uses this revision history when it propagates changes between two copies of a database. In Version 2.0, Notes checks the revision history to see if the version being saved is the direct descendent of the original, or whether an intervening copy has been opened by another user. If two users have edited a document at the same time, their versions are saved as responses to the original, and marked in views with a diamond symbol.

If the simultaneous revisions have taken place in separate copies of the database Notes will look at the revision history when it replicates the changes. The version that has been changed the most since the last replication will replace the original document, with any other versions becoming responses to it.

A minority opinion holds that overwriting is not in fact a real problem within Notes' frame of reference, and the reaction against it is simply a prejudice carried over from experience with conventional network database managers. According to this school of thought, Notes doesn't have to provide record or file locking because its designers didn't imagine that the kind of information Notes databases are intended to store (full text with associated categorization) generally would be open to editing by any user.

One edit overwriting another should occur infrequently, and it is best controlled by careful design of the application. If several people are likely to be editing documents in an application, the document each edits should be a response document—a new document that inherits most of its attributes, including its editable text, from the original, and is grouped with the original in a view. With access rights for the database set so that only the document author or the database manager can edit documents, overwriting problems shouldn't occur.

## Transaction Processing System

Notes' "seldom connected" networking makes it unsuitable for use as a transaction-based application—one in which many users constantly change and update data. Airline reservation systems are an extreme example of a transaction system, with a constant flow of reservations and confirmations and seat assignments for which the computer (networks of mainframes in these cases) must act as doorman and security guard.

But even much smaller database applications are built on transactional models. Small-business accounting systems that support order-entry or point-of-sale modules are transaction-based, processing individual orders and updating inventory records in real time, so that if inventory of an item is exhausted, the next order for it won't be accepted.

Notes lacks the record and file locking it would need to play traffic cop to such a centralized database. It also lacks the high-speed wide-area communications typical of large transaction-processing systems. While accounting systems typically run on a single LAN, the airline reservations systems are built on wide-area networks that use very high-volume communications technologies.

Notes' replication scheme wasn't intended to manage such real-time data communications over long distances. Rather, it was designed to eliminate the need for such communications by maintaining multiple copies of the information on the local area networks where it is used. The replication process that keeps two copies of a Notes database in synch with each other doesn't need expensive high-speed modems, multiplexers, and leased lines. It can run over dial-up telephone lines using off-the-shelf modems. As a result it runs relatively slowly: Replication is controlled by the Notes system administrators and can be run as often as necessary, but the time frames are more comfortably measured in hours than in minutes. Applications that call for minute-by-minute monitoring, transaction-by-transaction processing, are not what Notes is good for.

# Group Authoring System

The limitations of data protection and transaction tracking also make Notes an inappropriate choice for a group whose members must all work directly on a set of shared documents.

Group-authoring systems typically track changes in a document either by creating a variant version each time the document is changed, or by "redlining" the text—indicating by color or typeface which editor made which changes.

Notes does neither of these things. It doesn't automatically save all versions of a document—the winner in any conflict overwrites the original. Nor does the program provide redlining functions for comparing two documents to pinpoint differences. (Two versions of a document could, of course, be opened in side-by-side windows and compared visually, but this is tedious at best.)

Notes does work well for the kind of group authoring done in a discussion database. One member of the group drafts a document that becomes a main topic document in the application. The other group members contribute comments, critiques, additions, and revisions which appear in the database as response documents. The original author can then cut and paste among the documents to incorporate changes as she sees fit to produce a new version—and the comment cycle starts over.

# Group Calendar/Meeting Scheduler

There is no agreement on what groupware means, but many of the programs in this category include some form of calendar or schedule shared by the group: Each member enters his or her schedule into the program, and any member can see the schedule of any other member. (To preserve some privacy, the programs typically don't display the appointment list, but rather, a block chart that represents time committed and time free.)

These programs are most often used to help automate meeting schedules. The meeting organizer enters the list of invitees, and the program displays a chart of the combined schedules for the group, so that the convener can choose the time with the fewest conflicts. Then the program adds the meeting to each person's schedule, sends E-mail messages announcing the meeting, describing it, and requesting confirmation, and notifies the convener as the confirmations are returned.

Notes provides few of the functions of such automated scheduling systems. But whether a scheduling function is a major lack in Notes is another issue for discussion, much like its lack of record and file locking. Notes is simply oriented in another direction. Scheduling programs offer messaging and record-keeping functions that coordinate work-related communication. Notes provides an environment in which work can be done and shared, and the very necessary communication about the work can be integrated into the process rather than separated from it.

## Project Management Tool

Notes helps manage projects, as the Corporate Software example in Chapter 1 shows, but it is not a project-management package.

Project managers combine a database of tasks, dates, and durations with graphical output—the PERT and Gantt diagrams and similar chart formats. Project managers have two major uses, both related to their graphical nature. One is planning: Project management packages ease the process of identifying, ordering, and adjusting the component tasks of a project. The other is reporting: A Gantt chart is a good way to communicate work done—plans made and schedules met or missed.

Notes lacks the specialized database and charting functions of a project manager. Its discussion applications and electronic mail, its document management, and especially its status tracking can be woven together into an integrated system for executing an information-centered project. Just as with meeting schedulers, Notes provides tools for communicating the work itself, rather than for communicating *about* the work before and after the fact.

# Summary

The major functional areas of Notes—information management, workgroup communications, and security—are intended to support groups rather than individuals, and this added dimension makes these functions distinctly different from familiar examples of PC software such as word processors and database managers.

Notes applications, or databases, package information and the tools devoted to working on it. The information is created in forms, stored in documents, and organized in views. The fields in a document can be as short as a number or a name, or as long as a complex report with formatted text and graphics.

Notes doesn't create any barriers between information management and communication: Electronic mail is structured like any other Notes application, and any form can be designed to be sent as an E-mail message. As a result, Notes' communication and information management combine to make possible complex communication structures beyond the capabilities of simple electronic-mail systems.

All of this sharing of information takes place within an environment of security unparalleled among PC applications. Notes' security features work in many ways to insure the legitimacy of messages and their authors, as well as the confidentiality of applications and E-mail, by employing a complex arrangement of protected user IDs, encryption and decryption techniques, and access controls.

This combination of strengths makes Notes suited to roles in business that no other PC program can fill. But by the same token, there are familiar tasks filled by PC programs that Notes is not well suited for. Its "seldom connected" wide-area networking replicates databases in order to provide access to the same information in many places at once—exactly the opposite of transaction-processing systems based on instant communication with a centralized database, for such uses as airline flight reservations. Likewise, Notes is not well suited to project management applications, shared document authoring and editing, or group-scheduling and calendaring tasks.

# Section 2
# Using Notes

Notes provides new tools to groups by building on the benefits PCs provide to individuals. For individuals using Notes, the program is similar to other PC software packages—particularly such integrated programs as Microsoft Works or Lotus Symphony, programs with several functions that share a common command set and consistent interface.

But while these traditional integrated packages run on a single PC and aim at enhancing the productivity of individual users, Notes runs on a network of PCs, and aims at enhancing the productivity of groups. To accomplish this it adds functions—particularly communications and document management. These functions and the experience of learning and using them are examined in this section.

Chapter 3 covers the basics of using the program—how Notes appears to a user just beginning to work with Notes applications: creating and retrieving documents by using forms and views, sending and receiving electronic mail, using advanced editing tools to create complex documents, and running Notes remotely—either on a portable PC or a stand-alone desktop computer that communicates with a Notes server via telephone lines.

Chapter 4 reviews the application templates and example databases provided with Notes. The templates are a library of basic Notes applications. They are working applications, empty of data, that can be easily copied to quickly set up a simple application like a discussion database, or to supply a blueprint for the group-support functions within Notes. The example databases are more complex applications that indicate the possibilities of Notes: They indicate how the basic Notes functions can be customized and combined by users into applications that meet specific needs of organizations and take on familiar forms.

# Running Notes

**B**ecause Notes invites exploration, this chapter follows a new user of Notes as she explores, much the way any real user of Notes would. The new Notes user, Megan McDonnell, works for an insurance broker, Broward & Hastings. She has recently been promoted to a supervisory position at B&H, where she will lead a team working on some of the company's important accounts. Notes has recently been introduced into the company and Megan has been encouraged to use it to coordinate the work of her team.

The aim of this chapter is not to teach Notes, but to convey something of the experience of learning and using it. With that in mind, this chapter covers the basics of using Notes in a natural progression: Navigating the workspace, opening and using forms and views, creating and retrieving documents, sending and receiving electronic mail, creating complex documents, and running Notes remotely, on a portable PC or on a stand-alone desktop computer not connected to a network.

Considerable time is spent on the two main parts of any database, the forms and views, because understanding what these are and how to use them is important for new users.

Our new user also devotes time to reviewing a sample database called Sales Activity Report because it reflects the kind of tasks she envisions for the people in her workgroup—and the help she hopes Notes will give them. She also creates a database for her own team's use from the Client Tracking template. Megan felt that Notes would help her and her team in three main areas:

- Track their contacts with clients and maintain current information on them.

- Keep the group's superiors informed of its activities and issues it faced.

- Provide a forum for communicating information on clients, sales strategies, and the housekeeping details of meetings and events.

Although the Sales Activity Reports database does not exactly mirror this application as Megan envisioned it for her team, she found several of the forms and views similar to those she would need in her own reporting applications. The Client Tracking template was a good basis for keeping track of clients.

In the last section, when she uses Notes on a laptop that isn't connected to a LAN, Megan doesn't make major changes in what she uses Notes for — merely minor changes in the way Notes is set up. Using Notes remotely has implications for traveling employees, remotely located employees, and remotely located clients and vendors.

Even though what follows chronicles only Megan's early experiences with Notes and not also those of her team members, keep in mind that Notes is a group communications product: It is not meant to be used in isolation. In her exploration of Notes, Megan focuses on the kinds of group communications that she knows she will be part of. Many of the documents she creates and edits illustrate her desire to keep in touch with her team members and her superiors, to share information with them and to coordinate the members' work.

---

## Exploring Notes

As Megan began exploring Notes, she followed a progression common to new users:

- Exploring the Notes workspace and the special uses it makes of the standard Windows and OS/2 Presentation Manager interfaces

- Adding databases to the workspace and creating a new database from one of the templates

- Using views: Opening and closing documents, changing views, expanding and collapsing the view, and searching for text

- Using forms to create documents, learning types of keyword fields, editing and formatting Rich Text fields, printing

- Reading, creating, and sending electronic mail from her desktop PC in the office and from a portable while traveling

- Organizing the workspace and workpages

- Setting Preferences and View Icon options; using the Navigator

- Creating complex documents by means of Cut-and-paste, Dynamic Data Exchange (DDE), attachments, importing and exporting, DocLinks

# Beginning with Notes

Before Megan could begin to use Notes, the Notes administrator at Broward & Hastings had some work to do. He installed the program on Megan's PC, created her ID which automatically added her name to the Address Book, and he added the certificates she needed to access the servers. Much of his setup work involved commands on the Options menu: He used the User ID, New User, and Certify submenus to establish Megan as an authorized user and give her the certificates necessary to work on the network. She couldn't do this for herself, since certification must come from a Notes authority, not just any user. (Certification is discussed in Chapter 8.)

While the Notes administrator was still in Megan's office, he showed her how to do the first thing every new Notes user should do—create a password to protect her user ID (see Figure 3.1). Notes makes no compromises on security, even in details like the password. Its passwords are case sensitive (they can mix upper-case and lower-case letters), which makes them harder for unauthorized users to guess, but also harder for legitimate users to remember. And if a password is forgotten, the Notes account is lost—no one, not even the Notes administrator, can retrieve or change a password.

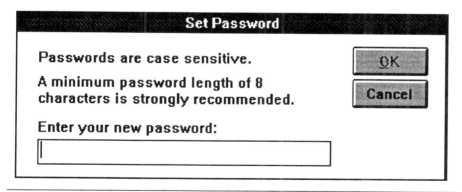

**FIGURE 3.1**   Setting a password in the Set Password dialog box is the first thing every new Notes user should do.

# Exploring the Notes Workspace

Megan was an experienced PC user, and it didn't take her long to notice that Notes adhered to the conventions of the Windows interface, but added a few details of its own. She discovered that it made its own use of the title bar across the top of each window. It also expanded the menu bar. The File and Edit commands were in their familiar places, but the commands that followed were different from those that appeared on the menu bars of the word processor and spreadsheet programs Megan had used (see Figure 3.2). Notes also added a third level of selection commands that Megan hadn't seen in any other Windows program: When Notes first started, up the screen displayed a row of six colored file folder tabs. Each tab represented a workpage. To select a workpage, the user clicks on a tab with the mouse.

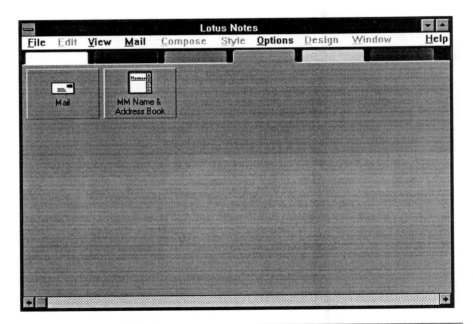

**FIGURE 3.2** The three major elements of the Notes screen are the title bar across the top of the window, the menu bar that lists the major commands, and the workspace—the rest of the window.

## The Title Bar

The title bar was always at the top of the screen while Megan was working in Notes, but it didn't always say "Lotus Notes." When Megan selected choices under the main menu items, the title bar acted as a Help system, displaying a brief explanation of the highlighted command. For example, when Megan selected the Open option from the Mail menu, the title bar text changed to display "Open your personal mail file." (This works only if Preferences are set for Menu Help. Preferences are discussed in detail below.)

Over time, Megan discovered that the title bar serves other purposes as well: When she ran Notes on a portable PC and dialed into a Notes server, the title bar displayed a message that indicates when communication has been established or disconnected. And very occasionally the Notes administrator at Broward & Hastings used the title bar as a minibillboard, a place to broadcast short, important messages to all users.

## The Menu Bar

The Notes menu bar is the user's tool for navigating, modifying, and designing Notes' databases. It also helps users access functions of Notes not directly related to the databases—printing, setting display and communications options, and security.

Not all the commands on the menu bar were familiar to Megan, but she understood the idea behind the menu bar itself from her experience with other Windows programs. Sandwiched between the title bar and the workpage tabs (see Figure 3.3), the menu bar offers a row of 10 commands beginning at the left of the screen with File and Edit and ending at the right with Help.

Selecting one of the menu options reveals a second level of related commands in the form of a drop-down menu (see Figure 3.3). The command groupings fall into logical categories. The File menu, for example, includes Browse, Copy, and Import commands that allow users to manipulate files. Because most of these commands require the user to make further choices, they open a third level, the dialog box. These dialog boxes may display information and accept data input. From the Options menu, for example, select Preferences, and the Preferences dialog box opens (see Figure 3.4), revealing directory, server, and file details and allowing the user to select from various run-time options.

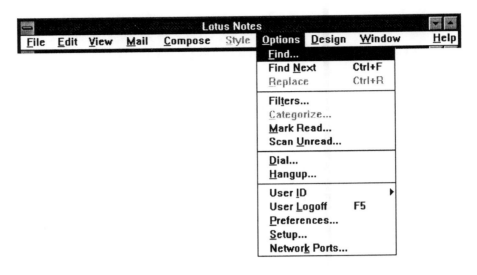

**FIGURE 3.3** The Menu Bar is always on-screen. Its 10 options represent groupings of Notes commands. Selecting an option reveals a drop-down menu that carries related commands.

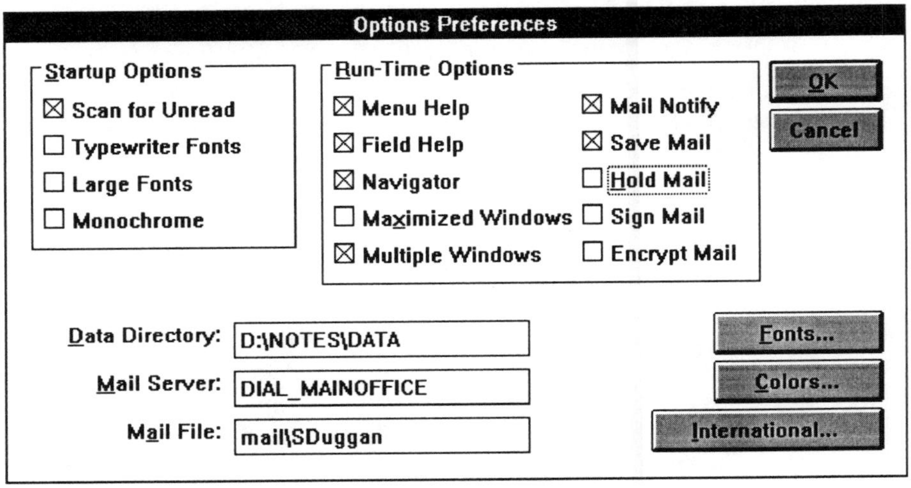

**FIGURE 3.4** The Options, Preferences dialog box displays option selections and user-specified data to be used by Notes.

---

## Choose Your Options

If you are working with Notes on a PC as you read this, take a minute to open the Options menu and verify some of the settings that affect your Notes screen display.

In the section headed Run-Time Options make sure Menu Help, Field Help, and Multiple Windows are selected, and Maximized Windows is not. An X in the box to the left of each choice indicates that it is selected.

Click the mouse once on the OK button when the settings are correct. The dialog box will close and you will be returned to the workpage display, with options set to match your screen display to the screen images in this book.

---

# The Workspace

The workspace with its six tabbed workpages was new to Megan but it took her only a minute to realize that clicking on one of the tabs was like opening one of a stack of file folders: A click on a tab brings that workpage to the top of the stack and makes it active. (The workpage tabs are gray, like the workspace, and blank when Notes is first installed; but they can be labelled and colored by double-clicking on the tab and entering a name in the dialog box that appears.)

When Megan added databases to her workspace, an icon appeared on the workpage open at the time. Each icon contained the application's title and a graphic device to identify it (see Figure 3.5).

**FIGURE 3.5**   This workpage includes the icons for Notes' example databases. The icons can also display the number of unread documents and the name of the disk file that holds the application.

Megan found she could easily move applications from workpage to workpage by selecting the icon and dragging it to the tab of the workpage where she wanted it to appear. The icon would disappear from the current workpage and appear on the new workpage when it was selected.

This flexibility of workpage names and icon groupings makes it easy for Notes users to customize their workspaces. A user may use all the workpages or only one. But most users will find that as they begin to work with several databases, it is helpful to group them by function, project, department, or area of responsibility. (When a screen fills up with icons, the workpage expands downward, and a scroll bar automatically appears to the right of the screen.)

# Adding Databases to the Workspace

No two Notes workspaces look the same because each user chooses the files that are on her desktop and adds or removes applications as needed. For example, Megan wanted to use some of B&H's existing databases and to create some new ones for her own use and for her group. To install the databases in her workspace, Megan clicked on the File, Database submenu (see Figure 3.6). She used the Add command to add files already existing on the network to her workspace and the New command to create custom databases for herself.

---

### 1 APPLICATION = 1 FILE

All the components of a Notes application are stored in one file. The file contains the forms, the views, and the users' documents, as well as more advanced tools such as filters that import, export, or reformat data.

These files are identified both by a file name used by the computer's operating system and by a title that appears in the application's icon box when it is installed on a user's workspace. Notes users tend to use the file names infrequently because the titles are more descriptive. However, there are times when it is necessary to know that actual file name. Both file names and titles show in the Database Add window.

---

Megan highlighted the names of the files she wanted to add and clicked on the Add Icon button. When she had added all the icons she wanted, she closed the window.

Megan also created a custom database for her group, using one of Notes' templates. The templates are ready-to-use files that include a range of forms

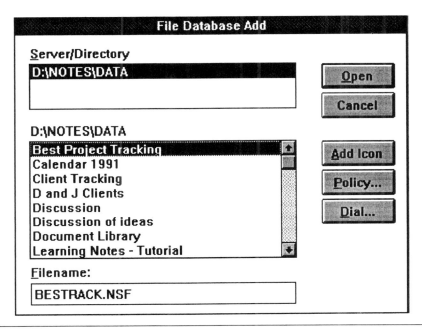

**FIGURE 3.6** The File, Database Add dialog window offers the list of servers and directories to which the user has access, as well as the application files in the selected directory.

and views but no data. They provide the basic structure for several types of applications, and serve as raw material for Notes users like Megan who tailor custom databases by copying a template and adding and modifying forms and views.

The available templates are listed in the File, Database, New dialog box. Megan chose the Client Tracking template and named her version "B&H Clients." When she selected New, Notes created the B&H Clients database, using the template as the basis for its forms and views (see Figure 3.7).

(Because templates provide the basic structure for an application, most Notes developers begin creating a new application by choosing the existing template most like the application they will create. Then they modify it, adding and changing views and forms. Megan added it to her own local hard drive. When she had modified it and was prepared to use it with her team, she notified the Notes administrator who would then add it to the server. Most Notes administrators find this is the best way to make sure servers do not become cluttered with test databases. They also work with the developers to make sure the databases replicate properly.)

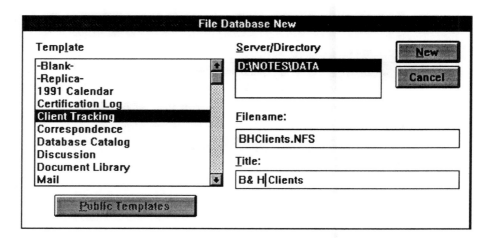

**FIGURE 3.7**   The application templates listed in The File, Database New window can be copied to start a new database.

# Opening and Using a View

Among the databases Megan had added to her workspace were a couple of the example databases that are provided with Notes. She opened the one titled Sales Activity Reports and read the Database Policy, the first screen to appear when a new user opens an application. The Database Policy is a brief statement about the application, its benefits, and how it works. When Megan closed the policy window, the Sales Activity application's default view appeared

The Sales Activity Reports database contains several sample documents related to a fictional software company. The default view, titled Executive View, sorts these documents into categories and subcategories (see Figure 3.8). It resembles an outline, with the topics of the individual documents forming the lowest level. By highlighting and double-clicking on a category, Megan could expand the view so that it listed the related subcategories; clicking on it again closed the list of subheadings and left only the main category headings. To open a document that interested her, Megan double-clicked on the topic.

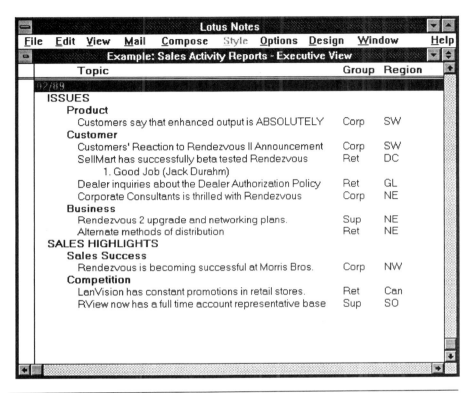

**FIGURE 3.8** The Sales Activity Reports Summary view lists documents in categories and subcategories, in a format that resembles an outline.

# The View Menu

The View menu provides a greater variety of ways to look at the data. It is divided into three sections (see Figure 3.9). The first is the Refresh command, which gives users an updated list of the database's contents. (When a user adds or removes documents, the view on the screen doesn't reflect the changes automatically. To update the view, the user must close and reopen the database—or use the Refresh command as a shortcut: by selecting it, users see the updated view without having to exit the database.)

The second section of the View menu controls the level of detail displayed in the view. The Expand, Collapse, Expand All, and Collapse All commands can reveal and hide subcategories and individual document listings in the view.

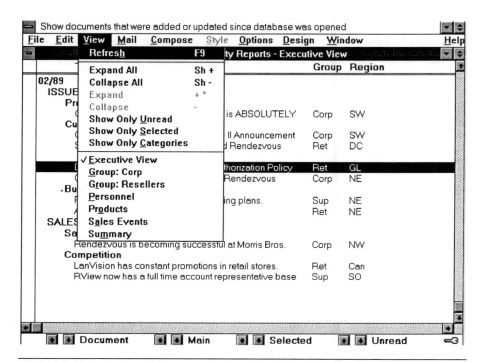

**FIGURE 3.9** The View menu includes commands that control which view is selected and how it is displayed.

Collapsing a view with many categories can make it much easier to find a particular document. With less to search through, Megan could find the general category and expand it until she found the document she was looking for (see Figure 3.10).

Megan quickly learned that many commands in Notes can be invoked in multiple ways. There are three ways to invoke the Collapse and Expand commands: by menu selection, with the mouse, or with the keyboard shortcut commands "+", "-", "SHIFT +", and "SHIFT -". Many commands within Notes can be invoked in these multiple ways.

The Show Only commands on the View menu work with categories of documents much the same way that the Collapse and Expand commands work with categories. They work like toggle switches—selecting a command once turns it on (and places a check mark beside it to indicate it's active); selecting it a second time toggles it off. The commands:

- **Show Only Unread** limits the view to documents not yet read by the user. It's a convenient way of checking a database for documents you haven't seen.

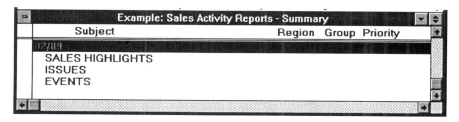

**FIGURE 3.10**  The Collapse All and Expand All commands have a major effect on the display of the view.

| Example: Sales Activity Reports - Summary | | | |
|---|---|---|---|
| **Subject** | **Region** | **Group** | **Priority** |
| **02/89** | | | |
| **SALES HIGHLIGHTS** | | | |
| **Competition** | | | |
| LanVision has constant promotions in retail | Can | Ret | Exec |
| RView now has a full time account represe | SO | Sup | Exec |
| SmartSoft was sufficiently immobilized by t | NY | Ret | High |
| LanVision is bringing their roadshow to the | NW | Ret | Med |
| **Sales Success** | | | |
| Rendezvous is becoming successful at M | NW | Corp | Exec |
| SI Systems has signed a Resellers Master | SO | Ret | High |
| Rendezvous-Unix continues to grow at Ban | NY | Corp | Med |
| Boston Trust Bank  has standardized on R | NE | Corp | Med |
| **ISSUES** | | | |
| **Business** | | | |
| Rendezvous 2 upgrade and networking pl | NE | Sup | Exec |
| Alternate methods of distribution | NE | Ret | Exec |

- **Show Only Selected** limits the view to documents selected either manually, by using the Find command, or by running a selection filter. The
  Find command, on the Options menu, searches for a specified text string
  in documents or views and marks every occurrence of a match. Selection filters are designed to select documents specified in a selection
  formula.

- **Show Only Categories** hides all documents and gives a bird's-eye view
  of the structure of the view. Megan found that, in a very large database,
  this command helped her zero in on the area of her interest.

The third section of the View menu lists all the views available in the active
database. The current view is always marked with a check. The Sales Activity
Reports application included seven views, which Megan moved among by

selecting the views with the mouse. Other databases have different numbers of views—the minimum is one, and the maximum is determined by the designer of the application.

As she worked with the View menu, Megan realized that its contents were context-sensitive: It listed one set of options when a database was open, another when all databases were closed (see Figure 3.11). In fact, this is true of many of the menus listed on the menu bar. As Megan opened and closed databases, items changed and some choices were deactivated. The View menu, for example, displays commands that affect the appearance of application icons when only icons are visible on the screen.

**VIEW MENUS**

| When database is open | | When form or document is open | | When databases are closed | |
|---|---|---|---|---|---|
| **Refresh** | F9 | Refresh Fields | F9 | **Refresh Unread** | F9 |
| Expand All | Sh + | **Edit Mode** | Ctrl+E | Edit Mode | Ctrl+E |
| Collapse All | Sh - | Show Ruler | | Arrange Icons | |
| Expand | + * | **Show Page Breaks** | | | |
| Collapse | - | | | Show Unread | |
| Show Only Unread | | Events | | Show File Names | |
| Show Only Selected | | Issues | | | |
| Show Only Categories | | Personnel | | | |
| | | Response | | | |
| Executive View | | ✓ Sales Highlights | | | |
| Group: Corp | | | | | |
| Group: Resellers | | | | | |
| Personnel | | | | | |
| Products | | | | | |
| Sales Events | | | | | |
| ✓ Summary | | | | | |

**FIGURE 3.11**  The View menu, like other items on the menu bar, changes as the Notes environment changes. With a database open it displays one set of commands, with a form or document open another, but with all applications closed it displays a different set.

## Searching for Text

Another way to show only a subset of documents is to use the Find command. Megan tried it out by searching for "resellers" in the Products view. First she typed "resellers" into the Options, Find dialog box (see Figure 3.12).

Next she chose the Search Selected Documents option and clicked the mouse on the Find All button. Because she hadn't marked any documents, a dialog box popped up asking if she wanted to search all the documents in the

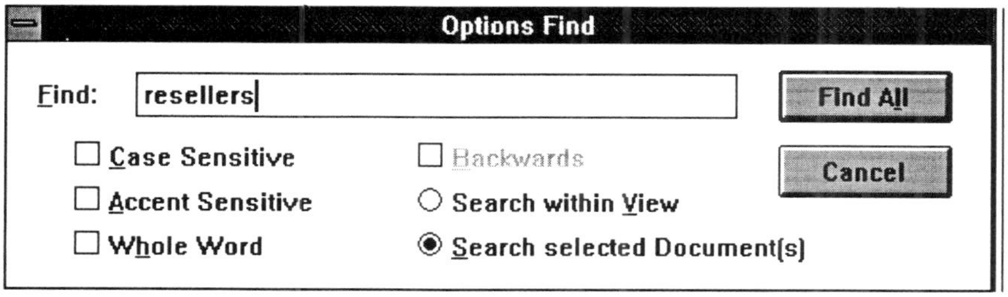

**FIGURE 3.12**  The Options, Find command searches for words or phrases. It can search just the text in a view, or all the text in all the documents included in the view.

view. She clicked OK. Notes searched through the text of all documents in the database and marked several which referred to resellers. Megan grouped the marked documents by choosing View, Show Only Selected. Only the marked documents appeared on-screen, which made it very easy for Megan to go quickly through them.

# Forms and Documents

The Sales Activity example database Megan had added to her workspace included a variety of documents. Each had been created using one of the forms listed on the Compose menu. To add a new document of her own creation, Megan clicked on Compose and selected the form called Issues. A new window headed Issues Form opened on the screen.

Notes automatically entered the date in the Date field, and put Megan's name in the From field. Megan tabbed through the rest of the fields filling in data. Relatively few fields required that Megan type in text (see Figure 3.13).

Several of the fields in the Issues form are keyword fields—one of several field types in Notes (see box, "Types of Fields"). A *keyword field* doesn't accept data entered by users. It presents the user with a list of choices. Using keyword fields makes it easy for the designer of an application to control what gets entered into fields that will be used as categories in views: It prevents misspellings and proliferating categories that might make the database less usable.

Megan tried to type into a text keyword field, but when she hit the first letter of a keyword from the list defined for the field, the entry would pop into the field. When she put the cursor in a field and hit the Return key, a dialog

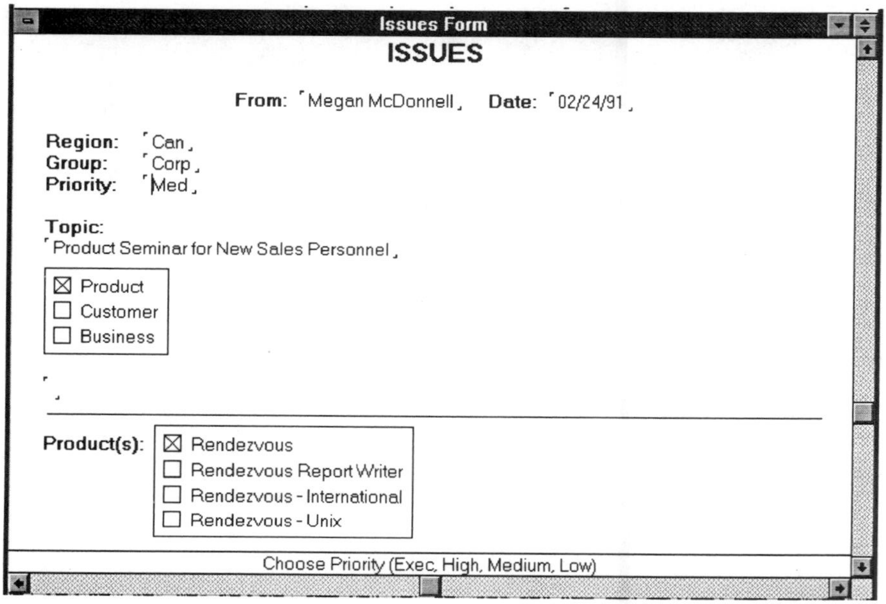

**FIGURE 3.13** Entering data in Notes doesn't always mean typing text. The Issues form uses check-boxes for some fields; other entries are selected from a list.

box opened containing the keyword choices for that field (see Figure 3.14). Or she could pop the available choices into the field one at a time by pressing the spacebar. Check-boxes and radio buttons look similar but work differently. Megan could make multiple selections in a block of check-boxes, but in a block of radio buttons, she could select only one keyword at a time—like a pushbutton tuner on a radio, when one button is selected, all others are "unselected."

## Changing the Style of Text

Megan noticed that when she selected "Issues" from the Compose menu, the Style option on the menu, which had been gray, turned black to indicate it was now active. But when she clicked on Style to display the Style menu, she found that none of its commands were active. She typed an entry *Organized Prospecting for New Business* in the Topic field, and opened the Style menu again, but it was unchanged. Only when she positioned the cursor in the issue

## Types Of Fields

Each field in a Notes form is assigned one of six data types. The types determine what may be entered in the field, how it is entered, or how Notes will use the data. The types are:

**Number**. The contents of Number fields can be used in mathematical calculations in views and formulas. They can include whole numbers, decimal fractions, scientific notation, and currency.

**Time**. A field type that enforces consistency in the entry and display of dates and times.

**Text**. Text fields can contain letters and numbers. Text fields are generally used for short bits of data — names, addresses, subject headings — that must appear in views. The text in a Text field appears in an assigned font and size; it can't be formatted by the composer of the document.

**Rich Text**. The Rich Text field type can hold a mixture of text, graphics, and charts. The text can be formatted in a variety of fonts, sizes, and colors. But text in a Rich Text field cannot be displayed in a view.

**Keyword**. Developers determine the list of terms allowed in keyword fields, and users are limited to those selections. Keyword fields are used where consistent spelling is important — for category names in views, or for the names of variable in formulas. Keyword fields can appear in the form of check-boxes, radio buttons, or standard blank fields.

**Document Author.** Notes automatically fills a Document Author field with the name of the user who creates the document. Author fields work with Notes security. Whenever a document is opened, Notes compares the current user's ID to any Author field in the document to verify the user's right to work with it. Document Author fields may be edited, but Notes will append "(alleged)" to the edited name to indicate politely that security may have been breached.

field itself, did the Style commands become active. She typed *IMMEDIATE action is needed*, highlighted the word *IMMEDIATE* with the mouse, and made repeated selections from the Style menu that made the word bold, underlined it, enlarged it two sizes, and finally colored it red.

Megan was able to do so much with the style of text in the Issue field because it is a Rich Text field. The contents of Rich Text fields can be extensively formatted in the Style menu — type font, type size and color, and the layout of the field can all be changed (see Figure 3.15).

There is a trade-off: Text entered in Text fields like the Topic field cannot be formatted with the Style menu. These fields are intended to hold a few words that will appear, like the Topic statements, in views. Rich Text fields cannot appear in views. (Designers can use the Style menu while they are

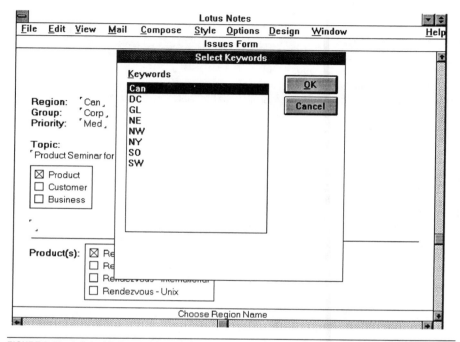

**FIGURE 3.14**   A dialog box for selecting the contents of a keyword field makes it easy to fill in the field consistently, without misspellings or mistakes.

creating new forms. For example, a text field can be formatted to appear in red boldface when data is entered, but users will not be able to change the formatting.)

## The Edit Menu

Megan found more commands for working with text on the Edit menu. Some of them she knew from other Windows programs—commands like Cut, Copy, Paste, and Delete. Others were unfamiliar—Paste Special, Links, Table, Encryption Keys (see Figure 3.16).

She was pleased to find a Check Spelling command, because she had learned to appreciate the convenience of the spell-checker in her word processor. The Style and Edit menus together provide Notes with all the necessities for creating and formatting text in Rich Text fields as either memos and

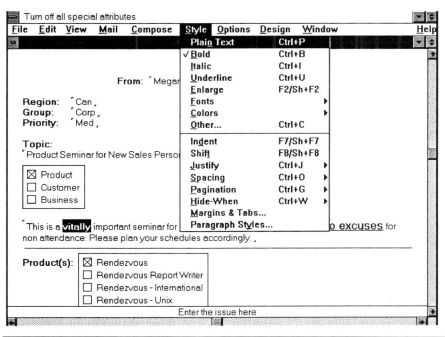

**FIGURE 3.15** The Style menu affects text entered in Rich Text fields. The commands in the top section change the appearance of text; those on the bottom control its positioning.

similar documents (the length of a Rich Text field is basically limited by available disk space) or, with the control over type size and color, and the importing of graphics, as presentations.

# Printing Documents and Views

Megan found all of Notes' printing controls under two entries on the File menu. She could choose a printer or change its settings under File Choose Printer, and from File Print she could print out either documents or views (see Figure 3.17).

With a view open in a window, she could print out the document the cursor was highlighting, the whole view, or selected document listings from the view. It took Megan a couple of tries before she learned that to print only selected lines in the view, they must be checkmarked in the far left column—either

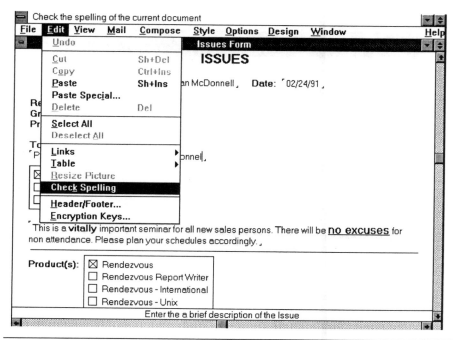

**FIGURE 3.16** The top of the Edit menu includes commands common to all Windows programs. Most of the bottom two sections are specific to Notes.

manually, or with a Find command, or by running a filter—before she selected Print View.

Two buttons in the File Print dialog box bring up other dialog boxes—one that controls some printer settings such as paper size and print orientation (portrait or landscape), and the Page Settings box (see Figure 3.18), which provides control over the appearance of the printed pages.

# Using Notes' Electronic Mail

Megan had used an electronic mail system before B&H installed Notes, so she found it very easy to make the transition to Notes E-mail. It not only worked like the E-mail she was familiar with (she could address messages to individuals or to groups, view an index of messages received, request a receipt to make sure the message was delivered), but it worked just like any other Notes

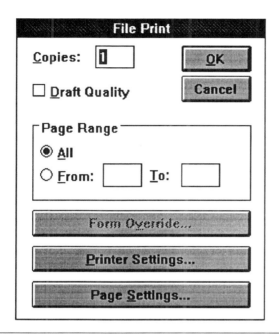

**FIGURE 3.17**  The File, Print, View box provides control over the number of copies to be printed, the range of pages to print, and printer and page settings.

database as well, using forms and views and menu commands. In fact, the only noticeable difference between her personal E-mail database and other Notes databases was that she was the only person with access to her E-mail. (This is configurable: The Notes user can grant another person access to his or her E-mail. Managers, for example, can give their secretaries access rights to their E-mail.)

Megan used Notes E-mail to communicate with her group, either in personal messages to individuals, or in messages addressed to the group as a whole. Megan also used E-mail to share documents with other people. For example, if she wanted one of her coworkers to look over a Lotus spreadsheet, she sent that spreadsheet file as an attachment to an E-mail message.

From the Mail menu Megan can open her mail database and view the documents in it (see Figure 3.19). She can also scan her mailbox for any unread messages. When she is composing a message, she can open a name and address book to check the name of a person or group by selecting an address. (This is especially helpful when she wants to send documents to someone whose name or spelling she cannot remember.) She can also forward a document to someone else.

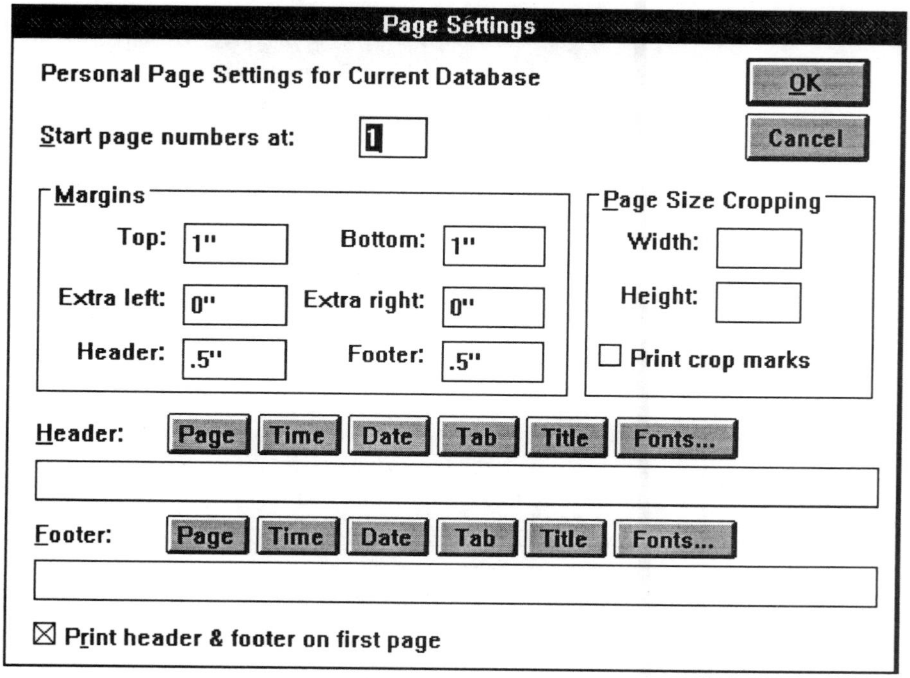

**FIGURE 3.18** The Page Settings dialog box provides control over the printed form of Notes documents: page numbering, margins, headers, and footers.

The last item on the Mail menu, the Send User ID command, is part of Notes' security system. Users can send three items: the Public Key part of their IDs that decrypts E-mail messages they encrypt; an encryption key that they have used to encrypt fields within a document; and a request to a Notes administrator to certify an ID so that they can log onto a Note server.

One of Megan's very first E-mail messages was a memo to the people in her work group urging them to attend an upcoming sales seminar. She selected Compose from the Mail menu, then New Memo.

The only field in the New Memo form (see Figure 3.20) that must be filled in is the "To" field. It must contain a valid Notes user or group name. Groups provide a very handy shortcut: Megan could have typed in the names of everyone in her workgroup. However, the Notes administrator had entered the names of these people in the Notes Name and Address Book as a group. All Megan had to do was to type in the group name, and Notes automatically distributed the message to all the group members. Every Notes user also has a personal Name and Address Book to enter names and create groups other than those in the Notes Name and Address Book.

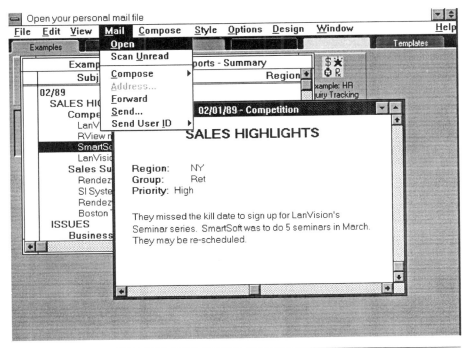

**FIGURE 3.19** E-mail is always available in Notes no matter what windows are open on the screen, just by selecting the Mail command on the menu bar.

Megan skipped the optional cc: and bcc: (courtesy copy and blind courtesy copy) fields and typed New Products Sales Seminar in the Subject field. She then wrote a short message asking everyone to attend the seminar.

The New Memo form had other fields Megan could accept or change. Because the members of her workgroup are all on the same server, they receive their mail as soon as Megan sends it. For this reason, she kept the default setting for the Delivery Priority field as Normal. For users who work on different servers connected by modem, Notes will batch the messages going to other servers until a predetermined time and send them all at once. If the message had been urgent, Megan could have changed the delivery priority to High. The server would then have dialed the recipient's server as soon as it received the message and sent it.

The other field Megan could change is Delivery Report. Its choices are No Report, Basic, and Confirmed. When Basic is selected, Megan receives a report on any messages the server cannot deliver. The report may explain that the message was addressed incorrectly, or that another server did not respond to a call. If the message went through correctly, Notes would not issue

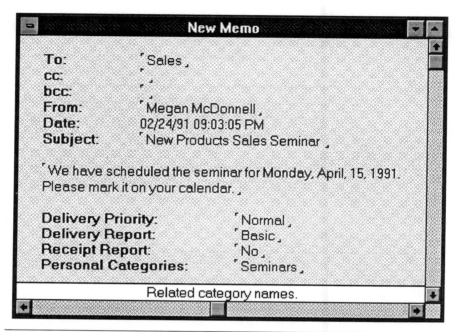

**FIGURE 3.20**  The New Memo form includes fields for carbon copies and blind carbon copies, and a Personal Categories field that can be used by the sender and recipient to help manage their mail.

any report. No Report means that Notes will not tell Megan if the message was undelivered. Confirmed, on the other hand, is like a return receipt. It notifies the sender that the message was delivered. (Confirmed cannot, however, report whether a user has opened and read the message.)

After she completed the memo form, Megan selected Send from the Mail menu. A small dialog window appeared offering her mailing options (see Figure 3.21). Sign adds an electronic signature to the message, which assures the recipient that Megan is the sender of the message. Encrypt encodes the document so that only the recipient can read it. Because the Sales Seminar message did not require these security features, Megan simply selected Send and the message was on its way. (Megan had already set her Preferences to Save Mail so that Notes would save a copy of everything she wrote in her own mail database.)

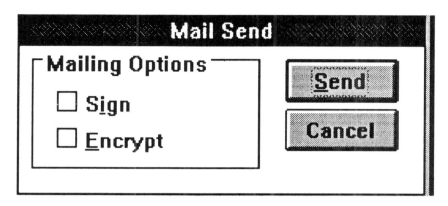

**FIGURE 3.21** The Mail Send dialog box includes two options, Sign and Encrypt, which increase the security of Notes electronic mail.

## Replying

When a member of Megan's team wanted to respond to her message, he chose the Reply form from the Mail Compose dialog box. This form has some special properties: If Megan's message was open or highlighted when he selected Reply, the To field automatically filled with Megan's name.

The Reply form is a different type of Notes document—it is a Response document. The New Memo form, in contrast, is called an Original or Main document. Most Notes applications include a form named Reply or Response. Differentiating document types helps Notes create the logical grouping of documents in views: an original document or E-mail message, followed by all the responses to it.

## Mail in Regular Databases

All any Notes form needs to become an E-mail message is a To field. This easy addition allows users to send documents to others who may not regularly use that database or have access to it, or to call special attention to a document (most users check their E-mail several times a day). Because Notes' E-mail can work with any document in any database, designers can build applications to do some very sophisticated things, such as mailing documents from one database to another. Some forms-tracking databases make extensive use of

E-mail for routing forms to the list of people who must approve them. Travel Authorizations, one of the example databases included with Notes, uses this capability.

# Customizing Notes

As Megan worked with Notes, she began to use more of the program's advanced features. When she had more than a dozen application icons in her workspace, she developed an organizational scheme that distributed groups of applications across several workpages. In addition, as other Notes users at Broward & Hastings became comfortable with the program, the number of new documents on the system began rising quickly. To help better organize the information, Megan began to use Notes commands that notified her of documents she hadn't yet read in important databases.

## Organizing the Workspace

As Megan looked at the applications in her workspace, she realized they fell into three categories: The first was her E-mail and applications devoted to internal communication within B&H. The second was databases related to activity reports and contact reports on clients and prospects. The third category was related to research—another group within her company was already distributing its reports in a Notes application and creating databases of information and news stories about B&H's clients and prospects.

Megan decided to set up three pages of her workspace to hold these three groups of applications. Megan opened the Workspace Page Name dialog by double-clicking with the mouse on the tab at the top of the page. She typed in a name for the page and chose a color for the tab. When she clicked OK, the tab appeared in the color she had chosen and with the name she had entered (see Figure 3.22). She set up the first three tabs as Mail, Clients, and Company News, each in a different color. The tabs don't have to be named and colored, but Megan found it helped her locate her files more quickly.

She moved the application icons to their appropriate workpages by clicking on each icon and dragging the mouse to the tab of the workpage where she wanted to place it. The icons disappeared from their former workpage and reappeared on the page to which she had moved them.

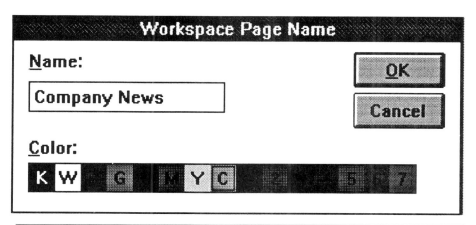

**FIGURE 3.22**  The Workspace Page Name window lets a Notes user set a name and a color for the workpage tabs.

## Setting Notification Options

As Megan became more confident with Notes, she learned how to use commands from the View and Options menus to tailor Notes to her preferences. Some of the commands affect the amount of information Notes displays. Others control how Notes notifies the user of new E-mail messages and unread documents in the applications.

When Megan selected the Show Unread option on the View menu, it displayed the number of documents Megan had not yet opened in each database (see Figure 3.23). Clicking on Show File Names displayed as much of the DOS filename for each application as would fit on a line across the bottom of each box. (This can be useful if you're trying to find a file to copy off to disk.)

A related command on the Options menu is Scan Unread. After clicking its Setup button (see Figure 3.24), Megan could use the Setup window to choose the applications she wanted to check regularly for new documents or messages.

After clicking on OK to save those settings, Megan could select Options, Scan Unread, and quickly step through the applications on the list. The dialog box's command buttons let Megan choose either to review the next database on the list or to skip to the next database containing unread documents (see Figure 3.25). She could click on another button to change all the unread documents' status to Read, or she could open the first unread document in the current database.

So that she would always be aware of new E-mail and documents, Megan selected Scan for Unread as a start-up option in the Options, Preferences

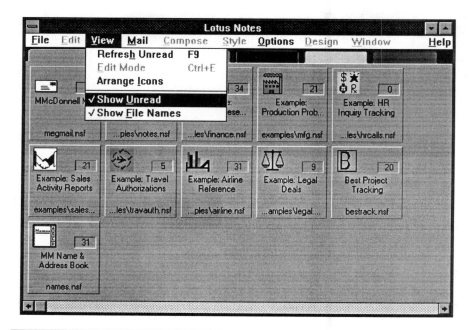

**FIGURE 3.23**   The two Show... commands in the View menu add information to the icon boxes.

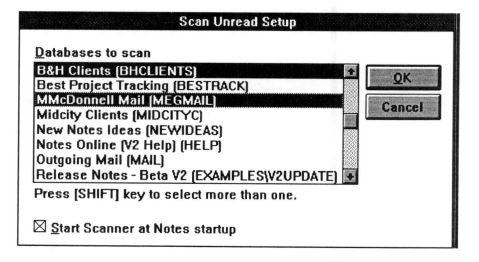

**FIGURE 3.24**   The Setup window for Scan Unread lets a user create a list of important applications to track for unread documents. The scanner can be set to run each time Notes starts up.

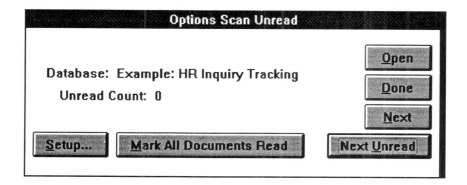

**FIGURE 3.25**   The Options, Scan Unread dialog box is the control panel for the scan function. It provides an easy way to check databases for new documents.

window (see Figure 3.26). After that, whenever she started up the program it automatically ran Scan Unread and informed her of new additions received since the last time she ran Notes.

# The Preferences Window

The Preferences window offers choices for modifying the Notes user interface. In this dialog window users most frequently modify the Run-Time Options (see Figure 3.26). Menu Help and Field Help determine whether Help descriptions appear in the menu bar as users move among fields. (Help for a menu bar command appears in the title bar; for a field, it appears at the bottom of the form window.)

Notes users who do not want more than one window to appear on the screen can select Maximized Windows, which opens each window to fill the entire screen. In some forms and views, this avoids having to scroll horizontally across the screen to see the entire view or document. Megan, however, liked opening more than one window at a time and decided to set up her screen for multiple windows. If she wanted to see a particular window in full screen, she could easily resize it.

Megan decided she wanted to keep a copy of the electronic mail messages she sent. She selected Save Mail, and Notes automatically left a copy of her correspondence in her mail database. Activating the Mail Notify feature causes Notes to beep softly and flash a message in the title bar when a user

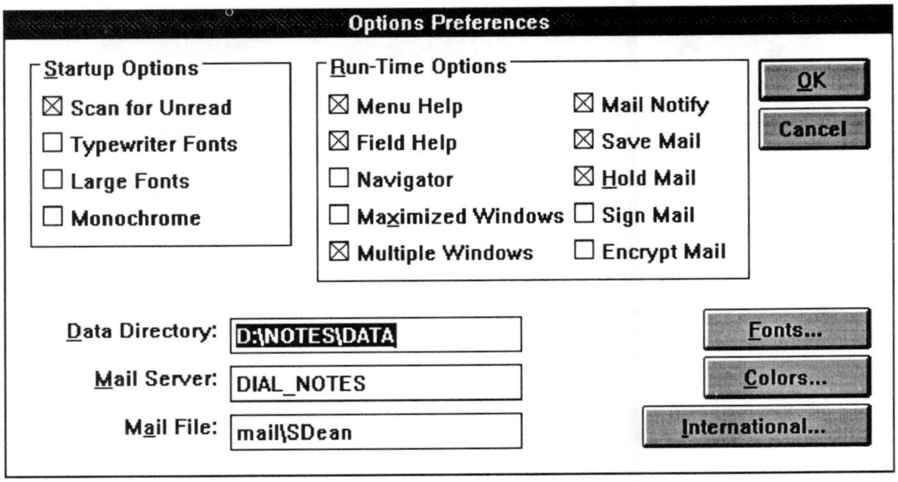

**Options Preferences**

┌─ Startup Options ─────────┐  ┌─ Run-Time Options ─────────────────┐
☒ Scan for Unread              ☒ Menu Help       ☒ Mail Notify
☐ Typewriter Fonts             ☒ Field Help      ☒ Save Mail
☐ Large Fonts                  ☐ Navigator       ☒ Hold Mail
☐ Monochrome                   ☐ Maximized Windows  ☐ Sign Mail
                               ☒ Multiple Windows   ☐ Encrypt Mail

[OK]
[Cancel]

Data Directory: `D:\NOTES\DATA`
Mail Server: `DIAL_NOTES`
Mail File: `mail\SDean`

[Fonts...]
[Colors...]
[International...]

**FIGURE 3.26**   The Options/Preferences dialog box is an important control panel for customizing Notes.

receives new mail. Hold Mail is important for laptop and remote users, because it holds all mail message a user creates in a mailbox file until she logs into the server via modem. Users on the LAN do not need this feature, since their mail is sent as soon as they finish it.

Megan didn't select Sign Mail or Encrypt Mail. Signing is a way of authenticating the name of the sender. Encrypting the message encodes it so that it cannot be decoded and read by anyone other than the person to whom it was addressed. Megan didn't feel that her correspondence would be confidential enough to require signing and encryption. For the few occasions when she wanted such security, it was always available from the Mail menu.

The path names in the Data Directory, Mail Server, and Mail File were automatically put in by Notes. She did not change them.

None of these decisions was irrevocable for Megan. Because the Preferences submenu is always available from the Options command on the menu bar, Megan could easily change the settings at any time.

## The Navigator

One of the options in Preferences is the Navigator, a bar which can be set to appear at the bottom of the screen whenever an application is open. The Navigator provides a set of mouse-selectable buttons that serve as shortcuts for moving among the documents listed in a view, without having to redisplay the view itself.

The four sets of buttons provide four kinds of movement forward and backward through a view (see Figure 3.27). Clicking on the "down" arrow beside "Document" displays the next document in the sequence listed in the underlying view: The "up" arrow brings up the previous document. "Main" jumps to the next or previous major topic document, passing over documents that are responses to topics. The "Selected" arrows work with documents selected by a Find command and "Unread" does the same for unread documents.

**FIGURE 3.27** The Navigator bar, on the bottom line of the screen, provides shortcuts for moving among documents in a view. The key is a symbol indicating the user's access level for the database.

# Creating Complex Documents

As their experience with Notes increased, Megan and her co-workers began to put Notes to work on tasks for which they had previously used other programs. For example, they produced complex reports that included text, spreadsheet data, and graphics. Notes easily imported data from other programs, whether blocks of text selected from open files or whole files that have been saved to disk.

## Cut, Copy, and Paste

Cut, Copy, and Paste are editing functions common to most programs that run under Windows. They use the Windows *clipboard*, which is a holding area in memory. Text, graphics, or charts can be copied to the clipboard in one program, then pasted into another program.

When Broward & Hastings put in Notes and Windows, the company also chose a Windows word processor as its standard. Megan's earliest experience with moving data across the boundary between Notes and other programs was using the Cut, Copy, and Paste commands. As she worked on a report, Megan could open a Notes document or E-mail message, copy text to the clipboard, open her word processor in another window, and paste that text into a file.

---

### Notes' Data-Gathering Tools

- Cut, Copy, and Paste move text, tables, and graphics among Notes documents, or between Notes documents and other programs.

- Import and Export move complete files. Import brings a file into a Notes document. Export saves all or part of a Notes document as a file outside of Notes.

- Dynamic Data Exchange (DDE) uses Windows and OS/2 functions to link two files, so that changes made in one are mirrored in the other.

- Attach and Extract, the Attachment commands, append a data file to a Notes document so that they can be stored or transmitted together, then separated again.

- DocLinks, found under Links on the Edit menu, don't copy or move text between Notes documents. They switch between documents. A DocLink symbol in text is an automated cross-reference. Click on it and whatever document the author wanted the reader to refer to, is opened.

---

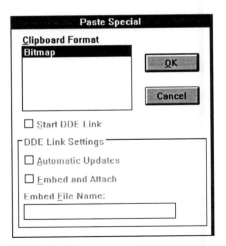

**FIGURE 3.28** Paste Special sets up a DDE link between a Notes document and a file created with another Windows program. Changes made to the file in that program appear in the Notes version, too.

# Using Dynamic Data Exchange

Cut-and-paste is a one-time operation: A user can make subsequent changes in the original text, but the pasted version does not change. It is possible to make copies that change as changes are made in the original by using Windows' Dynamic Data Exchange

Dynamic Data Exchange (DDE) connects files created by different Windows applications so that when changes are made in one file they are automatically reflected in the other. DDE offers a great connectivity advantage for people who work with applications designed to work under Windows 3.0, and it is fast and easy to use.

For example, if Megan used Word for Windows to create a proposal, and she wanted all or part of that proposal to appear in her Notes database too, she could create a DDE link by using the Edit, Paste Special command (see Figure 3.28). She could make changes to the proposal document in Word, and when she ran Notes and opened the version of the proposal included as a Notes document, those changes would also be made there. She would not have to switch to Word to see the proposal (but because the DDE link works in only one direction, she would still have to switch to Word to make changes). In a DDE link, one program acts as a server, maintaining the file and changes made to it, and another program acts as a client. The client can receive and display information from the server, but it cannot send that information to other programs. The Paste Special command makes Notes a DDE client. It cannot be a DDE server.

DDE can be a help in composing a Notes document, but once the document is distributed, the advantages of DDE are diminished. A DDE link includes a path statement pointing to the application that created the material in the document. Because the Notes replication process may send a document into a system very different from the system where it was created. The path specified in the DDE link is unlikely to be valid, and the link will be broken.

DDE was a first step toward a compound-document model for data in Windows. Version 2 of Notes can also work with a more advanced technology, called Object LInking and Embedding (OLE). OLE treats the components of a document—each block of text, each graphic, each table—as individual objects. Each object contains information not displayed on the screen but accessible to Windows, including the name of the application that created it. When the appropriate OLE server applications are available, for example, a user who wants to make changes in a graph included in a document would double-click on it and Windows would search the hard disk for the creating application. It wouldn't need a specific path, as it does now for DDE. OLE has other possibilities as well, such as building modular programs that can call on common functions: a spreadsheet and a presentation-graphics program might share a graphing module, for instance.

## Importing into a Document

Megan and her coworkers use Lotus 1-2-3 extensively to create worksheets documenting their recommendations for client coverage. Worksheet data and graphs are frequently included in reports, and the Notes users found that the Import function made it easy to import files.

Notes imports a variety of text, graphics, database and spreadsheet files. File format conversions are provided for ASCII text, 1-2-3 files, and 17 popular word-processor and graphics file formats.

Using the Import command requires a basic understanding of DOS filenames and directory structure. The File Import dialog window (see Figure 3.29) allows the user to set the directory and file to import on the left side of the box. The right side of the dialog box lists the format conversions available within Notes. When the user selects a file to import, Notes identifies its format and automatically highlights it in the conversion list box. For example, if the user selects a file created with PC Paintbrush, with the file extension .PCX, Notes highlights PCX Image in the conversion box.

Most word-processor files can be brought into Notes Rich Text fields with their formatting intact, and the text can be edited in Notes as well. Graphics files can be resized in Notes (using the Resize Picture command on the Edit menu) but they cannot be edited. Spreadsheet files come in as text only — they lose their cell formulas and macros, so they cannot be changed and recalculated.

## Using Attachments

Before Notes was installed, Megan and her coworkers shared their 1-2-3 work-sheets by "sneakernet" (passing floppy disks around the office by walking from desk to desk). Notes E-mail quickly became the favored means of circulating these worksheets: Staff members could jot an E-mail message and use the Attachments command on the File menu to electronically clip the worksheet to the message. The recipients would use the Extract command to copy the worksheet into a DOS subdirectory and then leave Notes and open 1-2-3 to view it.

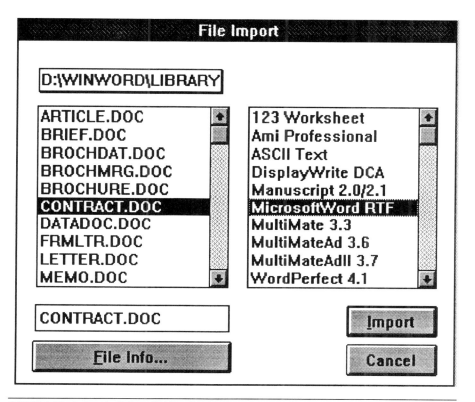

**FIGURE 3.29** To import a file into a Rich Text field in a Notes document, the user selects the file on the left side of the File Import screen, and the proper conversion on the right.

---

## From View to Database File

Import and Export work with Notes views as well as with forms, providing a way to move data between Notes and database managers such as dBASE. Notes doesn't directly import database file formats such as dBASE's .DBF files. These files must first be saved in delimited format, or as structured ASCII text. Notes works particularly well with 1-2-3 and Lotus Agenda: It can read and write 1-2-3's .WK1 files and Agenda's .STF files directly to and from Notes views.

---

Attachments are files created outside of Notes which are physically appended to a Notes document. The file can contain text or binary data—graphs and graphics files are easily attached to a Notes document (which can

make a Notes application   an easy-to-use database of materials that are otherwise hard to index).

The Attachments dialog box is opened from the File menu. The left-hand
window lists the files in a disk directory, and the right-hand window lists the
files attached to the selected document. A pull-down box lists the files and
directories available to the user (see Figure 3.30). The file is selected either
by bringing it into the list window on the left and highlighting it, or typing in
its path and filename. Clicking on the Attach button attaches the file. Its name
then appears in the list window on the right. The Compress option saves disk
space by compressing files as they are attached. Extracting a file from a
document automatically uncompresses it.

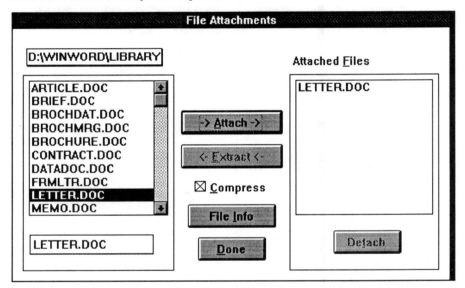

**FIGURE 3.30**   Files of any type or size can be attached to a Notes document for storage, then later extracted from it
using the File Attachments dialog box.

Attached files cannot be opened in Notes. The file must first be extracted
from the Notes document, and then opened using the application with which
it was originally created. This means that the recipient must be able to run the
program that created the file, but it also means that the program can be any
DOS or OS/2 application—it doesn't have to be a Windows or Presentation
Manager application.

For example, if one of Megan's clients sent her a WordPerfect 4.0 file that
Megan wanted to reference in Notes, she could attach the file to a document.
To use that WordPerfect document later, she could extract the file and open it

using WordPerfect. (Alternatively, she could extract the file and then use Import to bring it into a Notes Rich Text field for editing.)

Attachments are different from DDE-linked documents. DDE links are *dynamic*, and can be updated automatically or with a single keystroke as the originals are changed. Attachments are *static*—their contents do not change, once they are attached. As Windows-based programs that support linking become more widespread, Notes users will probably use the attachment feature less. However, attachments can be valuable historical records. Sometimes users want to see a document in its original form, not its updated form.

## Using DocLinks

DocLinks are very different from the other methods of assembling text. While those functions can copy or move text between two documents, a DocLink creates a link from one document to another (see Figure 3.31). To activate the link, the user double clicks on it with the mouse and the linked document opens in a separate window. To indicate a DocLink, Notes puts the symbol of a miniature window—a small rectangle—in the Rich Text field where the link is made.

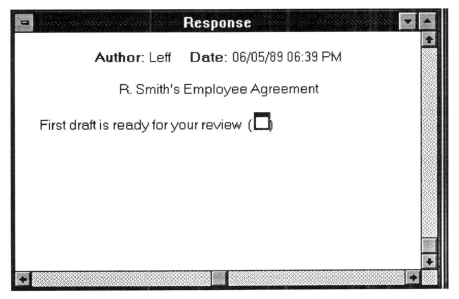

**FIGURE 3.31**   The DocLink symbol, a miniature window embedded in the text of a document, indicates a linked reference to another document. Double-clicking on a DocLink opens the linked document.

DocLinks provide a rudimentary *hypertext* function that can be especially useful in building databases of reference material. (Hypertext systems manage large numbers of documents, providing access by indicating links between related documents, or even related ideas in different documents.) DocLinks are best for providing easy access to a document, rather than pinpointing reference to a particular phrase or section—a DocLink points to a whole document, not to a specific text within a document. DocLinks work only within Notes. The two documents don't have to be in the same database, but both the creator of a DocLink and its user must have access rights to both databases and documents. One of the best examples of DocLinks is Notes' own Help database. It cross-references hundreds of related documents by means of DocLinks.

The great advantage of DocLinks is that they reduce the need to duplicate text. Information that must be updated can be stored just once in the database. When it is changed, the change is immediately available to anyone who opens a DocLink to it. This can save time updating several occurrences of the same text, as happens in procedures manuals or reference materials. A DocLink also saves disk space by avoiding document duplication.

DocLinks make it easy to refer readers to another document. Doclinks work like automated cross-references, providing a shortcut method of opening a document. Megan wanted one of her new staff members to read how B&H had arrived at a decision to issue fire insurance to a client. To do so, she opened the document containing the background on the decision and selected Edit, Links, Make DocLink. This resulted in a message from Notes in the title bar: DocLink copied to clipboard. Use Paste to insert it into a document.

Megan then opened a new Mail memo form and, in the Message field, she asked the staff member to read the document about the client's policy. She positioned her cursor where she wanted the DocLink icon to appear and selected Paste from the Edit menu. The DocLink symbol appeared there to indicate that a link had been established between the two documents. When the staff member opened the E-mail message, he could double-click on the DocLink to move immediately to the document Megan wanted him to read.

# Remote Notes

Megan decided to try Notes on a laptop computer when she was sent out of town to a two-week training seminar. She wanted to stay in touch with the home office and to continue to use electronic mail and the databases she shared with her group. She also planned to continue work on the tracking database she was developing.

The company provided Megan a laptop with Windows 3.0 already loaded. With the help of the Notes administrator, she installed Notes, setting it up as a dial-up workstation. Megan probably could have done this alone, but she asked the administrator for help because she was in a hurry and wanted to make sure she was doing everything correctly. The Dial-up (Laptop) Workstation option (selected in the Options Setup dialog box, see Figure 3.32) automatically configures Notes for remote use. It differs from a regular workstation setup in three ways:

- It sets up a replica mail database to duplicate Megan's mail on the Notes server to her laptop. (For workstations on a LAN, the user's mail file resides on the server.)

- It sets the COM port as the default for communications. (When a user is connected to a LAN, one of the LAN ports is selected.)

- It selects Hold Mail in the Option Preferences window. This creates a file on the laptop that holds all the mail messages she composes until they are transferred during dial-up. Users on a LAN do not need this file because the server routes mail as soon as it is received.

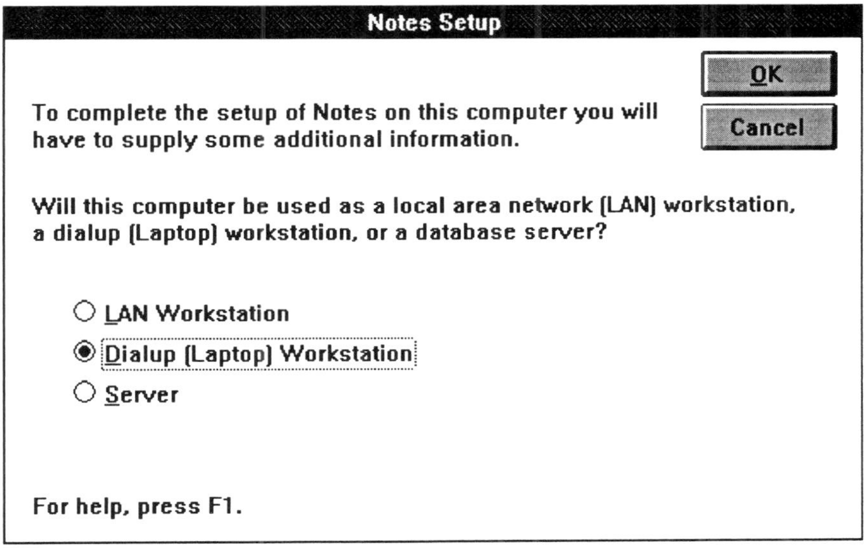

**FIGURE 3.32**  For remote use, Notes must be set up as a Dialup (Laptop) Workstation. This creates a local E-mail application and mailbox to store outgoing messages.

After she installed Notes, Megan copied her USER.ID file—the same one she used on the network—to the laptop. Then she went into the Name and Address Book and opened a Remote Connection document, in which she recorded the information Notes needed to connect via telephone lines to the server. She also opened the Options, Network Ports, Setup Modem window and selected the modem she was using from the list there. (If her modem had not been listed, someone could have created a command script for it, but that would have required more technical understanding than Megan had.)

The last thing Megan had to do was to choose the databases she wanted to replicate. Because the 40-megabyte hard disk on her laptop contained several other applications besides Notes and Windows, her storage space was limited. Also, she assumed that she would be busy enough at the seminar that she would only need the essential tracking and discussion databases. The discussion database had grown quite large and Megan wanted access just to the documents created in the last two weeks.

First, she had to create replicas on her laptop for the tracking and discussion databases which resided on the server. (The setup process created the replica for her E-mail.) A *replica* is an empty file that acts as a placeholder until replication occurs (see Figure 3.33). It identifies the name and location of the laptop file and the server and file name which it will replicate. It needs to be created only once.

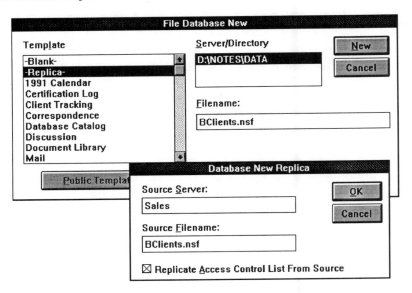

**FIGURE 3.33**   Copying a database to a portable PC begins with creating a replica file, naming it, and specifying a path to the source in the File Database New and New Replica dialog boxes.

Megan wanted to duplicate every document in the tracking database, but only recent the documents from the discussion database. To limit the latter to those created within the last two weeks, Megan opened the Database, Information, Replication window of the discussion replica and set up a purge interval and cutoff date for replicated documents (see Figure 3.34).

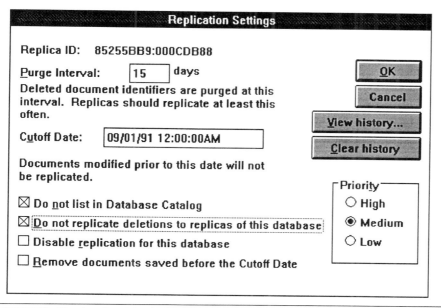

**FIGURE 3.34** Choosing a Purge Interval and Cutoff Date in the Replication dialog box instructs Notes to remove older documents—an advantage for laptops with limited storage.

As stated earlier, Megan didn't want anything older than two weeks in the discussion replica. Because the date she started using the laptop was September 15, she set the cutoff date to September 1. When she replicated for the first time, the server would transfer to the laptop only documents created or modified since September 1.

Next, she set the Purge Interval to 15 days, to reflect the two-week period she wanted documents to stay in her replica of the database. When she selected the command, Remove documents saved before Cutoff Date, she instructed Notes to automatically remove documents that had been in the database longer than the purge interval. Notes does this maintenance by comparing the current date, which it gets from the computer's operating system, with the Cutoff Date and the Purge Interval. Notes changes the cutoff date when one third of the purge interval has elapsed. (For Megan, this meant that on September 20, the cutoff date was reset to September 6.) The next time she replicated the database, those documents dated before September 6 were deleted.

To conserve space on her laptop's hard drive, Megan selected the command Do not replicate deletions to replicas of this database. This command allowed her to delete documents that she had read or did not want to save on the laptop, but kept the deletion from being propagated to the primary database on the Notes server.

For her tracking application, Megan chose different replication settings. She wanted to replicate all of the documents in the version of the database on the Notes server to her laptop. To do so, she set the purge interval at 0. This setting negates the cutoff date, because it works in conjunction with the purge interval. Megan knew that as the tracking database grew larger she would have to limit its size, but—for now—it would replicate everything. She did not select any other options.

Before she left the office for her trip, she dialed the Notes server from her laptop and selected File, Database, Exchange (see Figure 3.35). To replicate, she selected All databases in common. She also chose the option, Receive documents from server. In future replications, when she had added docu-

```
┌─────────────────────────────────────────────────────┐
│             File Database Exchange                   │
│  Server                              ┌──────────┐    │
│  ┌──────────────────────────────┐    │    OK    │    │
│  │ Sales                        │    └──────────┘    │
│  │                              │    ┌──────────┐    │
│  │                              │    │  Cancel  │    │
│  │                              │    └──────────┘    │
│  └──────────────────────────────┘                    │
│  ┌─Replicate──────────────────────────────────────┐  │
│  │ ☒ All databases in common                      │  │
│  │ ☐ Selected databases                           │  │
│  │ ☒ Receive documents from server                │  │
│  │ ☐ Send documents to server                     │  │
│  └────────────────────────────────────────────────┘  │
│    ☐ Transfer outgoing mail                          │
│    ☒ Hangup when done                                │
└─────────────────────────────────────────────────────┘
```

**FIGURE 3.35**   The File Database Exchange box controls which databases are replicated, which server the remote PC connects to, and whether documents move in only one direction or in both directions.

---

### Taking Notes on the Road

Running Notes on a laptop or notebook PC requires a machine that meets the minimum requirements for a Notes workstation. For dial-up interactive access to Notes databases, a 9,600 bps modem is best, but for replicating electronic mail and database documents, Notes will work with a modem as slow as 1,200 bps.

*Hardware requirements*:

- 80286 or 80386SX processor

- 2 megabytes of memory required for Windows 386 Enhanced mode; 1 megabyte required for Windows Standard mode (2 megabytes is recommended).

- 40 megabyte or larger hard disk

- LAN adapter card: needed only if you are switching between a LAN and a remote connection or if the PC will always connect to the LAN. A network card isn't necessary for workstations that will be used only for dial-up telecommunications.

- Graphics display: The monochrome VGA-compatible screens on many notebook PCs work well with Windows and Notes.

- Pointing device: a mouse or a device especially designed for portables, like the Logitech Trackman Portable or Microsoft BallPoint.

- Modem: 1,200 bps minimum, 9,600 bps recommended.

---

ments to the laptop resident databases and had composed mail, she would also select the options, Send documents to server, and Transfer outgoing mail. By simply choosing File, Database, Exchange, Megan would be able to replicate her databases and send and receive her E-mail whenever she choose.

If Megan wanted to look at a database on her server, one which was not replicated on the laptop, she could use the Option, Dial command to connect to the server via phone line—just as she would across a network back at the office. She could also use the Exchange command without selecting the option, Hangup when done. In that case, Notes would replicate the databases and transfer the mail. It would then stay connected to the server while Megan worked with applications.

There is one caveat to using Notes on a remote PC: Using a laptop with a 1200 bps or 2400 bps modem to replicate E-mail and a small number of documents with a Notes server works well, but for working interactively with databases on the server, a 9600 bps modem is recommended. At slower speeds, the Windows screens redraw too slowly to be practical.

## Notes for Remote Desktops

Working in Notes from a remote workstation varies so little from being directly connected to a LAN that no one should feel intimidated or inconvenienced by it. Lotus made many improvements in version 2 of Notes to make it easier to use on a laptop. The changes also make Notes a strategic product for tying workstations in small, isolated offices into a companywide communications system. An office with one or two workstations hardly justifies its own Notes server, but by using Notes remotely and dialing into a server in a larger office, employees in small offices can overcome their isolation.

Several companies are exploring a related strategy: They are setting up remote Notes terminals in the offices of clients or vendors who are not running Notes themselves. These remote workstations can keep companies in touch in a very timely fashion and make available all the features of Notes to facilitate their communication.

There are three ways of working with Notes on a laptop or remote workstation: off line, interactively, and switching between remote usage and a direct connection on the LAN where the server resides.

- **Off line**.   This is the way Megan McDonnell used Notes on her portable. Replication is the key to success in this mode. Users will put all their important databases on the laptop and dial into their servers to replicate the changes in those databases and transfer mail. When replication and mail delivery are finished, Notes can automatically disconnect, and the users can work off line on their newly updated databases.

- **Interactively at a remote location**.   Some remote users may find they want to work *interactively*—that is, they want to stay in constant communication with their server, working much as they do when they are on a LAN. They can replicate and also work directly on databases to which they have access. The advantage is that a remote user can keep up with high volumes of rapidly changing data in real time, or use databases too big to store on a laptop hard drive. However, this approach can be very expensive if users are calling long distance—or frustrating if the phone lines are not dependable. Anyone who works this way should have a 9,600 bps modem.

- **On site/off site.** More and more PC users work with portable machines that spend some time on a desktop connected to a network, and some time on the road. Notes makes this transition easy. The Notes user who returns from a trip can have his portable back on the LAN by connecting the to the network and making two quick changes in Notes: (1) switching the setting for the communications port Notes uses from a COM port to a LAN port, and (2) disabling the Hold Mail option. When he leaves the office, he resets those two changes and Notes is again ready for the road.

# Summary

Notes' consistency minimizes the time and effort required to become comfortable with the program: It is based on a graphical user interface, either Windows 3.0 or the OS/2 Presentation Manager, which enforces a uniform implementation of commands and builds on users' familiarity with other programs running in these environments.

Notes adds to this consistency with its own structure of forms and views that is common to all applications. (Its electronic mail is implemented as a standard application, as well.) The result is that navigating the workspace, opening and using forms and views, creating and retrieving documents, sending and receiving electronic mail, creating complex documents, and running Notes remotely on a portable PC or a stand-alone desktop computer—even installing and modifying applications created from templates—are all activities easily performed by new users with only a few hours of experience in Notes.

# The Example Databases and Templates

Notes comes with two collections of applications that offer working examples of the program's capabilities. They demonstrate the different types of applications that can be developed in Notes. They also provide a sense of the kinds of workgroups that can use Notes and the benefits they can derive. In addition, each application is a case study in the techniques of developing a Notes database and serves as a jumping-off point for developers to customize them for particular tasks and for particular workgroups.

The applications are of two types—templates and example databases. The eight templates cover the most basic types of Notes applications, including a discussion database, a document library, and a client tracking application (see Figure 4.1). The templates are empty shells, applications with views and forms but no data.

The example databases are more complex applications, more closely focused on particular tasks. Also each example includes documents that show off the application's capabilities—in views, the categorization; in forms, the design.

## The Templates

When developers create databases, they often start by selecting the template most similar to their design and modify it. The templates listed in the File, Database, New menu cover a variety of functions:

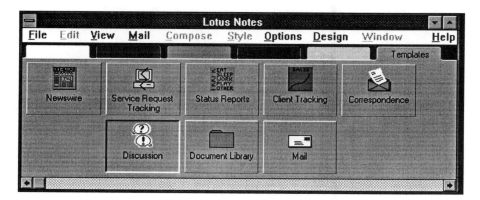

**FIGURE 4.1** The desktop icons for applications created from the templates shipped with Notes. The templates provide a quick, easy way to create the most common types of Notes applications.

- **Newswire** is a simple database used to disseminate information to a group. It has two forms, News Item and Response. A news item can be entered by the user or imported into the form—it doesn't have to come from a wire service. A Newswire application would be useful for a group that wants to build a set of reports and share comments on them. More complex applications that feed high volumes of news stories through a gateway into Notes start with such a basic template.

- **Service Request Tracking** allows users to enter requests for repairs, orders, or support. It contains a form for making the request and another for responding to it. The requests can be viewed by assignments, dates, and completion time. Many organizations have used this template as the basis for their internal PC support and helpdesk operations, and for requests to vendors.

- **Status Reporting** keeps the group informed of the activities of its members. Its three forms—Objectives, Response, and Status Report—can be displayed in several views: Issues, Objectives, Divisions, and Status Reports. This template's project-management features make it useful for coordinating a group that shares the subtasks of a larger project.

- **Client Tracking** is for salespeople and anyone else who needs to record information about contacts with clients and related activities. One form, Client Information, creates a profile of the client; another, Meeting Report, details client meetings. The Update/Response form allows users to add comments. Documents can be sorted by client, account manager, location, or status.

- **Correspondence** shows off Notes' mail-merge capabilities. It has two forms: The Person form is a detailed address book in which users record business and personal data. It includes space for a photograph and a scanned copy of the person's signature. The second form, called Quick Letter, copies address information from the Person form into a blank letter form.

- **Discussion** is one of the simplest and the most widely used templates. It contains forms for creating a topic document or a response and is frequently used without modifications. In five minutes, a Notes user can create a new discussion database from the template, assign user access to a few individuals or a group list, write a brief policy stating the application's purpose, and have it ready to run.

- **Document Library** has been adapted by companies to serve as a centralized repository in which users store information they may later need to retrieve. It is not meant for timely information as Newswire is, but for any information a company wants to file for future reference. Although it contains only one Main View, designers may create other views by categories.

- **Mail** creates a standard E-mail database. It is a useful example of a well-structured application with a variety of forms and views, and a good starting point for an application developer.

Just as applications can be created from the templates, templates also can be created from applications. The File, Database, Copy command allows users to create a template from an existing application (see Figure 4.2). Selecting the Forms and Views Only radio button creates templates which reproduce all the forms and views, formulas, and filters of the original file without the data that has accumulated in it.

Templates also can be used to change the structure of an application. Using the Design, Redesign Database command, users delete the database's old forms and views and replace them with those from a different template.

# The Example Databases

Lotus provides several example databases with Notes. Unlike the templates, these files include sample documents, and they are intended to be tutorials.

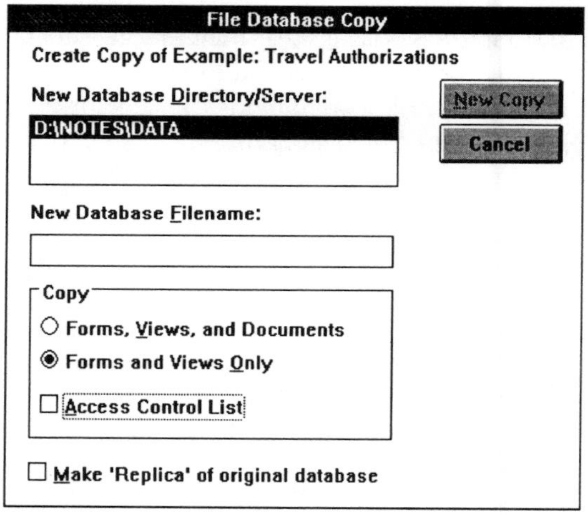

```
┌────────────────────────────────────────────────┐
│              File Database Copy                  │
│  Create Copy of Example: Travel Authorizations   │
│  New Database Directory/Server:      ┌─────────┐ │
│  ┌──────────────────────────────┐    │New Copy │ │
│  │ D:\NOTES\DATA                │    └─────────┘ │
│  │                              │    ┌─────────┐ │
│  │                              │    │ Cancel  │ │
│  └──────────────────────────────┘    └─────────┘ │
│                                                  │
│  New Database Filename:                          │
│  ┌──────────────────────────────┐                │
│  │                              │                │
│  └──────────────────────────────┘                │
│  ┌─Copy──────────────────────────┐               │
│  │ ○ Forms, Views, and Documents │               │
│  │ ◉ Forms and Views Only        │               │
│  │ ☐ Access Control List         │               │
│  └───────────────────────────────┘               │
│                                                  │
│  ☐ Make 'Replica' of original database           │
└────────────────────────────────────────────────┘
```

**FIGURE 4.2** The File, Database, Copy window allows users to make templates from existing applications by choosing the Forms and Views Only radio button. It makes a new copy of the database without the data.

New users will find them very helpful in gaining an understanding of how Notes works.

While the templates are intended to be working samples of the most generalized functions of Notes, the example databases are more complex applications (see Figure 4.3). They are versions of applications developed to meet the needs of real working groups. Frequently, they combine the functions of two or more templates.

The example database files are usually loaded in a subdirectory on the Notes server. Users can check with the Notes administrator to find out where the files are stored. The remainder of this chapter examines these example databases.

## Electronic Mail

The Electronic Mail example database includes sample mail messages for use in tutorials and training sessions on using Notes E-mail.

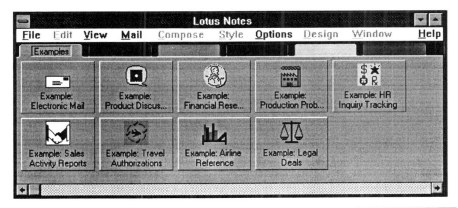

**FIGURE 4.3** The desktop icons for the example databases. These databases include sample documents, and are useful for learning to use Notes, and for studying the structure of applications.

# Product Discussion

The Discussion database is the simplest type of Notes application, yet it clearly demonstrates Notes' ability to structure information. In this example only two forms are needed, Main Topic and Response (see Figure 4.4). The Main Topic form contains only three fields to fill in: the topic, the category the message falls into, and the message text. Three views use this information to list documents by author, by category, or by creation date for a historical record of the discussion.

Discussions are one of the most democratic ways to use Notes because they have no hierarchical structure and encourage participation from everyone who has access to the database. In this example, it is interesting to see the number of responses to every Main Topic document. The responses demonstrate the collaborative process of the workgroup as it shares knowledge, solves problems, and builds a record of the process.

# Financial Research

Developed for an investment bank to help track companies that might be takeover candidates, this application merges news from outside sources with internally generated analyses and daily status reports. The forms ease the collection of many types of information. One form, for use with the File Import

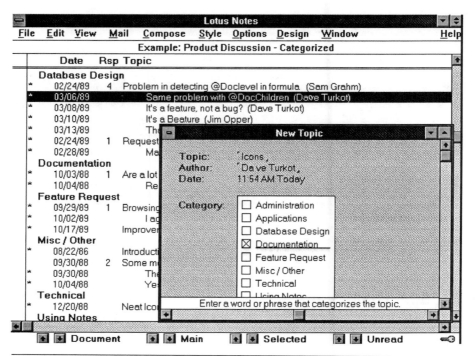

**FIGURE 4.4**  A New Topic form overlays the Categorized view of the Product Discussion database. Selecting a check-box in the New Topic form includes the document in that category in this view.

command, brings news into the database: stories, analysts' reports, and publicly available financial data from Lotus One Source, a CD-ROM-based information service on publicly traded companies. Other forms record meetings, share suggestions, report project status, or respond to any other form. Views provide indexes to daily status reports, financial reports, or news analyses on each company the bank is following.

In the Daily Status view, the line for each document's subject also includes in parentheses the name and location of its author. The authors work in widely scattered offices but are able to exchange information in this application as if they were all in one place. A database like Financial Research is useful for any company that needs to gather and disseminate information daily. Pertinent news is extracted from outside sources and made available company wide, for reference and for comment (see Figure 4.5).

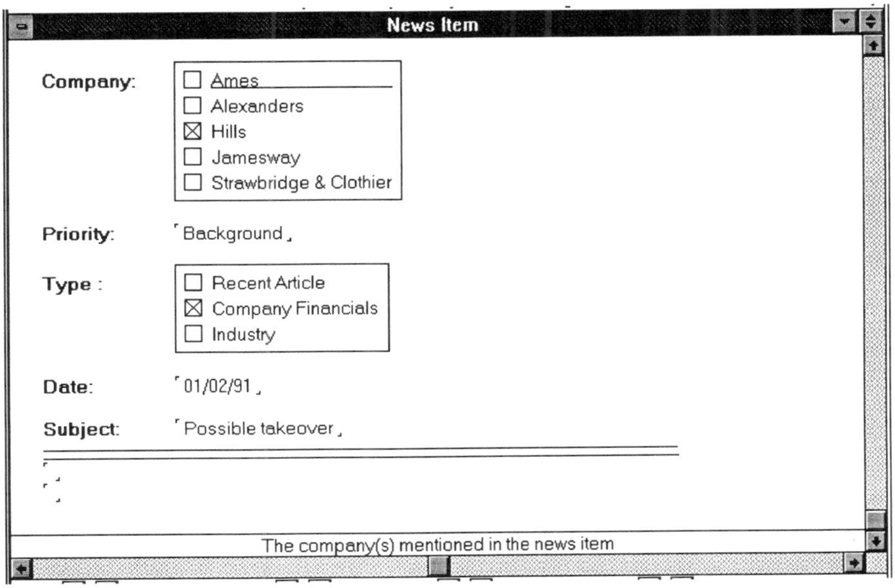

**FIGURE 4.5**  The News Item form uses check-boxes to categorize the document, and includes the empty fields at the bottom of the screen for entering or importing data.

## Production Problems

This application tracks production problems in a manufacturing environment. It serves groups in several different divisions that share their expertise with each other. Because users of this database would want to examine the particular documents that relate to their current difficulties, the application is very tightly structured (see Figure 4.6). There are only two forms, Production Problem Report and Response, and four views which cross-index the problem reports by date, department, part number, and type of problem.

The Production Problem Report form enforces this structure by presenting the user with radio buttons for selecting a problem type and production department, and check-boxes for specifying the part or parts involved.

This kind of tracking database is useful at all management levels. Production supervisors can see the status of problems reported on previous shifts. Upper-level managers can get a timely overview of the plant's activities. Access to a database like this can be extended, through Notes' replication capabilities, to include suppliers, who often find out late about problems on which they could have offered solutions.

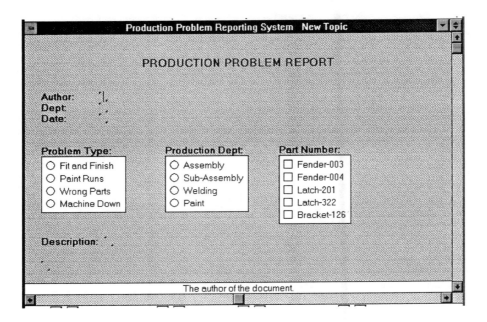

**FIGURE 4.6**  In the Production Problems database, the radio buttons and check-boxes in the Production Problem Report form make possible a very tight categorization scheme in the view, Reports by Dept.

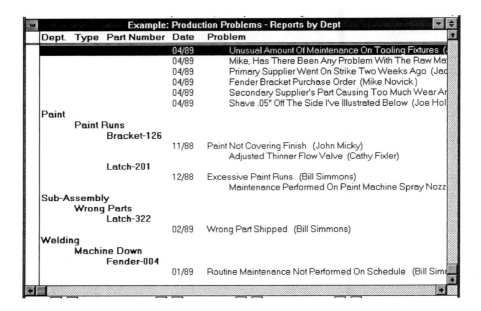

# HR Inquiry Tracking

This database helps a Human Resources department manage inquiries from employees. It is a more elaborate tracking application than the Production Problems database. Its basic input form, the Inquiry Log form, collects much more information, including a keyword field which identifies whether the inquiry is unresolved and therefore still open, or closed. Views are included to list open inquiries by date and by the staff member assigned (see Figure 4.7). Other views list inquiries by category and by region. The views provide the department managers with an overview of the types of questions employees are asking and the department's performance in addressing them.

The application builds a historical record of inquiries and solutions that can serve as a reference database. The inclusion of a Response form lets the department's staff swap expertise or special knowledge.

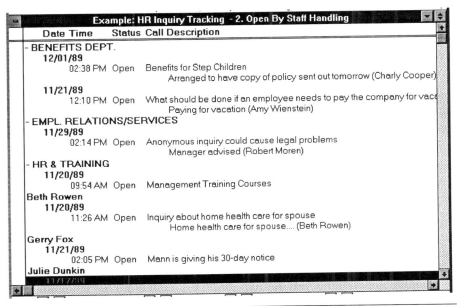

**FIGURE 4.7** The HR Inquiry database combines two functions in a single view. The detailed inquiry tracking is joined by response documents that let staff members share expertise.

# Sales Activity Reporting

Sales Activity Reporting is structured for a more hierarchical workgroup than are the Production Problems and Financial Research applications (see Figure 4.8). It informs executives of marketplace issues, sales highlights, and events reported from the field. Regional sales personnel enter information which is categorized and sorted into the views executives use. (Of course, executives can enter data and responses, too.) On the basis of the information entered, the forms can be categorized by priority, sales region, product type, customer, and competitor, to name only a few categories. The executives are always looking at the most recent information from the field. They can stay up to date on the competition's activities, customers' reactions to new products, and issues that seem important to their sales force.

The database's personnel form records new hires, transfers, promotions, and terminations. But access to the Personnel view which lists these documents is restricted to management by the database's User Access list. Security is assured by granting separate privileges to management, sales, and marketing. Attaching privileges to a view means that only those who belong to the group with the named privilege may look at the view. If you do not have

| Example: Sales Activity Reports - Executive View | | |
|---|---|---|
| **Topic** | **Group** | **Region** |
| **02/89** | | |
| **ISSUES** | | |
| **Product** | | |
| Customers say that enhanced output is ABSOLUTELY | Corp | SW |
| **Customer** | | |
| Customers' Reaction to Rendezvous II Announcement | Corp | SW |
| SellMart has successfully beta tested Rendezvous | Ret | DC |
| 1. Good Job (Jack Durahm) | | |
| Dealer inquiries about the Dealer Authorization Policy | Ret | GL |
| Corporate Consultants is thrilled with Rendezvous | Corp | NE |
| **Business** | | |
| Rendezvous 2 upgrade and networking plans. | Sup | NE |
| Alternate methods of distribution | Ret | NE |
| **SALES HIGHLIGHTS** | | |
| **Sales Success** | | |
| Rendezvous is becoming successful at Morris Bros. | Corp | NW |
| **Competition** | | |
| LanVision has constant promotions in retail stores. | Ret | Can |
| RView now has a full time account representative base | Sup | SO |

**FIGURE 4.8** The Sales Activity Reporting example presents reports from the field to executives at the home office. Therefore, it includes information on the source of the report on the subject line.

the privilege of looking at a particular view, it will not even appear on the pull-down View menu.

This database demonstrates how one Notes database can serve several levels of management that need to swap some, but not all, information with each other. It also opens communication between the managers at headquarters and the employees in the field, helping to ease the isolation field workers often experience. In addition, field workers spend less time filling out forms and writing reports, because the views tailor the information for different management groups.

## Travel Authorizations

The Travel Authorizations application is the most complex of the example applications, even though it may seem the easiest to use. This example of a forms-routing application allows users to initiate, approve, and track travel requests (see Figure 4.9). Like most Notes applications, the complexity is hidden from the user. Travel Authorizations uses the E-mail routing built into Notes to send requests up the line for approval, automatically sending the request from the first approval level to the next until all the managers have

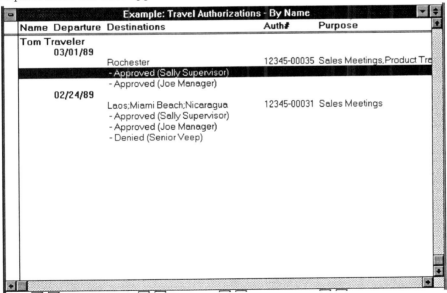

**FIGURE 4.9** The Travel Authorizations application submits a request to the supervisors who must approve it, routes it automatically, and reports on its status to the person who originated it.

signed off. It also notifies the requester each time the request is routed to the next manager in line. The views organize the information by request number, department, name, purpose, and travel date.

This type of application serves a hierarchical group structure or one in which disparate divisions of a company use forms to communicate. It could be adapted to handle purchase orders, for example. From properly designed forms and views that include numerical data—days of travel, ticket prices—information could be exported to a spreadsheet for cost and budget analyses, or to a word processor for inclusion in reports.

## Airline Reference

Airline Reference is a ready-reference database of financial information on airline companies. As in the Financial Research application, one of the forms facilitates importing information from external sources such as Lotus One Source and Reuters—balance sheets, ratio analysis, competitive analysis, and high-low-close graphs of stock prices are included among the information available. The views vary widely in their construction and purpose. Several views provide catalogs of the research documents, including lists sorted by company or by type of report. Other views work more like database reports, extracting data from documents and presenting it in summary tables for quick reference. Figure 4.10 shows a table of key data by sales volume.

This kind of database is extremely useful for groups which research an industry or a client group. Importing the data from outside sources where it has already been compiled saves time and centralizes the data in one place. The structure of the views makes it easy to manage the data and quickly identify missing reports or information needs updating.

| Example: Airline Reference - Key Data by Sales Volume | | | | | | |
|---|---|---|---|---|---|---|
| Company | Date | Sales | Gross Profit | Int Exp | Income | ROS |
| UAL | 9-30-88 | $9,502 | $6,011 | $271 | $1,053 | 11.1% |
| Texas Air | 12-31-87 | $8,474 | $4,473 | $622 | ($466) | -5.5% |
| AMR | 12-31-87 | $7,198 | $2,914 | $213 | $198 | 2.8% |
| Delta | 6-30-88 | $6,915 | $2,729 | $97 | $306 | 4.4% |
| British Airways | 3-31-88 | $3,756 | $1,896 | $31 | $151 | 4.0% |

**FIGURE 4.10**   When the information to be displayed is numbers, Notes views can resemble spreadsheets or database reports.

# Legal Deals

Legal Deals is an example of an application for a collaborative workgroup. The group in this case is a law firm's partners and staff. The documents in the database cover the sale of properties owned by two clients. The group working on these deals must be kept informed of due dates, bank financing, environmental issues, and concerns of employees in the companies being sold. Problems, concerns, and information related to the sales are entered into the database.

The structure of this database and its forms and views is not hierarchical (see Figure 4.11). Rather, it conforms to the way its users work together on a task as peers. Therefore, it does not contain forms which require authorization, as in the Travel Authorizations application, for instance.

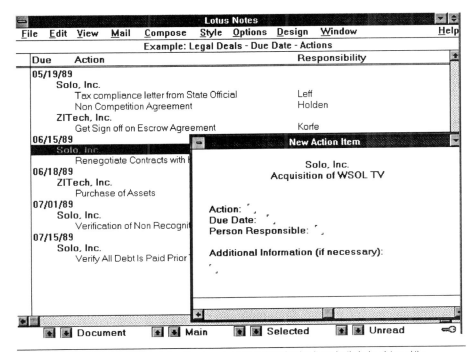

**FIGURE 4.11** The uncluttered New Action Item form overlays a view of action items by their due date and the company. Such simple forms encourage use and are filled in quickly.

# Summary

The example applications and templates in Notes deserve to be investigated more thoroughly, but even this brief introduction should give a sense of the variety of applications Notes can be used for. It can be adapted to the hierarchical structures of the organizations that use Travel Authorizations and Sales Activity Reports. And it can serve the more egalitarian organizational structures represented in Legal Deals and Production Problems.

Most importantly, these applications are only a starting point. They are readily adaptable building blocks for many of the basic functions of workgroup information management. And they can just as readily be customized by Notes administrators and designers—and even users—to become even more specifically suited to a group's specific needs, its patterns of communication, and its ways of getting work done.

# Section 3
# Creating an
# Application

The success of Notes in an organization depends on creating applications that not only have relevance to the work that must be done in a company, but to the ways that a company prefers to do its work.

Creating successful applications requires knowledge of much more than the commands on the Design menu. The first chapter in this section, Chapter 5, begins with a look at the background for any computer application development. The corporate culture should influence the developer of a Notes application—how the group communicates and shares its work product, the sensitivity of the information it handles, and not least, its experience with computers and its expectations for Notes.

The development process itself follows a clearly defined series of steps that are applied to a sample application—a Notes database for a company called Pegasus Public Relations. The chapter concludes with an examination of the analysis and design steps. Chapter 6 continues with the building, testing, and documenting steps.

The final chapter in this section, Chapter 7, looks at some application design tools and techniques that depart from the traditional development process (using filters, privileges, encrypted fields, and masks) and help designers and administrators deal with the most non-traditional aspect of Notes—setting up applications for use by groups.

# 5

# The Development Environment

The history of PCs, brief as it is, has two lessons to teach Notes application developers. The first and most obvious is that just as the PC has furnished the individual user with not just one application, but a toolkit, so each Notes application should be regarded as part of a system or a toolkit. The second lesson is that Notes, like the PC, is more smoothly integrated into an organization when end users have an active voice in the process.

When the PCs atop their desks perform only one function, users have a tendency to ignore them. The same applies to Notes. Users are much more likely to take the time to learn the program when they can put it to use in several ways. Electronic mail is a Notes function most users begin to use very quickly. As other applications are added to their Notes toolkit—and as they create Notes applications themselves—their understanding and their involvement with the program grows.

Notes fits into a larger set of applications, as well. It is meant to be used with other products. Many organizations are introducing Notes as part of a conversion to Windows 3.0 as a standard PC operating environment. Several companies run Notes with such Windows programs as Word for Windows, Lotus Ami Professional, and Microsoft's Excel, PowerPoint, and Project. Users can easy switch from one program to another and take advantage of Windows' Dynamic Data Exchange (DDE) and Object Linking and Embedding (OLE), which link data and documents across different Windows programs.

Additional ways to link Notes applications to other programs on the PC include using filters to manage the import and export of data, or developing external programs which address the Notes application programming interface (see Chapter 9). For example, one company has written an external program that uses Notes' application programming interface (API) to tie Notes to its relational database. When certain transactions occur in the database, the custom software generates a message that is sent to the appropriate Notes database or user.

## Notes and the Democratic Process

Another lesson from history concerns the PC's role in encouraging democracy within the organization. Many experts feel that PCs, by providing increased access to information, contribute to a flattening of organizational structures. They point to increased communication between the higher and lower levels of the company structure, and a diffusion of decision making as a result. Other experts see PCs as a symptom of this structural change, not the cause. They think organizations that decide to be more democratic have turned to PCs because they support the new structure's needs for information and communication.

Whichever theory proves correct, the spread of PCs in organizations has resulted in a more active role for end users in selecting the hardware and software they use. No longer does an MIS department dictate where computer terminals will be placed and what they will be used for. PCs and local area networks in fact gave the line departments in a company an alternative to MIS, a way to put computer power to work on their own terms, running the applications they wanted.

If Notes is to succeed in an organization, the developers of applications must encourage the group members' participation in the planning and implementing process. A large financial institution that was one of the earliest Notes customers learned that lesson the hard way: Despite a first failed attempt at a Notes installation it made a second try, this time including end users extensively in the planning process. The installation worked the second time. The system administrator later cited the initial effort's lack of user involvement as the reason for its failure.

# The Design Environment

In addition to understanding the tasks people want to accomplish, the person who develops an application must take other factors into account, as well. He needs to study the corporate culture and interpersonal relationships in an organization, the office politics, and the casual as well as the formal behavior of the group. The designer must understand whether the Notes application will support an existing structure or make radical changes to it.

But understanding the working patterns of a team or department is even more difficult than it sounds. Few groups can actually articulate their structure and collaborative process. A designer who comes from inside may have the advantage of an intimate knowledge of these inner workings of the group. An outsider must spend some time observing and understanding the dynamics of the group that will be using Notes. In both cases, the person who sets out to document a group's work must examine eight important factors:

## Corporate Culture

In many ways the group will mirror the attitudes and practices of the larger organization. Does the company function democratically as a community of peers that freely share information? Or is it a rigid hierarchy, with several layers of management that control information flows on a need-to-know basis? Does management control office procedures and policies tightly or does the group have freedom of movement? Are the group's membership and structure fixed or fluid?

## Physical Proximity

How are the offices laid out? Are some group members in different locations? Are some going to be connecting by modem from remote locations? Does the current layout of the office enhance or hinder communication? Do many informal discussions take place in the hallway or around the coffee pot? These are all clues to how the group works.

## Computer Usage

How much previous experience does the group have with PCs? Are they comfortable using a keyboard? A mouse? Do they use an electronic mail package other than Notes? Many companies are finding that they have the most success getting new computer users to understand Notes by starting them out on E-mail. They then graduate to a simple discussion database. Training is also a major issue.

## Communications

How much information is shared among the members of the group, and how is it transferred? Do group members document phone calls, faxes, and memos?

How do they document meetings? Who creates their reports and how are they done? What communication problems do they identify now?

## Workflow Patterns

If the Notes application is to be modeled on an existing paper-based application, what forms does it use? Where does it start? Who initiates a project? Who oversees it? Does it progress in stages which must be signed off by a manager as they are completed? What is the path from the beginning of a project to its end? Where does the process bog down?

## Access to the Work

Is much of the work highly confidential, or open to any and all employees? Will some information be accessible to management exclusively, while other information is shared among the rest of the team? Who makes decisions based on the information? What kinds of reports must be generated from the information and for whom?

## Who Will Benefit?

Is Notes to be used primarily to create reports for management? Are the people creating the information a different group from those using it—and if so, what is the perceived benefit of Notes to each group?

## Expectations for Notes

Introducing Notes into the office introduces change, which always brings with it some anxiety and resistance. How receptive to Notes is the group? How well have the people in the group been prepared for Notes? Does the group recognize a need for Notes? Do most members feel it will help them do their work better? Have they been a part of this decision, or do they feel that Notes is being forced on them?

# The Organization's Support for Notes

The size of a workgroup determines the level of support and management that its applications need. An individual user can certainly create useful applications, but databases that reach across departments or whole companies may need more than seat-of-the-pants design and occasional maintenance. Appropriate support may mean designated help from a corporate MIS department, or even an outside consultant. Notes application support generally falls into the three categories examined below.

**Individual Notes users** and small groups can create and customize Notes applications for themselves without special help. Working from a template as a starting point, it's easy to add a different view of the information, alter the layout of a form, or add an additional field or two to capture specific, personal data.

Applications to be shared by a group are not inherently any more difficult to develop than applications used by only one person. There is no code to write, for example, to make an application work on a network. The most difficult part lies in the planning: in determining who may make use of the application, and what access they will have.

**Workgroups** need a resource person to help create Notes applications that meet the needs of the group. This development resource person may be the Notes administrator, but it may also be an enthusiastic Notes user. The resource person's level of experience depends on the size of the group (or groups) using Notes, the number of applications to be developed, and their complexity. Some workgroup applications benefit from the involvement of an experienced developer with a programming background.

Complex applications that depend on information from outside the group —data imported from company accounting records, or sales reports from branch offices across the country—need support from corporate MIS staffs. They develop the database reports and manage replications schedules and telecommunications systems that will give the Notes application its value.

**Large-scale applications** crucial to an organization's business goals may require help from outside the company. Lotus sponsors two programs aimed at providing this expertise—value-added resellers (VARs) and the Alliance Partners.

The VARs sell, install, and support Notes, and the value they add can run a wide gamut from installing networks, to training, to custom application development, to management consulting.

The Alliance Partners are consultants and software developers who specialize in writing programs to Notes' API that do such things as get information from a mainframe or access an SQL server. Other Alliance Partners have created separate products and services that work with Notes such as SandPoint's Hoover, a database-access tool, and Desktop Data Inc.'s News-EDGE, which manages Notes databases of wire-service news. Other Alliance Partners, such as Quality Decision Management, develop specialized applications. (For more on VARs, the Alliance Partners, and their services, see Chapters 9 and 10.)

# Application Development

The process of developing a successful Notes application has much in common with any software-development project.

Mainframe computers are barely four decades old, but already time and the traditions of data processing have honed program development to a highly structured process, just as they have formalized the structure of Management Information Systems (or MIS) departments in large companies. The personal computer has brought many changes to this environment, and Notes brings many more — it breaks down the rigid distinction between programmer and end user of a database, for instance, by offering tools that greatly reduce the knowledge required to produce a useful application.

But Notes doesn't eliminate the underlying principles or the discipline of programming. The process of creating a Notes application is considerably less rigid than, say, programming in Cobol for mainframes, but they both have the same major steps in common: Analysis, design, building, testing, and documentation (see box, The Five Steps of Application Development). A clear understanding of such things as conditional logic and program flow makes for a more efficient Notes developer — and more sophisticated Notes applications. But while Notes rewards the experienced programmer by yielding polished applications, it also rewards the nonprogrammer. Any user who has a clear understanding of a business problem can create applications of critical importance to the business. And these applications can become polished through constant use and reworking.

To illustrate how application development in Notes works, this chapter and the next will chronicle a development project for Pegasus Public Relations, a large public-relations company with clients and branch offices spread across the Midwest. Although Pegasus is a fictitious company, the problems it faces and the way it deals with them are based on experiences of real companies. The example begins with a description of Pegasus and its situation, then follows the project through the five steps of application development.

---

### The Five Steps of Application Development

A good way to ensure that the Notes application development process focuses on these needs of the organization is to follow the steps prescribed by classical mainframe program development—analysis, design, building, testing, documenting.

- **Analysis**. In the traditional MIS environment, an analyst works with the intended users of the application to establish the parameters of the project, identify the data needed, and specify the format of the program's output.

- **Design**. Choices about programming language, data structures and programming algorithms are made, and the designer uses tools such as decision trees to outline the structure of the application.

- **Building**. A developer creates the program, following the design. This step is often called "coding," a bow to the computer's early days, when programmers wrote software in the processor's own machine-language code. (With its graphical interface, Notes reduces much of the labor of coding to pointing and clicking with the mouse.)

- **Testing**. This is frequently the most tedious part of a programmer's responsibility—creating test data sets big enough to exercise the application, then looping through the process of compiling the program, running it until it breaks, finding the bug and fixing it, and starting over.

- **Documenting**. Computer programs need documentation that serves several purposes: manuals, reference and training materials for users of the application, for maintenance programmers, and (in the case of mainframe programs) for computer operators.

---

# An Application for Pegasus Public Relations

Pegasus Public Relations decided to install Notes when it became apparent that the divisions among the staff, as well as the distance between the branch offices, were beginning to impair the company's ability to serve its clients. The company's goal was to improve communications among the branch offices and among the company's three major home-office divisions: Administration, Client Services, and Creative Services.

Ben Lewis, an account representative in Client Services, was tapped to develop the first major Notes application. He had worked on several projects for the agency, most recently an effort to set up the agency's multi-user accounting database to generate client-related reports for the agency's management. But the system had flopped. Producing the new account plans and activity and budget reports had required the Client Services and accounting staffs to enter more data into the computer. But since the reports were used only by management, the two staffs received no benefit in return for the extra work. As a result, data entry became a low priority for both departments. Because the information was often out of date, the reports had little value to management. Eventually the system fell into disuse.

Ben was wary of more computerization, but he had been exposed to Notes early in the agency's evaluation process, and he was enthusiastic about its potential.

The success of the Notes application for Pegasus Public Relations depended not just on Ben's knowledge of Notes, but also his knowledge of his company and the way it works. Because Notes minimizes the mechanics of development—the building, debugging and documenting—Ben was able to devote his time to the analysis and design.

Ben began his work by talking to people in all three divisions, gathering ideas, working to get a clear picture of each division's goals.

- **Administration** is Pegasus' management division, including the partners and the financial and accounting staffs. The top managers spent much of their time pitching new business and servicing Pegasus' best clients, but they felt removed from the daily office activities. They wanted to make sure that the account reps were servicing clients properly and not overlooking opportunities to enhance Pegasus' standing among those clients. The twice-weekly client status meetings were essential, but increasingly inefficient and taking up too much of the reps' time. The Creative Department's chronic problems with budget overruns concerned top management, and it wanted to track the department's use of time and materials. Ben heard repeatedly from the managers that they wanted to improve communications within the company.

- **Client Services** consists of the account representatives who work directly with the clients. The account reps wanted to control client information and keep it current. Their goals were to coordinate their work and organize, share, and track data more efficiently. They needed the information stored in a central location, a tracking mechanism to record client contacts and activities, a way of generating and sharing action items and tickler files, and the ability to generate letters and notes to clients.

- **Creative Services** is the other large division within Pegasus. Its staff writes, designs, plans events, and produces all kinds of print and electronic communications. Creative often contracts for the services of outside professionals—writers and graphic designers, photographers, video producers, directors, and stylists. The Creative staff, feeling pressure from management about their cost overruns, wanted to use Notes to track their time and expenses.

Ben's solution combined elements of a status reporting application with time/billing and materials/tracking functions. He gave the account reps a way to create and manage contact reports and historical information on clients. He gave Creative Services an overview of active projects assigned. And he gave management a view that showed time and expenses charged against each project as a percentage of its budget.

Ben's work followed the five steps of classical application development: analysis, design, building, testing, and documentation. Altogether, Ben invested 60 hours of work in creating his application. Two-thirds of that time he spent not working at a computer keyboard, but talking with the application's intended users and sketching its forms and views, performing the very necessary analysis and design.

# The Analysis Step

In the analysis step, Ben devoted about half his time across a couple of weeks to gathering people's ideas for the database. When the interviews, questionnaires, and brain-storming sessions were finished, he had a good idea of what information was needed. Next, he had to identify a source for it—would it come from the existing accounting system, or would it be entered into Notes by the Client Services and Creative staffs? Finally, he spent a couple of days turning the ideas he had collected and his knowledge of Notes into rough drawings of six forms and five views that would be the framework of the application.

Ben began his analysis by initiating several information-gathering projects at once: He conducted formal interviews, collected written suggestions, and engaged in informal chats in the coffee room. It was a familiar routine to Ben, depending as much on sensitivity to office politics—who should be consulted, who should be kept informed—as data-processing knowledge.

---

### Developing Notes in Notes

For Notes applications, the analysis can be supported in an interesting way by Notes itself: If Notes is already installed at users' workstations, set up a Notes discussion database and give everyone who will use an application, from managers to entry-level employees, a place to record their needs and desires and ideas for the application.

---

At this stage, Ben and his coworkers were drawing rough sketches, samples of the forms and views they wanted to see in the finished database. Ben's goal was to learn as much as possible about the staff's expectations for Notes. As he did his analysis, it became clear that Pegasus' divisions were asking for a system that made four kinds of information readily available:

- A record of each client's address, phone numbers, and contact names.

- Detailed qualitative information on clients' preferences, perceptions, and reactions.

- Information on plans and commitments made by Pegasus, including formal project plans and less formal action items.

- Performance records of the billable time spent by the account reps and Creative Services staff on client-related activities.

# Defining the Views on Paper

Ben took these four areas as questions, and sketched out a preliminary set of five views that would provide the answers (see box, Views First, Then Forms). As he worked on the views, Ben realized that they served different purposes. The first four were indexes, providing quick access to a variety of information. The last view was a summarizing tool: It would gather information from the company's operations and calculate summaries of billable time and materials.

---

## View First, Then Forms

In a Notes application the views are the primary output, while the forms are the input, the data-collection vehicle. Although a developer builds forms before views, he must know what he wants the views to contain before he creates the forms, since all information is ultimately derived from the forms. Views are similar to database reports, and much as a database developer has to know what kind of reports an organization wants before she can design the database, so Ben had to design the views first and then move on to design the forms.

---

# The By Client View

The simplest view is an index of Pegasus' clients (see Figure 5.1). It presents each client's name, address, telephone number, contact person, and Pegasus rep. It serves as a quick reference tool. For example, a Creative staffer might use this view if she needed to telephone a client about a current project.

The alphabetical listing of clients provides the organizational scheme for other views in the application. Each of the forms inherits data from the client records to identify and categorize the letters, memos, status reports, project descriptions and contact reports that relate to that client.

The data presented in this view would be entered into Notes in documents created in a form Ben called Client Information, which is discussed with the other forms below. The view, By Client, provides the most frequently needed information from those documents—a name, a phone number—without requiring the user to open the document. Yet the view also serves as an index to the more complete Client Information forms.

When a form is filled in and saved, the saved data becomes a document in the database. The documents are listed in the views: Each line in a view represents a document, and each column is the contents of a field in that document or is calculated from field contents. Data cannot be entered directly into a view—it must first be entered in a document using a form.

Pegasus Public Relations
View 1

By Client

| Client | Phone # | Contact Person | Acct Rep Assigned |
|--------|---------|----------------|-------------------|
|        |         |                |                   |

**FIGURE 5.1** The simple view called "By Client" lists each client's name, phone number, contact person and account rep.

## The Current Projects View

Current Projects identifies all the client projects (see Figure 5.2). It allows the Creative Services staff to easily track project assignments and due dates. The view's Date Started and Date Due columns help management and Creative Services balance workloads.

Just as the By Client view displays information from documents created in a form called Client Information, the Current Projects view rests on a set of documents created in a Project Description form. The view provides ready reference to the documents' most important contents, and serves as an index.

## Pegasus Public Relations
## View 2
### Current Projects

| Client | Project Name | Date Started | Date Due | Employee |
|--------|-------------|--------------|----------|----------|
|        |             |              |          |          |

**FIGURE 5.2** The Current Projects view indexes all of Pegasus' client projects. It displays the beginning and due dates and the project team members.

# The Next Contact Date View

Next Contact Date is a tickler file (see Figure 5.3). The data it presents comes from Action Item and Contact Report documents, short forms for users to enter tasks for which they or someone else is responsible.

This view is intended mainly for the use of the account reps, although anyone can use it. Sorting this view by date helps the reps prioritize their activities and plan ahead. It also helps management keep abreast of what is happening with the clients and reps so that they can offer assistance or advice about clients with whom they are well acquainted.

View 3

Next Contact Date

| Date Next Contact | Client | Action Item | Employee | |
|---|---|---|---|---|
| | | | | |

**FIGURE 5.3** The Next Contact Date view displays action item documents by the due date assigned. This view helps account reps keep track of their responsibilities to clients.

## The Action Items View

Action Items (see Figure 5.4) is a variation of the previous view, Next Contact Date. It changes the order of the columns, making the employee the second sort criterion.

While the Next Contact Date view serves as a particularly useful tool for management, the Action Items view, by grouping tasks according to the employees responsible, is especially helpful to the employees. (The account reps might find it helpful to create their own private views, discussed later, which list only projects assigned to individuals, and personal items that they didn't want to appear in the public views.)

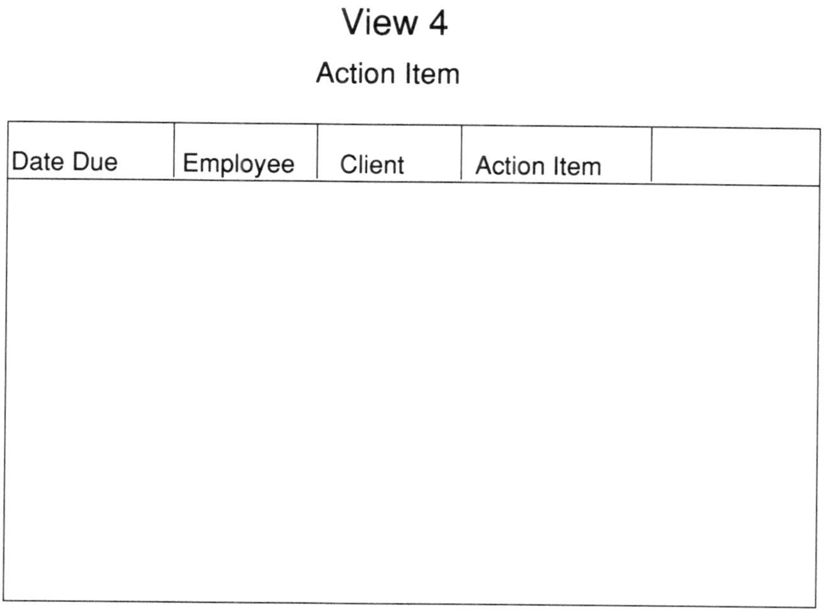

## View 4
### Action Item

| Date Due | Employee | Client | Action Item | |
|----------|----------|--------|-------------|---|
| | | | | |

**FIGURE 5.4**   A variation on the view Next Contact Date, this view arranges items so that each employee can see what his or her assignments are by date.

# The Cost by Client & Project View

Ben created the Cost by Client & Project view (see Figure 5.5), to serve a purpose different from that of the others. The first four views were intended for use as reference and a forum for sharing information. This view consolidates financial information and uses Notes' summary math capabilities to calculate a bottom-line summary of project costs.

The view is a daily tally of each project's materials costs. It extracts information the Creative staff enters in the Project Status form (discussed later in the chapter) and presents it in a spreadsheetlike structure.

## View 5
### Cost by Client & Project

| Client | Project Name | Employee | Date | Labor Cost | Material Cost |
|--------|--------------|----------|------|------------|---------------|
|        |              |          |      |            |               |

**FIGURE 5.5** Creative Services requested this view to track the cost of each project. The view draws on Notes' ability to perform limited mathematical operations within views.

# Defining the Forms

Once Ben had finalized the views on paper, he was ready to define the forms. The forms provide the data from which the views draw their information. Ben needed to consider not only the fields that each form would contain, but also the appropriate data type for each field, and which fields would be repeated throughout the forms.

Ben created six forms for the Pegasus application. Just as the views serve multiple purposes, so do the forms. Data entry is the most obvious, but Notes forms aren't just utilitarian instruments for data collection. They can be designed to display data in special ways on-screen or to format it for printed reports. In fact, a different form can be created for each of those purposes — data entry, display or printing — for the same data.

# The Client Information Form

The basic form in the Pegasus application is the Client Information form (see Figure 5.6). Because many other fields in other forms inherit data from the Client Information form, it is the first form used to create a document that identifies a client in the database.

Pegasus Public Relations

Form 1

Client Information

| Client | Account Representative |
| Address | Contact Person |
| Phone | Contact's Phone |
| Type of Business | |
| Comments | |

**FIGURE 5.6**  The Client Information form is simple and short. The comments field, which can grow to as much as four gigabytes, provides plenty of room for entries to accumulate over time.

Client Information documents are available to anyone in the company who wants to find a phone number, or check on the nature of the business. New personnel at Pegasus will use it to acquaint themselves with the clients, and it will be updated from time to time as the client's personnel change, too.

## The Project Description Form

The account reps use the Project Description form as they create proposals for their clients (see Figure 5.7). The form offers a detailed description of a project, including time frame and estimates of materials and labor costs.

Many of the fields in this form are inherited by the Project Status form used by account reps and Creative Services people to report on their progress. Project Description documents are indexed in the View By Project.

## The Project Status Form

The Creative Services staff uses the Project Status form to document their billable hours for each client project (see Figure 5.8 on page 124). Employees enter a description of their day's work, the hours they worked, and the materials cost. Despite its cluttered look, the form takes very little time to fill out because the contents of many fields are either inherited or computed by Notes.

Information saved in Project Status documents appears in the Cost by Client & Project view, an overview of all current projects and their status. Employees and their supervisors can use this information to help balance workloads and improve efficiency.

## The Contact Report Form

The Contact Report form, and the Action Item which follows, are for the use of the account reps. A rep fills out a Contact Report form each time he or she contacts a client (see Figure 5.9 on page 125). The Client, Date Contacted, and Employee fields are filled in automatically. In designing this form, Ben duplicated an existing paper form that was already used by the account reps.

When a contact requires follow-up action, the account rep can describe that action in the Comments field, enter a name in the Assigned to: field and a

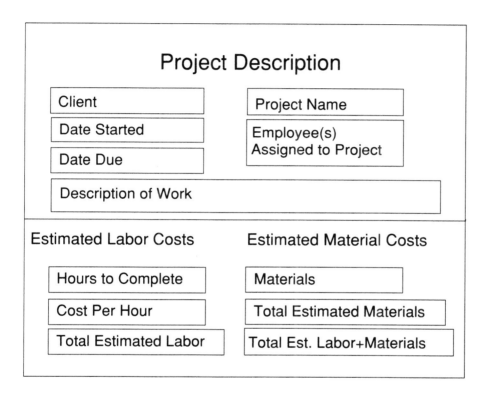

Pegasus Public Relations
Form 2

Project Description

Client

Project Name

Date Started

Employee(s)
Assigned to Project

Date Due

Description of Work

Estimated Labor Costs

Estimated Material Costs

Hours to Complete

Materials

Cost Per Hour

Total Estimated Materials

Total Estimated Labor

Total Est. Labor+Materials

**FIGURE 5.7**   The Project Description form inherits the client's name from the Client Information form. It includes computed fields that calculate totals for estimates of materials and labor costs.

due date in "Date Next Contact." Then the document becomes an action item: It appears in the views called Next Contact and Action Items.

As the contact reports accumulate, they form a historical record of Pegasus' relationship with the client and serve as invaluable background material to help new account reps familiarize themselves with a client.

Pegasus Public Relations

Form 3

| Project Status |
| --- |

| Client | | Project Name |
| --- | --- | --- |
| Date | | Employee |
| Description of Work | | |

| Labor Costs | | Material Costs |
| --- | --- | --- |
| Hours worked | | Materials |
| Cost Per Hour | | Cost of Materials |
| Total Labor Cost | | % of Total Materials |
| % of Total Estimated | | Total Cost-Labor/Materials |

**FIGURE 5.8**  The Project Status form records the daily work an employee devotes to a specific project. Many of the fields in this form are computed automatically by Notes.

# The Action Item Form

Documents created with the Action Item form (see Figure 5.10) are used in two views, Next Contact Date and Action Items, which function as electronic to-do lists, appointment calendars, and tickler files for the account reps. The Action Item form inherits fields so that the reps have to key in only a description of the action, the due date, and any comments.

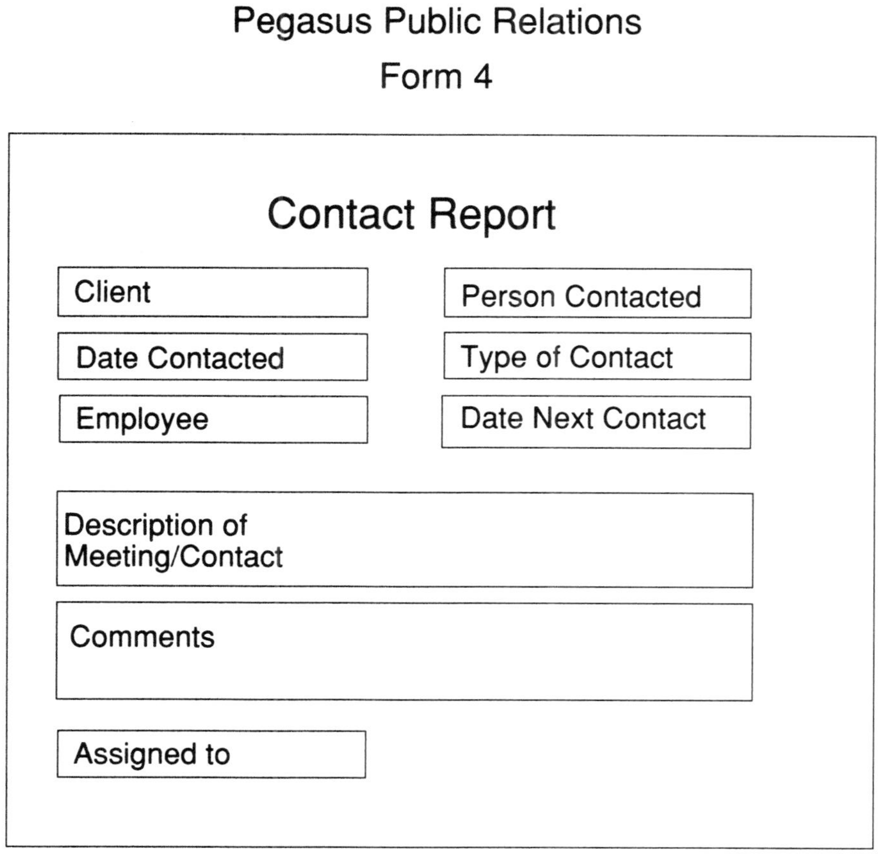

Pegasus Public Relations

Form 4

## Contact Report

| Client | Person Contacted |

| Date Contacted | Type of Contact |

| Employee | Date Next Contact |

Description of
Meeting/Contact

Comments

Assigned to

**FIGURE 5.9**  The Contact Report is filled out by the account reps. The Date Next Contact field, picked up in the Next Contact view, turns the contact reports into a tickler file.

# The Letter Form

Ben included the Letter form in the Pegasus application for a variety of reasons. The form quickly and simply creates a letter or note to a client. The user enters data in only two fields—the salutation and the body of the letter. The date is automatically filled in and the address is inherited from the Client Information form. It works like a mail merge file, incorporating selected fields from one document into another (see Figure 5.11).

---

### Private Views and Documents

While Ben was still a long way from actually building the forms and views of the application in Notes, already he was getting feedback on how the Notes application would affect work patterns at Pegasus. The account reps, for example, were concerned about the Action Item view. They wanted the convenience of using the Notes application for reminders to themselves. But they weren't happy with the idea that everyone on the company could see all those reminders. Ben realized that he could write a selection formula so that the Action Item and Next Contact Date views would display only documents that included a due date or a contact date. The account reps could create private views for themselves, using other selection criteria to display items without due dates. (And to further insure their privacy, they could encrypt documents they wanted to keep purely personal.)

---

The Letter form is very different from the other forms in Notes: Its primary purpose is information output, not input. Ben hoped the Letter form would spark users of the Pegasus application to suggest other ways of making the application more convenient, more useful.

The form has special value for Client Services because it captures client correspondence into the database. The resulting body of information can be helpful to supervisors and new personnel.


# Verifying the Analysis

Ben sought feedback throughout the analysis process. He distributed his sketches among the management and staff. He assembled some sample views and documents so that Pegasus' management could better visualize Notes' benefits for them. He also conducted walk-throughs of the application for groups from Client Services and Creative Services to help them understand how a Notes application would fit into their jobs. Ben's goal was to stress Notes' advantages to the staff and to calm some fears about how much extra work it might cause. In fact, as he showed them, much of the application mirrored work they already were doing. Ben further refined the sketches based on the staff's comments and concerns, and then moved on to designing the application.

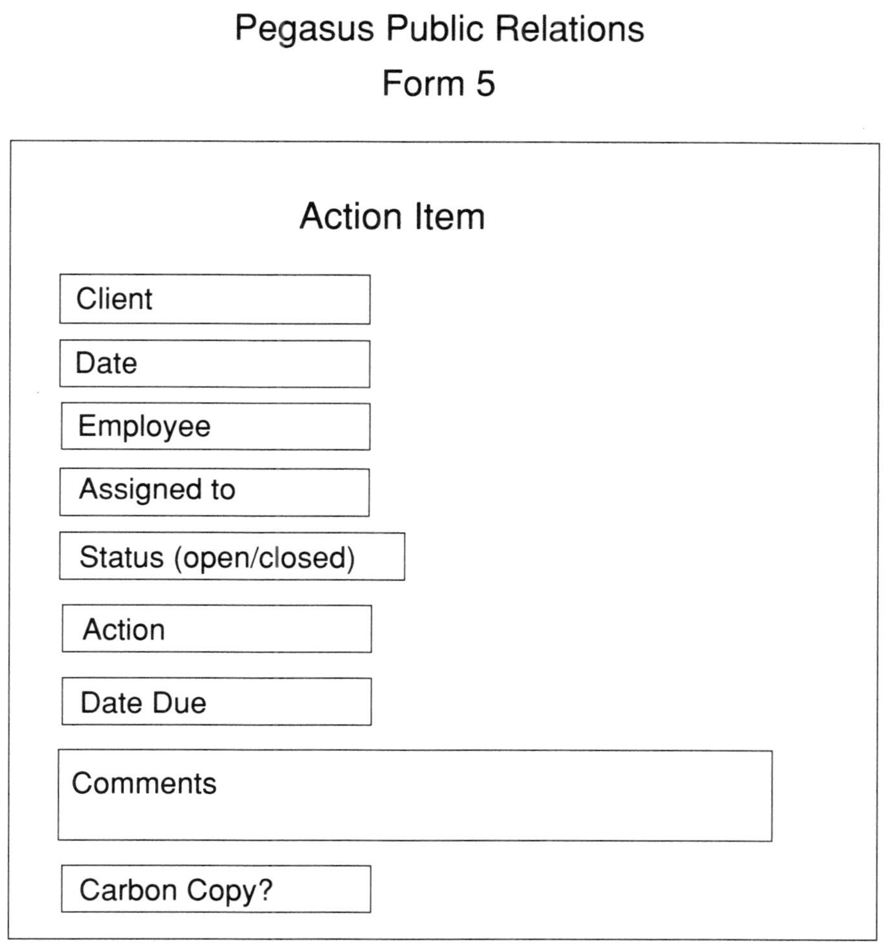

Pegasus Public Relations

Form 5

Action Item

Client

Date

Employee

Assigned to

Status (open/closed)

Action

Date Due

Comments

Carbon Copy?

**FIGURE 5.10** The Action Item form is intended for managers and account reps to make assignments or convey client requests.

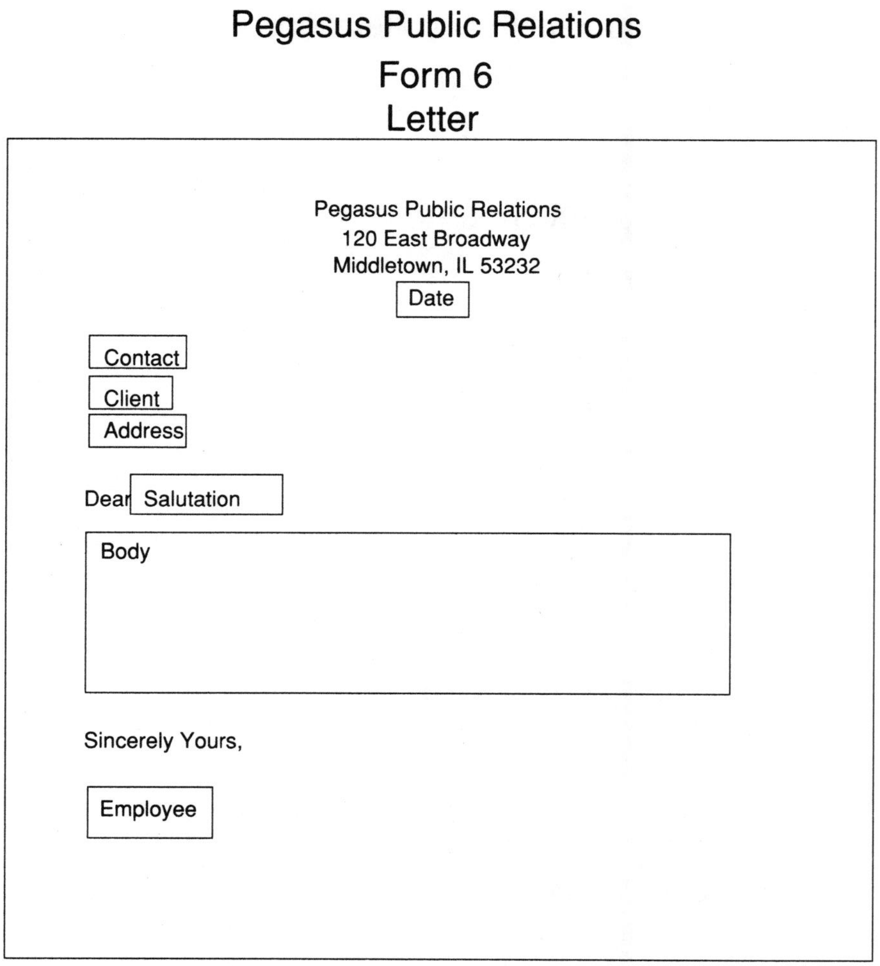

Pegasus Public Relations
Form 6
Letter

Pegasus Public Relations
120 East Broadway
Middletown, IL 53232

Date

Contact
Client
Address

Dear Salutation

Body

Sincerely Yours,

Employee

**FIGURE 5.11** The Letter form is intended as a convenience for users — and as a way of capturing information in the database that might not otherwise be preserved.

# The Design Step

If the application had been a simple one with a single form and a couple of views, Ben probably could have gone straight to work creating them onscreen in Notes. But the Pegasus application was considerably more complex, and the sketches he had prepared in the analysis step weren't adequate preparation for building the application's forms and views in Notes. A design step was required to describe the Pegasus application in terms Notes could understand. Ben had begun his analysis by focusing on the views, which allowed him to work backward from the desired output. But he had to start his design work with the input, and assign the data items names and characteristics Notes would use to manipulate them.

To do this, he spent a vitally important couple of hours breaking down the sketches into a list of data fields, giving each field a descriptive name and deciding the field's data type and field type. He determined which fields would be calculated and considered the formula that would perform each calculation. He identified the fields that would inherit their contents from other documents and made sure he had used the same field names in both places.

At this stage, too, Ben began making decisions about the appearance of the forms and views. He chose typefonts and colors and laid out his sketches of the forms and views with an eye to their ultimate use. He tried to design forms that would work well on both the computer screen and the printed page.

Throughout the process of analysis and design, Ben was aware that he was constantly balancing the features and functions that Pegasus wanted in the application against the capabilities of Notes. Because Notes is good for handling unstructured information, but not good for split-second updates of data (these points are discussed in Chapter 2), a key part of the development process is answering the question: Is Notes an appropriate platform for this application?

# Forms and Fields

Forms require more planning than views because forms are the heart of the database. Views are the user's point of entry into Notes, but views are derived from forms. Views can be created quickly, almost *ad hoc*, if the underlying forms have been well prepared. Views reveal the relationships among documents and data. That is the real power of views—they give a mass of material

---

# Designing the Forms

---

Ben's analysis had determined what data items would be included in each form. His next task was to build a profile of each data item, specifying its attributes and its relationships with the other elements of the form. He had several steps to follow:

- **Match data items with field names**. Each data item must have a field in a form to receive it, and each field must have a unique name, so that when Notes uses that name in a formula the right data will be selected.

- **Create a naming convention**. This was necessary for the all fields in an application. It's easier to remember the names of fields, to write formulas for selection and inheritance, if a consistent, descriptive set of names has been applied to the fields.

- **Assign a data type to each field**. The data types (Text, Number, Time, Keywords, Rich Text, Document Author) determine what Notes can do with the contents of the field.

- **Assign a field type to each field**. The field types (Editable, Computed, Computed for display, Computed when composed) determine where the field contents will come from. Editable fields are filled in by the user of the form. Computed fields are filled in by Notes based on a formula the designer writes for the field. Fields that inherit their contents from other documents are computed fields.

- **Design the form**. The developer of an application has extensive control over the appearance of forms. She lays out the graphic elements of the forms, chooses typefonts and sizes for the static text in the forms and colors for the text and backgrounds.

- **Manage the application's security**. An important part of designing any Notes application is deciding who will have access to it, and what limitations should be put on their use of particular views and documents.

---

a manageable, comprehensible shape. But it is the forms that make collecting all that data possible.

Ben had to make many decisions about the fields, the type of the data they would contain, the naming conventions he would use, and the graphic design of the forms (see box, Designing the Forms).

# Naming Conventions for Fields

The first thing Ben Lewis did was to assign a name to each field in each form. He tried to make field names short but descriptive. Notes field names are usually written in "proper case"—that is, spelled with an initial capital letter followed by lower-case letters, like a proper name. Spaces are not allowed, but two words describing a field can be run together as in FirstName or connected by an underscore mark as in First_Name. In the Pegasus application, Ben used the first alternative, running together capitalized words where complex field names were clearer and more specific than single words: HoursToComplete, CostPerHour.

# Data Types

Next, he identified the type of data that would go into each field (see Figure 5.12). The choice of data type depends on what the contents of the field will be used for, and where and how it should appear. A Notes field can contain one of six types of data, which will be examined next.

**Text**      The simplest options are for text and numerical data. The data type Text is used for fields that contain only a few words and are to appear in a view, such as an address or a title.

**Number**    The Number data type allows the developer to set the formatting options for the field to include decimals, dollar signs, or percentages. Data in Number fields can be used in formulas and aggregated in views.

**Time**      The Time data type stamps a field with the date and time of a document's creation. Several Pegasus forms, including Project Status, have fields which enter the current date automatically using a field formula that consists of a single function, @Created. Because the system can't backdate the forms, it encourages the Creative Services employees to fill out their Project Status reports daily.

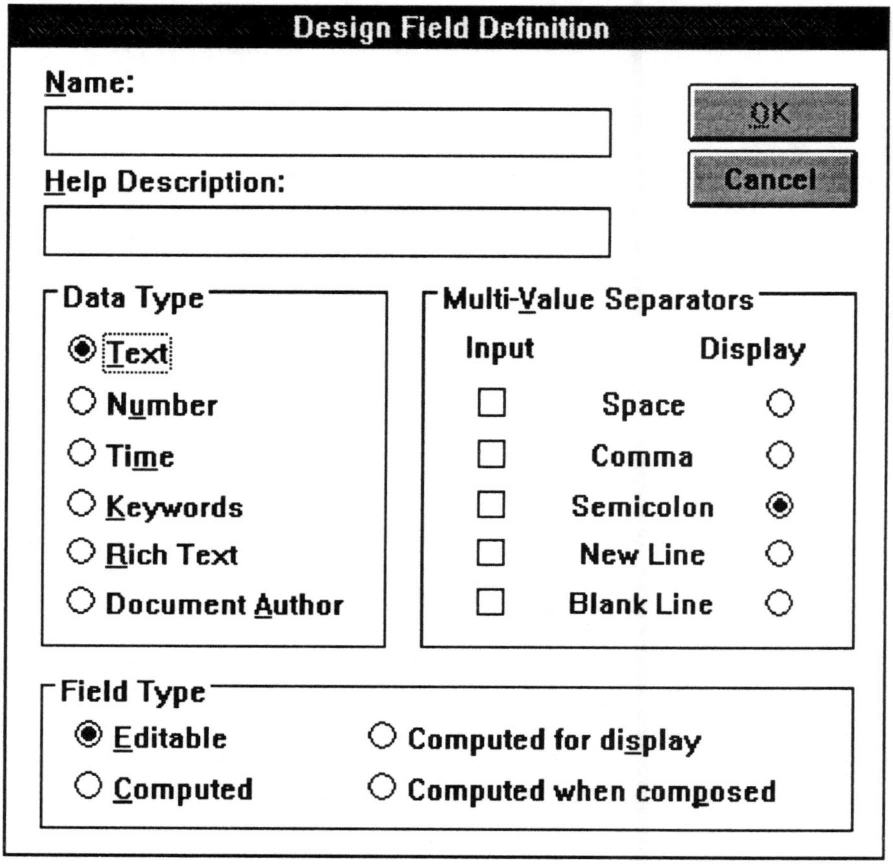

**FIGURE 5.12** Data Types are selected from the Design Field Definition dialog box, as well as the field name, help description, field type, and separator.

**Document Author**   Similar to the Time data type, the Document Author option fills the specified field with the name of the person who created the document. Notes picks up the name of the logged-in user from the ID file. Ben Lewis chose the Document Author data type for the fields labelled Employee in the Project Status, Contact Report, and Action Item forms. In Action Item, he made the field editable so users could assign the action to another individual. (In this case, the word "alleged" appears after the name to indicate it is not the actual author of the document.)

**Keywords**     The Keywords data type limits the user's choices in filling in a data field. The developer of the database provides a list of choices that appears in the form as a set of check-boxes or radio buttons or a list the user moves through by hitting the spacebar. The advantage of using Keywords is consistency: If a field containing a company name in a form is made a category in a view, for example, the same company could become three categories if users had spelled the name three different ways.

For example, in the Client Information form, Ben made the field for Business Type a Keywords field. Users identify the client's business type by selecting from a list of seven choices. If the management of Pegasus wished in the future to do studies on the percentage of business that came from each type, they could create a view categorized by business type. Selecting choices from a Keywords list insures the consistency of data entry this process needs. For example, without a Keywords list, the choice Automobile Dealership could have been typed in as Car Dealership, Ford Dealership, Used Car Dealer, or some other variation.

**Rich Text**     The Rich Text data type makes it possible for a field to contain whole documents as large as four gigabytes. Rich Text fields can also hold charts, graphs, and scanned images. Rich Text fields formatted with text in several sizes and graphics inserted bear little resemblance to database entries and often look more like desktop publishing documents.

# Field Types

While the data types define the nature of the field, the five field types put restrictions on the fields. The types are Editable, Non-editable, Computed, Computed-for-display, and Computed-when-composed.

For those fields that hold information users can enter and edit, the field type must be Editable. Text, Number, Time, or Keywords fields can be either Editable or Computed. Rich Text and Document Author fields only have two Field Type options, Editable and Non-editable. Ben Lewis set the Employee field in the Pegasus forms to Non-editable to insure that the author of each document was reported accurately; users weren't able to change the contents of the field in documents they created and thus pretend to be someone else. Even if a field of the data type, Document Author, is left Editable, Notes imposes a security safeguard: It prints the changed contents of the field, but follows it with [alleged]).

Fields that Notes fills in must be one of the three Computed field types: Computed, Computed-for-display, or Computed-when-composed. Pegasus's Project Description and Project Status forms use several computed field types. On the Project Description form, the Total Estimated Labor field is computed from a formula that multiplies the values in Hours to Complete by the Cost Per Hour. In the Project Status form, % of Total Estimated is computed by dividing the value in Total Labor Cost by the Total Estimated Labor field from the Project Description form. Both these fields are of the Computed type: The value they contain is calculated each time the form is displayed, and the result saved. If a manager decided to lower a client's fee, he could change the Cost Per Hour field and resave the document in order to get the new amount.

The Computed-for-display field type calculates the same value, but does not save it when the document is closed, so that the value is not available to be inherited into other documents. Using this field type saves disk space. The Computed-when-composed field type designates a value that is calculated when the document is created, but not updated each time it is resaved. In the example above of the change in the hourly rate, if the field had been a Computed-when-composed field type, the answer computed at the time the document was composed would not change even if the hourly rate were lowered at a later time.

## Inheritance

Like the Keywords data type, inheritance is a way to enforce consistency in Notes. As the name suggests, inheritance works by transferring data from a field in one document, called the controlling document, to a field in another. The controlling document is the document that was opened or highlighted in a view at the time the user chose the form from the Compose menu.

In the Pegasus application, each form inherits the client's name from the Client Information form, which is the first form Pegasus fills out for a new account. Because the client's name is typed into Notes only once no matter how large the database grows, it is always spelled consistently.

Inheritance was important to the Pegasus application for another reason, too. In their conversations with Ben, staff members emphasized that they had little time to spend keying data into a computer. They wanted the forms kept short and simple and, whenever possible, able to pick up data already in the database.

In addition to providing consistency and convenience, inherited fields help orient a user to the form. The Client field from Pegasus's Client Information form is inherited in many other forms as a guidepost, a visual reminder to the user of which client he is working with.

## Hidden Fields

Fields can be included in forms but not displayed. There are several reasons to do this. First, a field can be hidden to avoid cluttering the screen with information the user doesn't need to see, such as her own name or the date. A hidden field might be used in a formula, but not displayed because it has no meaning by itself. A field might be hidden because it contains information that has no meaning by itself or that the database manager doesn't want the user to see — an intermediate value in a complex calculation, for instance, or a value not used in the form but required so that it can be inherited into another form. Finally, a field can be hidden under certain conditions but displayed under others. For example, a document might include a field called Date Created which would be filled in by Notes but not displayed when the document is created.

The Pegasus forms include several hidden fields. For example, Ben discovered that to compute the value of the % of Total Estimated field in the Project Status form, he needed to inherit the Total Estimated Labor field from the Project Description form. However, since users didn't need to see it, he made it a hidden field.

## Synonyms

Notes allows forms and views to have multiple names — or, more properly, a name and multiple synonyms. It's a good idea to assign a name and a synonym to each form and view. For example, the view Projects has a synonym called Current Projects. Notes uses the first name (in this case, Projects) on the list in public places, like the Compose and View menus. The second name is kept private for the use of the application designer in formulas like a view's selection formula, which specifies that only documents created in a particular form will be listed in the view. The advantage is that the first name can be changed for cosmetic reasons — to change the mnemonic initial that can be keyed in to make the selection, or to reorder the listing of items on a menu — without forcing the designer to hunt down and rewrite every formula that refers to that form or view.

# User Access and Privileges

User access is another major element of the application design. The manager of a Notes application controls two kinds of access to it. The right to use the application is governed by the User Access Control list (see box, User Access Levels). The right to use specific views and forms is controlled by assigning a privilege to a form or view, and granting a user, or a list name from the Name and Address Book, the same privilege. All applications make use of User Access Control to assign access, while privileges are used only in more complex databases, or when especially sensitive data is involved (see Figure 5.13).

User access for Ben's database was very simple: All the users were assigned Editor access, which allowed them to edit any document in the database (see box, User Access Levels). After the application had been in use for some time, changes made it more complex. Ben then assigned privileges which restricted certain views and forms to use only by Pegasus managers. That process is described in Chapter 7.

# Summary

Notes can produce applications that not only do exactly the work the groups using them want to get done, but that also reflect the corporate cultures of those groups—their patterns of communication, their emphasis on security, their use of PCs. To take advantage of this adaptability, however, the developer must understand more than just how to create forms and views. A Notes application is most likely to succeed if it is developed in a democratic atmosphere that includes its potential users, and is designed to provide some benefit to each of the groups that uses it.

The development of Notes applications needs a level of support that matches the scope of the application. Individuals and small groups can develop their own databases. Applications that span departments and computer systems need support from the corporate MIS department. And for companies developing strategic applications, there are specialized consulting services and information-management add-on products available from value-added resellers of Notes and a group of consultants and developers united by Lotus under the banner of Alliance Partners.

A good way to ensure that the application development process focuses on these needs of the organization is to follow the steps prescribed by classical

# User Access Levels

Access to a Notes application is not just a matter of "on" or "off." There are seven levels of access, and each level has progressively more control over the database and its contents. Every database has a default access setting, as well, and Notes users who aren't named on the User Access Control list for that database are limited to the rights assigned the default setting. The seven levels:

- **No Access**. If the default user access is No Access, then only those people specifically named in the access list may open and use the database. While users who have No Access to an application can't place it on their workspace or open it, they may read the policy statement. Since every policy statement should name the manager of the application, Notes users may contact her and request access.

- **Depositor**. A user with Depositor access may mail documents into a database, but may not open it and read in its contents. This makes possible applications where information must be kept private, such as the collection of personnel reviews, or ballot box applications.

- **Reader**. A Reader may open the database and read in it, but may not to create new documents nor edit existing ones.

- **Author**. An Author may read all the existing documents, create new ones, and edit documents he created. He may not edit documents created by others.

- **Editor**. To edit the work of others, a user must have Editor level access to the database. Then he can create new documents and read and edit all existing documents in a database. Editors cannot change the structure of the forms or the views or change the access list itself, however. Editor access is a common default setting, because it allows the user the most scope in working with the contents of the application.

- **Designer**. The Designer can do everything an Editor can do with existing documents and the document-creation process. In addition, a Designer may add, delete, or change forms and views. He may not, however, make any changes in the User Access Control list.

- **Manager**. The Manager is the gatekeeper of access to the application, and she also has the power to permanently delete the application from Notes. (There is typically more than one manager assigned to an application, just as a security precaution.)

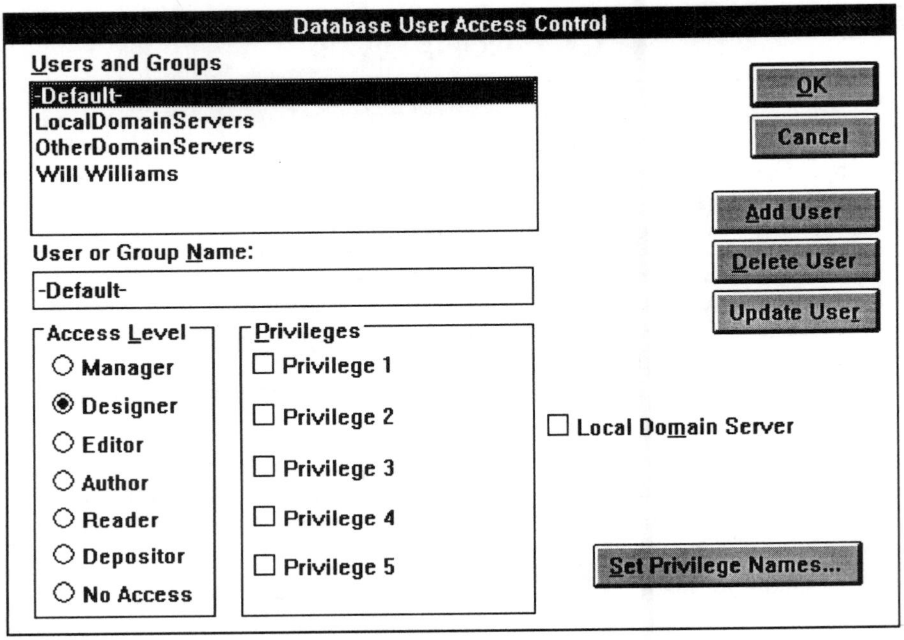

**FIGURE 5.13** Database security depends on the Access Level managers assign users in the Access Control List. Here, also, users are added, deleted, or updated and privilege names are assigned.

mainframe program development: Analysis, design, building, testing, documenting. A sample application for a company called Pegasus Public Relations illustrates this process.

The application's developer drew on his knowledge of the company as much as his knowledge of Notes. He began by analyzing his company's intentions for the application—who would use it, what work they did, what information they would put into the database, and what they wanted to get out. These inputs and outputs became rough sketches of the application's forms and views.

The design step put the inputs and outputs of the analysis step into terms Notes would understand in the building step: The developer turned the sketches into lists of fields with assigned names and types. He worked out the flows of data through the database's forms as information was inherited into one document from another. He formulated the graphic design of the application, and its security structure—who would be given access to the application, and limitations on their use.

# 6

# Building an Application

**W**hen his planning was complete, Ben was ready to begin building his application in Notes. With the forms and views laid out on paper and the data and field types assigned, much of the hard work was done. What followed was often mechanical. Working largely in the Design and Style menus, he attended to the many details involved:

- **He created a new database**. He did this using the File menu, following much the same procedure as a Notes user adding an existing database to his workspace.

- **He created the forms**. This took the most time, as he assigned each new form's attributes, created its static text and data fields, and put a final polish on its layout appearance and function, adjusting text fonts, sizes, and colors, and field structures and placement.

- **He created the views**. Creating a view also required several steps—assigning attributes, columns, and categories, but it was generally easier and faster than creating a form.

## Creating the New Database

Ben began by selecting the workpage on his desktop in which he wanted the database icon to reside. Ben built the database on the hard disk of his own computer and transferred it to the Notes server only after it was finished and had gone through some initial testing. He created a new database using the File, Database menu (see Figure 6.1).

Ben named the disk file Pegasus and the desktop object Pegasus Clients and Projects. The file extension .NSF was automatically appended to the name, Pegasus, to identify it as a Notes application file. Since he was creating

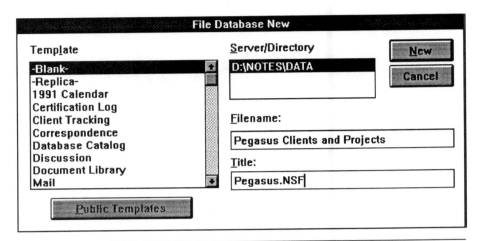

**FIGURE 6.1** A database is created in the File Database New dialog box. The filename must meet DOS's eight-character limit, but the title that appears on the desktop can be more descriptive.

the file from scratch, not using a template, he left Blank highlighted in the Template list box. When he selected New, a blank icon appeared on his workpage containing just the title of the database.

Ben discovered that when you create a new database without using a template, no forms or views are defined. By clicking on Pegasus Clients and Projects, he could open the application, but all that appeared was a nameless view with only one column labelled "#", the default column for document number.

To create the forms and views, Ben worked in the Design menu. The Design commands are reserved for designers and managers who can make structural changes to the database. This restriction prevents users from accidentally or purposefully changing the application. Since Ben had created the Pegasus database, he was automatically granted manager access to it.

# Creating the Forms

In the design phase, Ben had laid out the views first, in order to specify the outputs required from the application. Then he had designed the forms, working back from outputs to inputs to make sure that all the necessary data was gathered and managed correctly. In building, however, Ben created the forms first, then the views. He did this because Notes knows nothing about a data field until it has been defined in a form. Once defined, the fields appear on a list maintained by Notes in the application, and they can easily be selected for inclusion in a view.

Notes does not require the developer to follow a precise order in building a form. The developer is free to make changes in a form at any point in the process. Forms can evolve over time as users request different features. In building a database from scratch, Ben found he worked most efficiently by first laying out the general structure of the form, then progressing to the details. By following a routine for each form, he was able to avoid repetitious switching from menu to menu and window to window (see box, Building a Form, Step by Step).

---

## Building a Form, Step by Step

The work of creating a form follows steps that involve graphic design, defining fields, and setting security:

- **Establish the form's attributes**: its name and synonym, its background color, its type and other options.

- **Lay out the static text** and create the data fields on the screen. Position text and graphics; select colors and sizes of text.

- **Define the fields**. Select the data and field types, write format and value formulas, and set security features.

- **Create the Window title** for the form, writing a formula if necessary.

- **Test the form** to make sure any data-formatting, validation, and calculation functions work properly.

- **Assign User Privileges** and other security restrictions if the form will be restricted to only a few users of the application.

---

The first form Ben built was the Client Information form. Ben used the Design menu to create his form (see Figure 6.2). From it, he selected Forms; and then, in the Design Forms menu, he clicked on New. A new form appeared as a blank, white screen. Before he began entering text and creating fields on this clean slate, he returned to the Design menu and selected Form Attributes.

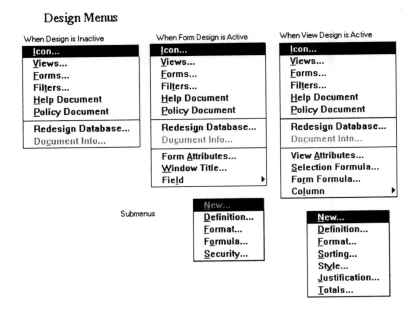

Design Menus

FIGURE 6.2 The Design menu choices change as forms and views are created. Most of the work of building forms and views takes place in this menu.

# Establishing the Form's Attributes

Ben began by setting the form's most basic attributes, its names and its type, in the Design Form Attributes dialog box (see Figure 6.3.).

Each form needs a name. When the application is finished, the names of the forms appear under the Compose menu. Form names may also be used in views and filters. In the Name text box, Ben entered two names for this form, separated by a vertical stroke: 1. Client Information|Client Information. The first name is the one that will appear when a user highlights the Compose Menu to see the list of forms; the second one is a synonym which the designer may use behind the scenes to identify forms in views, filters, and formulas. Ben started the visible form name with a numeral because Notes sorts menu entries in alphanumeric order. Using a numeral before the name meant that he could change the order of the appearance of entries in the menu simply by renumbering them. The second name, Client Information, was the one Ben intended to use in formulas that referred to the form.

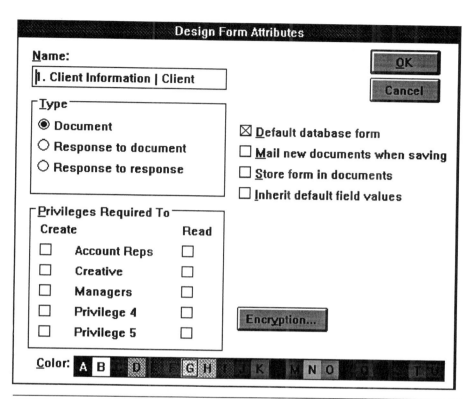

**FIGURE 6.3** The designer assigns the form's name, its type, privileges needed to use it, if any, and other default settings in the Form Attributes screen.

The form's type was Document, and Ben decided that it would be the default form for the database. Every application needs a default form. Notes displays a document in the database's default form if the form in which it was created cannot be found in the database. If any of the field names in the document matched the field names in the default form, the contents of those fields will be displayed. A more common use of a default form occurs when data is imported. Notes uses the database's default form as the pattern for storing the incoming information. Any fields in the imported data that aren't matched in the default form are thrown away. Designers who know ahead of time that documents will be imported from another application often make the default form match the documents in the external database field for field.)

After consulting with the art director Ben decided to use different background colors on different forms to help identify them. He chose yellow, color

G, for the Client Information form. He put off assigning privileges or encryption options until later, when he would address user access issues.

## Data Fields and Static Text

At this point, Ben's form was a blank yellow window. To lay out the form's fields, Ben worked in the Design, Field menu and the Style menu. To place a field on the screen, he positioned the cursor where the field would start and selected the Design, Field, Definition menu. After he named and defined a field, it appeared in a rectangular box (see Figure 6.4).

He could place the cursor anywhere on the screen and enter and format text. This text, labels for the fields and instructions to the users, appears every time the form is opened, no matter what data is entered, so it is called static text.

Ben's original sketch of the Client Information form looked much like a printed form, with the fields placed side by side, in two columns. He quickly discovered that the way Notes treats fields caused problems with this arrange-

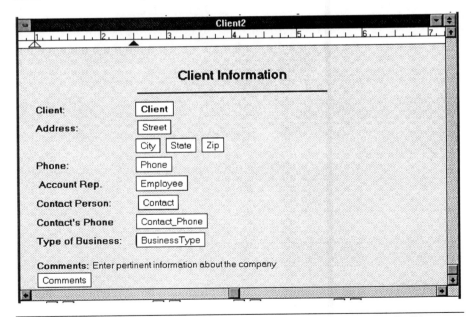

**FIGURE 6.4**   In a form, fields (in the rectangles) and static text can be placed anywhere and displayed in all the variations of typeface, size, and color.

ment. Notes fields have no fixed length. Normally, as data is keyed in, the field expands to the right. When it reaches the right margin of the form window, it starts a new line, pushing any text it encounters ahead of it. Unless the layout of the form allows for this expansion of fields, the clarity of the design can quickly be lost as data is entered.

Ben's solution also addressed a request from some of the Notes users at Pegasus. Some people had found that when using Notes, if they put multiple windows on the screen, the right side of the form—in smaller windows—frequently was cut off. He vertically rearranged the static text and the fields and aligned them on the left, so that they would fit conveniently in a small window and could grow without disturbing the appearance of the form.

He also altered the design of the address field. Because he intended to import the agency's client records from dBASE files into Notes, the form's fields and field names had to match those of the dBASE records. In those records, the Address field was split into four fields—street, city, state, and zip—so that four corresponding fields were needed in Notes (see Figure 6.5).

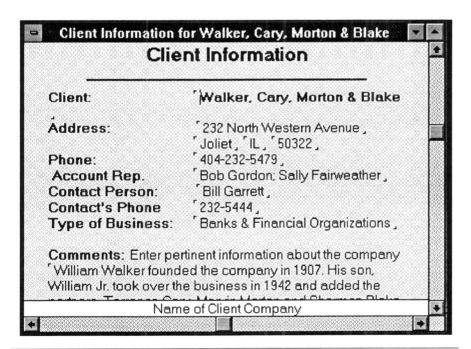

**FIGURE 6.5** The Client Information form is designed to display well in a small window, so that users can open multiple windows and still see the information in documents created with the form.

To add text to a form, he moved the cursor to the position where he wanted it to appear and began typing. If he decided to move the text to another location, he used the Cut and Paste commands. He left the ruler turned on (the Show Ruler command is on the View menu) so that he could set margins and tabs to line up the fields and their static text.

After adding several more fields, Ben began to refine the form's appearance. He embellished the forms with choices from the Style menu and put considerable effort into making them look good. For example, he centered, boldfaced, and increased the size of the heading and boldfaced all the static text which identified the fields. After showing some of his first efforts to the agency's art director he reworked and simplified them, reducing the numbers of colors and lines he used, making the forms less cluttered.

## Defining the Fields

When the layout seemed satisfactory, Ben began working on the fields. Each field had to be defined so that it would function correctly. To work on a particular field, Ben highlighted it with the mouse and double-clicked to open the Field Definition window from the Design menu. This screen was the same one he had used to name the field, but now he was returning to it to fill in all the other specifications (see Figure 6.6).

Many of the fields needed a Help Description, a short explanation or instruction that appears at the bottom of the form window when the cursor is positioned on the field. The Help Descriptions guide users as they enter data. As a user tabs from one field to another to enter the various parts of a client's address, the Help Description changes accordingly to prompt for the expected input: Enter the street, Enter name of city, Enter a two-letter abbreviation for state, and Enter 5-digit zip code. The Help for the Business Type field (which is a Keyword field) directs the user to Press Enter or Spacebar for choices. The Help Descriptions are a major part of the application's documentation for users, and Ben was careful to write one for each editable field.

Each field needs a data type. In the Client Information form, the fields are all Text except Business Type, which is a Keyword field, and Comments, which is Rich Text. (See Chapter 5 for an explanation of field and data types.) Remember, Text and Keyword fields can appear in views, but Rich Text fields cannot be put into views. This limitation is seldom a problem in application design because most Rich Text fields are too long to be displayed in the tabular form of a view. And in the case of Pegasus, most comments are far too long and unspecific for a column in a view.

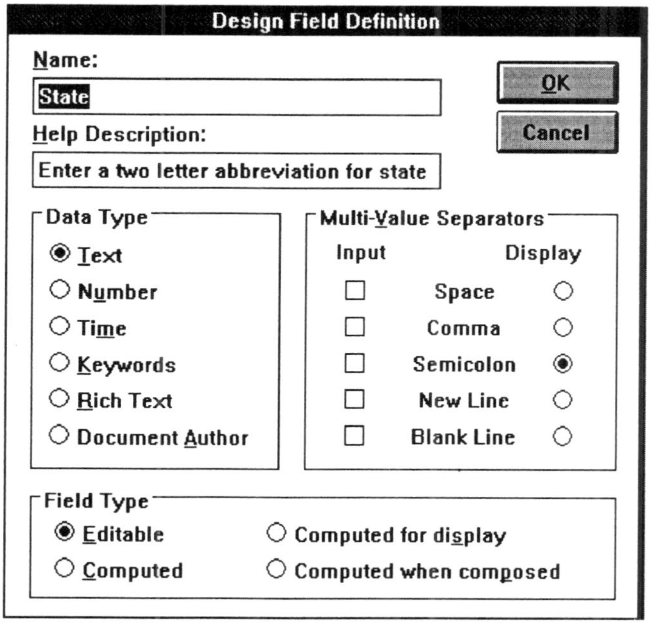

**FIGURE 6.6** Several parameters must be specified for each field in the form. The Help Description shouldn't be ignored — it appears as a prompt for users when they tab into that field in the form.

Each field also needs a field type. The Client, Address, Phone, Employee, Contact, and Contact Phone fields are of the Editable field type — that is, they can be changed by the user and do not contain predetermined values. Editable and Text are the default values because they are most often used.

Users can change the style only of Rich Text fields, but designers can edit all the data types — Text, Number, Time, Keywords, and Document Author — to appear in a variety of styles. Because Ben wanted the Client's name to appear in bold type when the document was open, he highlighted the field and selected Bold under the Style menu. When he was finished with the field name, Client appeared in the field box in bold.

In Ben's application, Business Type is a Keywords field that lets the user assign one of a list of business types — retail store, manufacturer, and so on. The Keywords data type is selected in the Design Field Definition window. Then the list of keywords and the format of the field are set in the Field Format dialog box (see Figure 6.7).

The format can be one of three user interfaces — Standard, Check Boxes, or Radio Buttons. The User Interface box itself uses the radio button interface, a set of selection buttons that allows only one choice — when one button

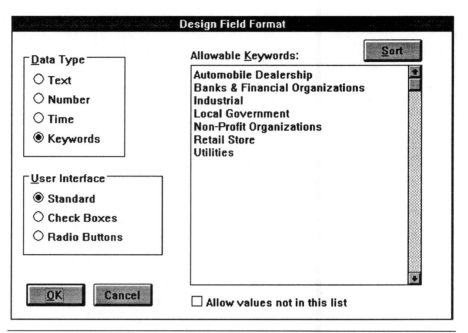

**FIGURE 6.7** The Design Field Format window lists Keyword choices. The entries in the Allowable Keywords box can appear in the form as radio buttons, check boxes, or a standard text field.

is selected all the others are deselected. Check boxes presents a list of the choices, each with a small square box to its left. (The list and boxes appear whenever the form is opened for editing or display, but not when it is being designed.) Unlike radio buttons, check boxes allow users to select as many choices as they want. But both check boxes and radio buttons restrict users to the choices listed and do not allow them to type in any other value.

The standard interface offers the greatest flexibility of the three interfaces but is the least intuitive. The standard interface for a Keywords field appears in a form as an empty field. Users have three ways to set the field to the value they want. Pressing the spacebar rotates available choices through the field as if it were a window with the list of choices behind it. Typing in the first letter of a key word causes it to appear in the field. Selecting the field and pressing the Enter key pops up a dialog box with the list of choices to select from. If none of the choices is correct, the standard interface allows users to type in another value.

Ben selected Standard for the Business Type field because he wanted users to be able to enter other key words if none of those in the list fit. He also felt the list was too long to appear on screen and that most employees would know the categories well and would not need to see them all listed. Figure 6.17 shows the finished list of key words with the standard interface selected.

The other field that needed changing was Comments. Ben made it a Rich Text field and selected Editable as its field type. This field contains client information. Ben wanted to give users the range of text formatting tools they were familiar with from using a word processor—underline, boldface, italic, margin controls, multiple type sizes, and even colors. In Notes, these are available only in Rich Text fields.

## Creating the Window Title

The first form was almost complete. The final touch was the window title, the text that appears in the title bar at the top of the window when the form is opened.

Window titles, like the field Help descriptions, are a small but important piece of Notes' Help system. The titles orient the user by presenting information about the active document. The window title is not static text; it can change to reflect the status of the document. The changes are governed by a formula created under the Design, Window Title menu.

Ben wanted the window title to reflect whether the user is working in a new form (by displaying New Client Information) or editing a saved document (by displaying Client Information for and the name of the client that had been saved in the document). The formula he wrote used two Notes @functions: @If and @IsNewDoc (see Figure 6.8). @If sets up a condition and @IsNewDoc specifies that condition. The @IsNewDoc function checks the document to see if it has been saved (in which case, it isn't considered new). If the condition is true (the document is new), then the first of the two clauses bracketed by semicolons is put into effect. If @IsNewDoc is false, the second clause is executed: "If this is a new document display the words 'New Client Information' as the window title. Otherwise, display 'Client Information for' and the contents of the field named Client."

## Testing the Form

Notes checks each formula as it is entered and doesn't accept any that contains a syntax error. If Ben made a mistake, such as leaving out a closing parenthesis in a formula, Notes beeped and flashed an explanatory note on the screen when he tried to save the formula. This built-in troubleshooting

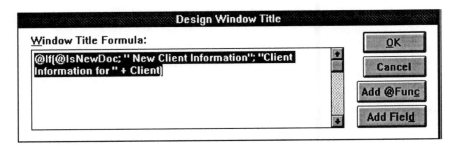

**FIGURE 6.8** This formula governs the text in the window title for the Client Information form. It adjusts the title to reflect whether the active document has been saved or is being created.

saved time by pointing up errors as he made them rather than forcing him to track down the source of mistakes later on.

Ben created several sample documents to make sure the form was accepting and displaying data correctly. More extensive testing would wait until other forms and views were created.

## Creating the User Access List and Privileges

For this relatively simple application, which would be open to many Notes users, Ben chose not to assign any user privileges. He gave everyone Editor rights, and reserved Manager access for himself and one other Notes user. All users could then create new documents and read, edit, and delete existing documents. Only the managers could change forms, views, or add new users to the User Access Control list. (For an explanation of User Access levels, see Chapter 5.)

## Inheriting Values in a Form

The item of data most frequently included in the documents in Ben's application is the name of a Pegasus client—one appears in every document in the database. Yet each client name is keyed into the application only once—when the Client Information document is created. After that, it is inherited by each new document from a predecessor.

To set up these inherited fields, Ben followed a sequence of steps. First, he checked the setting, Inherit default field values, on the Design Form Attributes screen (see Figure 6.6). Next, he set the Field Type to Computed in the Design Field Definition window. In the Design Field Formula, he wrote a formula that was simple but necessary: Client.

He used inheritance in another form, Letter. In that form he needed to inherit from the Client Information form not only the client's name but the also the address.

To make inheritance work, Notes performs several checks when a user opens a new form. It determines whether inheritance is enabled and from which document the new form will inherit data. Then, it searches for fields with the Computed field type and Editable fields with a Default Value formula, and it computes their contents by executing their field formulas. Where the formula indicates inheritance by including a field name Notes searches the proper document for the proper field and transfers its contents into the current form.

# Computed Fields

The formulas for computed fields will look familiar to any spreadsheet user. In a calculation, a field in a Notes form behaves just like a cell in a worksheet. In editable fields, the user fills in the data. In computed, fields field formulas specify data cells (by name, not by location—one difference from a spreadsheet) and the operations to be performed on their contents. In effect, each field is a named range of one cell.

The purpose of the Project Description form is to establish the cost of a project for the creative team and the account reps as well as the clients. For example, it takes data from fields named HoursToComplete and CostPerHour and calculates a value for TotEstLabor.

# Hidden Fields

Fields that contain computed values are usually hidden while the document is open for editing because they have no contents until the document is saved. A designer can choose to hide fields when the document is being edited, when it is being read, or when it is being printed—or at all these times, to make some fields completely invisible to the user.

Ben made the TotEstLabor field hidden while Project Description documents are in editing mode because the value is not computed until the document is saved. When in reading mode, after the document is saved, or in printing mode, the values of the computed fields appear. A user who wanted to see the computed values could open the saved document and read them or print them out.

Hidden fields are often used in Notes forms to hold intermediate results, values that result from one calculation and that will be used by another, but which by themselves have no significance to the user. Although the Project Status form, for example, contains fifteen fields, the user only needs to enter data in five of them. The others are inherited, automatically entered, or computed values (see Figure 6.9).

Two of these inherited fields are TotEstLabor and TotEstMatCost. They are hidden at the bottom of the form and used to calculate the percentage of the total project labor and materials costs represented by the current form. The two values themselves are unseen by the user, and their results, the percentages of total estimated labor and materials reported on this form, appear only when the document is read or printed.

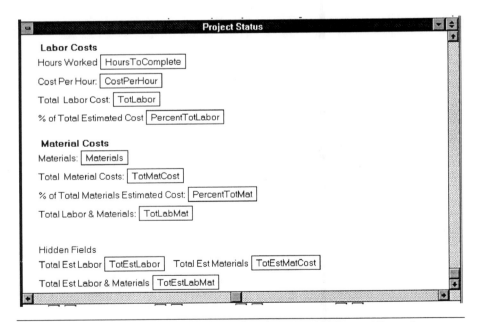

**FIGURE 6.9**  The hidden fields at the bottom of the Project Status form are used only in computations — they are hidden from users whenever the document is edited, read or printed.

# Response Documents

To make the Pegasus Notes application a forum for communication, Ben needed to provide a way for it to respond to documents, so that the staff could add information, make a suggestion, or expand on an idea. Notes makes it easy to build this response capability into an application. Response forms add a greater dimension to any database by giving every group member the opportunity to be a transmitter as well as a receiver of information. Including a response form in an application is one of the basics of good programming practice in Notes.

Ben developed a simple form named Response. It automatically picks up both the name of the form from which it was launched and the client's name (see Figure 6.10). It does this by using inheritance. The date and user name are entered automatically. The only field the user must fill in is the Comment field.

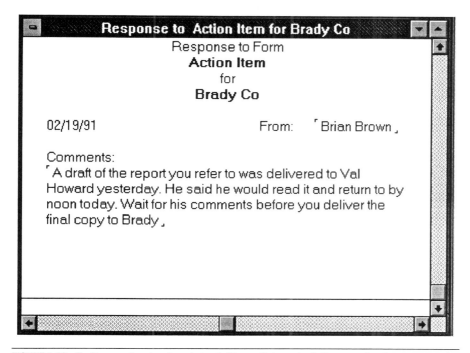

**FIGURE 6.10**    The Response form is an important part of the way Notes works. It allows users to enter responses and comments that appear in views along with the document they respond to.

## Forms Management

The last form that Ben created was the Letter form. This form has a very different purpose from the other forms in the Pegasus database. Most Notes forms are input tools; they gather data which is used within Notes. The Letter form serves as a way of exporting data from the electronic environment of Notes to the outside world. With this output capability, Notes can offer many of the functions familiar to users of forms-creation and forms-management software.

The Letter form is not as formal as an invoice or an application, but it gives some indication of what might be done with forms in a Notes application. It inherits much of its contents, eliminating the need to retype addresses. It automatically prints out in the Times Roman 12 point font Pegasus uses in all its correspondence and proposals. It lets the users work within Notes using simple cut-and-paste to include text from other documents, rather than making them export files and leave Notes to work in a word processor. Most importantly for the group, it captures the communication with the client in the database, where it can be used as example or as reference.

The Letter form includes Pegasus's address as static text at the top and automatically fills in the date. The address fields their contents from a "Client Information" document. The Salutation field is left blank. The body of the letter is created in a Rich Text field, so it can include formatted text, imported data and even graphics. Finally, the user's name is automatically filled in.

## Sending E-Mail from an Application

The walls between Notes' applications and its electronic mail system are very low. Fields that are standard to every document in Notes provide almost all the routing and categorization information of a typical E-mail message — author, date, subject, message text, attachments. Because the only thing missing is a To field, Notes provides a way to include one: include a field named SendTo in the document. To E-mail a copy of the document, a Notes user fills in the SendTo field, then clicks on the Mail menu and Send.

Ben took advantage of this capability by adding a SendTo field to the Action Item form. The inclusion of the field made it easy to forward the information in a way that assured it wouldn't be overlooked. Remember, the static text may be different from the field name. In the Action Item form, the SendTo field is labelled "Assigned To" (see Figure 6.11).

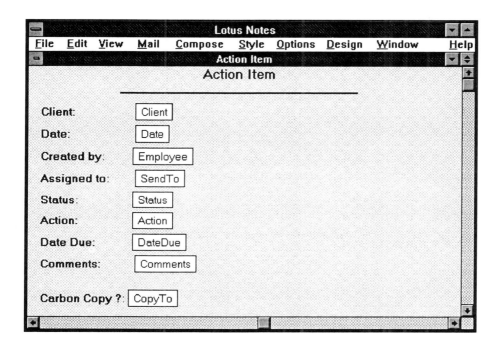

**FIGURE 6.11** The Action Item form in Design mode shows the field named SendTo. A user name entered in this field will receive a copy of the document as an electronic-mail message.

# Creating the Views

There is no prescribed order for creating the pieces of a Notes application: Developers can build all the forms, then all the views, or they can alternate between forms and views. Ben chose the latter method. As a way of testing each field to make sure it functioned properly, he first created a form, then used that form to create several documents. He checked to make sure computed fields calculated values as they were supposed to; that formatted fields, such as Client, appeared in the proper typeface and size; that fields inherited the values they were supposed to; and that hidden fields worked properly. He needed several documents to test the views that he intended to create. After he had created several documents, he built the view that drew its information from those test documents.

In Ben's application the By Client view listed the documents created using the form, Client Information. The By Client view served as a quick reference for account reps who wanted to check a client's phone number, or managers who wanted to see which employee was assigned to an account. Just as in creating a form, Ben followed the same set of steps to create each view (see box, Creating a View).

---

## Creating a View

There is less work to creating a view than creating a form because the developer has limited control over the appearance of a view. Those controls that are available influence the structure of the view, rather than the graphic design. There are no text formatting controls, and only limited controls over colors. The design of the view is primarily influenced by the positioning of its column and the use of category headings. The steps involved include:

- **Create the view**, name it, and select its attributes such as background color.

- **Define the columns** for the view, set their format and their sorting order.

- **Write a selection formula** to determine which forms the view will draw data from.

---

## Creating and Naming Views

Ben began by selecting Views, New from the Design menu. An empty, untitled view appeared with one column labeled with a "#" sign to indicate the number of the document. (Notes assigns a sequential number to each document as it is created.) He selected Design again. In the View Attributes screen, he named this new view, By Client (see Figure 6.12).

On this screen, he selected who could use this view, when it would be displayed, and how it would look when opened. The "who" was simple: By leaving all the check boxes blank under Privileges Required to Use, he made the view public for anyone who had access to the database. Since the purpose of this database was to foster communications among Pegasus' three divisions, he felt that each group should be able to access any document about a client. He set the "when" by selecting Default View: This would be the view displayed the first time a user opens the application. To set the view's look, he chose Expanded in the Categories Initially box. This setting insured that the view

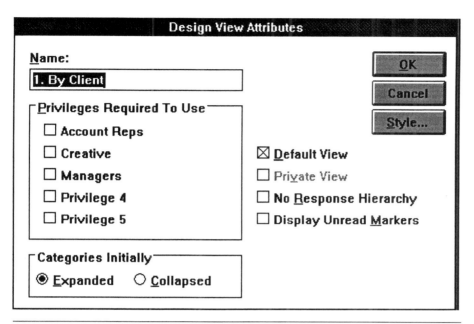

**FIGURE 6.12**  In the View Attributes window, the developer names the view, assigns privileges to it, indicates whether it is to open expanded or collapsed (main headings only), and sets defaults.

would display a line of information for each document it indexed, rather than category headings only.

Clicking the Style button in Design View Attributes opened the Style Attributes window. In this window, Ben selected colors for the view. Notes automatically displays views on white backgrounds, unread documents in red, and other text in black. Here, in Style Attributes, Ben could change the background color from white to the same light yellow he had used for the Client Information form.

# Creating and Defining the Columns

The view By Client is a simple one. Its only purpose is to provide access to the documents it indexes. Its columns contain data drawn entirely from the documents. As a result, Ben did not have to write formulas to calculate the contents of a column, or create a multilevel categorization scheme with hidden columns to organize the view. All Ben had to do was create the columns and specify which field in the form would provide the data in each of them (see

Figure 6.13). He did this by following his sketch. He began with the column defined by default as "#". He changed this definition by selecting Column, Definition from the Design menu.

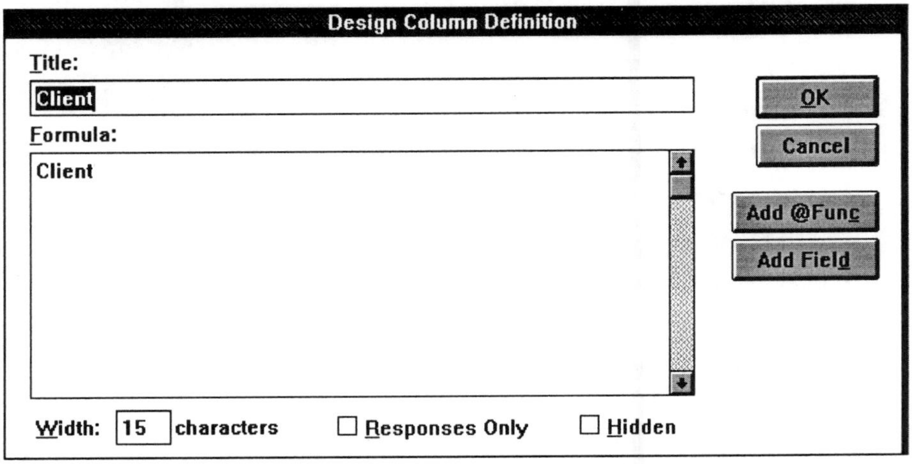

**FIGURE 6.13** Each column in a view is assigned a title and a formula — in this case, the name of the field that is to appear in that column.

He renamed the column, Client and changed the formula that defined its contents to Client, the field name from the form. He changed the width of the column to 15 characters to display the whole name.

Once Ben defined a column, he could then format it, sort it, change its style by selecting colored and boldfaced text, justify it, and, if it were a number field, total it. He chose some of these options for each column. Since the Client column had originally been formatted for the document number, Ben changed the Design Column Format choice to text.

Ben created additional columns by positioning the cursor in the empty space to the right of the column he had created for Client. Once again, he chose Column New from the Design menu and created the second column called Phone # with the field, Phone. In additional columns, Contact Person used the field, Contact, and Acct. Rep. used the field, Employee. When all the columns were in the view, Ben adjusted their widths by using the mouse to move the column division lines, since it was much faster than opening each column definition and typing in the width.

To polish the view's appearance, Ben ordered the view by highlighting the Client column heading and selecting alphabetical order in the Design Column, Sort menu. Under Column, Style, he chose a blue color for text in the Client column and marked it for boldface, to make the client names stand out from the rest of the information (see Figure 6.14).

| Lotus Notes ▾ ▲ |
| File    Edit    View    Mail    Compose    Style    Options    Design    Window    Help |
| Pegasus Clients and Projects - 1. By Client ▾ ⬍ |

| Client | Phone # | Contact Person | Acct. Rep. | ▲ |
|--------|---------|----------------|------------|---|
| Brady Co | 617-898-9876 | Charles, Jordan | Robert Savin | |
| Crocker Motors | 502-244-5454 | Fred Moore | Sally Fairweather | |
| Donut Inn | 343-343-7745 | Cherrie Roberts | Robert Savin,Kevi | |
| Fidelity Industries | 617-823-7623 | Margot Carson | Henry Jackson | |
| Riverside Industrial | 412-343-3434 | Bud Bronson | James Wilson | ⬍ |
| Walker, Cary, Morton & | 404-232-5479 | Bill Garrett | Bob Gordon,Sally | |

**FIGURE 6.14**   The finished By Client view sorts the clients in alphabetical order and displays the most frequently used information from the Client Information forms.

## Creating the Selection Formula

Selection formulas limit what shows up in a view. The formulas can select documents created with specific forms, or documents which contain specific fields, in any combination. For example, SELECT @All selects all documents. SELECT Status = "(169)Open" selects all documents which contain a field called Status with a value of Open. In the case of Pegasus, Ben had used the field named Client as a selection formula, which meant that when documents were added to the database, any document with a Client field would be indexed in this view. This wasn't what Ben wanted. Every status report and action item would include a client name, but Ben didn't want them to appear in the By Client view. He wanted to limit this view to showing only data that came from the Client Information form. For this reason, he wrote a selection formula (see Figure 6.15).

The formula box originally had the formula SELECT @ALL, which would have selected all documents created in the database for possible inclusion in the view, no matter which form was used to create them. Ben changed the formula to SELECT Form = "Client Information."

When his design was finished and saved, Ben had completed his first view.

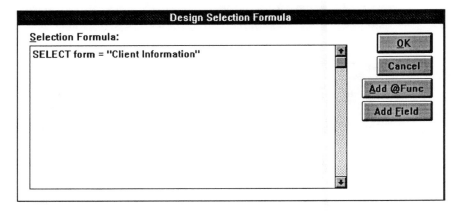

**FIGURE 6.15**   Selection formulas limit the documents which display in a view. In this example, only documents created with the Client Information form will display in this view.

## Totaled Columns in Views

The Design Column, Totals command brings similar spreadsheetlike capabilities to views, but it works differently: There is no formula to write. Because views can be structured in only a limited number of ways, the possibilities for doing column totals and subtotals can all be covered by a brief menu window (see Figure 6.16).

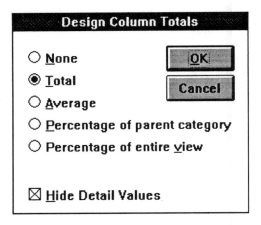

**FIGURE 6.16**   The Column, Totals feature allows the user to figure column totals, averages, or percentages for the column as a whole and for categories within it.

Ben used column totals in the Cost by Client & Project view to calculate Labor Cost and Material Cost columns. This view (see Figure 6-17) is built on the Project Status form. It categorizes all the projects in progress by client name and by project and lists each employee's daily labor and materials costs. It displays the costs for each project as a subtotal, and gives a grand total of all costs at the bottom of the list.

| | Pegasus Clients and Projects - Cost by Client & Project | | | | | |
|---|---|---|---|---|---|---|
| ■ Project | Employee | Date | Total | Labor Cost | Materials | |
| **Brady Co** | | | $3,422 | $1,130 | $2,292 | |
| Brady Fall Catalog — Project Estimate: $ ; To date: | | | $827 | $535 | $292 | |
| | Walt Donon | 09/28/90 | | $275 | $45 | |
| | Gordon Jones | 10/02/90 | | $260 | $247 | |
| Brady Fall Catalog — Project Estimate: $21500 ; To date: | | | $2,595 | $595 | $2,000 | |
| | Gordon Jones | 10/02/90 | | $595 | $2,000 | |
| **Fidelity Industries** | | | $16,173 | $3,543 | $12,630 | |
| Fabulous Fidelity — Project Estimate: $ ; To date: | | | $2,543 | $792 | $1,750 | |
| | Walt Donon | 09/29/90 | | $325 | | |
| | Susan Somes | 09/28/90 | | $137 | | |
| | Susan Somes | 10/10/90 | | $330 | $1,750 | |
| Fabulous Fidelity — Project Estimate: $15000 ; To date: | | | $140 | $140 | $0 | |
| | Henrietta Partridg | 10/02/90 | | $140 | | |
| Fidelity Finest — Project Estimate: $ ; To date: | | | $12,691 | $1,811 | $10,880 | |
| | Charles Casey | 09/27/90 | | $220 | $455 | |
| | Susan Somes | 10/02/90 | | $550 | $10,000 | |
| | Robert Slack | 10/02/90 | | $450 | $300 | |
| | Robert Slack | 10/02/90 | | $6 | $125 | |
| | Andy Good | 10/02/90 | | $585 | | |
| Fidelity Finest — Project Estimate: $448000 ; To date: | | | $800 | $800 | $0 | |
| | Tim Pennington | 10/02/90 | | $800 | | |
| | | | $19,595 | $4,673 | $14,922 | |

**FIGURE 6.17** The Cost by Client & Project view uses the Design Column Totals functions to generate subtotals and totals using time and cost data taken from the Project Status forms.

The view was designed for both management and the creative team project managers. Updated as employees fill in "Project Status" forms, it allows managers to see at a glance the status of a whole project. Using this information, they can avert cost overruns or, if overruns are inevitable, at least alert management in time to prevent them.

If employees needed to see tallies of their own work, a similar view could first categorize the employee and then the project, so that employees could see an overview of how they were spending their time.

# Graphic Design of Forms and Views

Good taste in designing forms is difficult to define, but important to achieve. Awkward, amateurish graphic design can make an application unpleasant to use—and unused, as a result.

There are several components to the graphic design of an application, and they all should be used with restraint: titles and labels; type styles and colors; graphics and illustrations; and layout.

## Titles and Field Labels

The static text in a form—the field labels, form titles, and other words—offer instruction, description, and explanation when needed. Even though it is not data, it is very important. Labels must be visually distinctive guideposts to the fields in the document, as well, but they shouldn't be so prominent that they overshadow the data in the fields, making it difficult to locate or read.

## Typefaces and Colors

Both static text and the data within fields in a form can be formatted using all the available type fonts, sizes, and colors. Ben showed some early samples of his forms to the agency's art director and got some useful pointers. He learned, for instance, that he should use features such as italics, large text, and underlining sparingly, as they provide emphasis when carefully employed, but can easily be overused. The art director also pointed out that using different background colors for different kinds of forms would help users locate themselves more readily in the application. But background colors must be chosen carefully so that they don't clash with colored text.

The graphic design of the views is far more rigid than the forms, but background colors and a limited amount of text formatting can be used in the views.

# Graphics

Graphics—logos, illustrations, even scanned photographs —can also be put into Notes forms. But these, too, should be used with restraint. On slower PCs, graphics may slow down the display and scrolling of a document.

# Form Layout

The layout of the form—placement of the static text and fields—requires planning and some experimentation. Designers must consider whether users are going to open the form in a full-screen window, or will they be using a window that covers only part of the screen? Window size can't be built into a Notes form, since each user controls her own Preferences. While most users tend to use multiple windows, the Preferences menu allows them to select Maximized Windows if they prefer to see everything in full-screen mode (see box, Designing for Windows).

# Testing the Database

Notes is so interactive that design, building, and testing all happen at once. For Ben Lewis, the process of testing and debugging the Pegasus application went along with the creation.

Ben tested the database by entering sample data and making sure all the forms and views displayed the proper information in the proper places. He created enough sample documents to make sure inheritance was handled properly, and the column totaling function in the Cost by Client & Project view was working. With Notes' text-oriented applications, it's not hard to tell whether they're working properly: either the text is where it should be or it isn't; and if it isn't, it's usually easy to figure out why.

Even if problems are found after the application is put into service, Ben will be able to make fixes without destroying the data users have already entered.

# The Documenting Step

Documentation is just as critical in the development of a Notes application as it is for more traditional programs. With Notes, documentation is just much

---

# Designing for Windows

The graphic design of forms must take into consideration the contents and intended use of the forms, and the way the majority of Notes users in the organization prefer to work with them.

- **Multiple windows**. Because most Notes users like to use multiple windows of varying sizes, forms must be designed so that a small window covering only a portion of the screen is as easy to use and understand as a full screen.

- **Window size**. Layouts that have been designed for a full screen, with fields placed side by side, may look strange and be inconvenient in a small window. Some fields will seem to disappear partially or to wrap awkwardly to fit into the window. It is sometimes difficult to match the static text with the field it identifies.

- **Vertical or horizontal?** Fields arranged vertically on a single column work well in a small screen. On the other hand, if users want all the fields in a form to fit on one screen so that they do not have to do a lot of scrolling, they may have to use a full-screen window.

- **Emulating paper forms.** Notes forms that are supposed to duplicate the appearance of paper forms may require a full screen to maintain their familiar appearance to users. Likewise, forms that are intended to be printed out may require a layout that makes them fit awkwardly into a small window. One solution is to build a separate form used just for printing the documents with the Form Override feature.

---

easier. Users don't need instructional manuals for each new application, because all Notes applications work alike. Similarly, programmer documentation to help other developers who might have to maintain the database doesn't need to be extensive, because Notes applications are largely self-documenting —field names and formulas, for example, are always available through the Design menu to the developer working on the application.

For the Pegasus application, documentation was minimal. Some was in the forms themselves. As Ben created the forms, he carefully entered a Help description for each field—a line of text that appears at the bottom of the screen to explain the purpose of a field as it is selected.

Ben also wrote a database policy, a brief text document which described the purpose of the application and characterized the data it collected. The policy document, a standard part of every Notes application, also indicates who may use the application. It also names the application's manager, so that users who don't have access to the application know who to contact to request it. This works because the policy document is the only piece of an application that can be seen by a Notes user not on the application's user access list. (The policy can be displayed from the File, Database dialog box.) The policy also appears on the Help menu, and is automatically presented the first time the application is opened by a user.

The Pegasus policy statement was divided into three parts, according to department. Each section identified and explained the purpose of the forms and views as they related to that department and the work of its employees. For example, Creative Services' Project Description and Project Status were designed to track projects closely. For this reason, the policy statement stressed that those forms should be filled out by each employee daily. A final section explained how the application coordinated the separate departments' work.

The policy statement should provide users of the application with administrative information. For example, if a database is purged on a regular basis, this information should be documented—otherwise, a user might wonder what happened to documents she had read earlier. Applications which are connected to external programs and data sources through Notes' application programming interface (API) should be documented, especially if conditions exist which might confuse users. For example, to save connection fees an external program might batch queries to an online information service and run them only at night. Unless users know this fact, they might think that the application is not working.

Standards should also be included, mainly for the benefit of a developer who might have to make additions or changes to the database. To be able to read a list of standard field names in the policy document, rather than open all the forms to find out what they are, would save time and effort.

Ben could also have written an extensive Help file for the application which would have appeared on the Help menu (because this was a simple application, such an effort wasn't necessary). In the case of a database that contained forms requiring users to import external data, a Help document could describe in detail the steps to follow to get the data into Notes. Help databases are also a good place to explain how to send a document in a group database to a user's mailbox.

# Summary

To build a Notes application, the developer created the database and defined its forms and views, following the design drawn up in Chapter 5. The process uses the development tools of Notes, from field types to user access levels to the selection formulas that govern what documents appear in a view.

Because the creation of a Notes application is very interactive, testing is not a separate step in the development process. Debugging a Notes application is straightforward: entering sample data quickly shows up flaws in a form, and a handful of sample documents will do the same for a view. And no flaw is fatal—changes can be made in forms and views without destroying data already entered in an application.

In Notes, the final development step, documenting, is almost as simple as testing. Applications need very little documentation for either users or maintenance programmers. What they do need, and the developer of the Pegasus application provided, is a thorough database policy document which explains the purpose of the application, who has access to it, and administrative information—how the application works, why it behaves as it does.

# Advanced Application Techniques

S ome of the most intricate aspects of creating a Notes application involve setting up procedures that sift old and unused documents out of the database, creating access controls that reflect the complex authority structures of organizations, and using the basic tools of forms and documents to shape an application that is easy to use yet secure.

Most of these operations require cooperation between developers and Notes administrators. Giving a group access to an application, for example, involves creating a group in the Name and Address Book (usually done by the Notes administrator) and setting user-access levels and privileges in the database (usually the responsibility of the developer). Other functions covered in this chapter involve different divisions of effort, but any shared responsibility and consultation between developer and administrator have a high pay-off, because these are areas where Notes can be unforgiving when mistakes are made.

The first part of this chapter covers filters, those programmable agents that act on fields within documents. Filters can change or update the contents of fields, sort out documents which meet certain criteria, or makes copies of selected documents and change their contents. Filters are seldom included in the design of a new database, but they can become indispensable timesavers when an existing application needs maintenance.

Replication is the subject of the second section. Replication is much more than the simple-minded passing of new documents from one copy of a database to another. Notes includes controls that turn replication into a tool for maintaining the database, purging aged documents, managing some copies of an application so that they contain only a small number of current documents, while others are inclusive and archival. A variety of options make different patterns of replication possible, as well.

A third section covers those parts of Notes' security that function at the database level—privileges, encryption keys, and form formulas or masks. This security is built into the databases by the designers, and sometimes (as in the case of encryption keys) by the end users. Properly set up, these features and database structures can make an application easier to use while providing the security organizations need.

# Using Filters

Soon after Ben launched the Pegasus application, an account representative, Laura Smith, left the company. Management assigned Laura's accounts to a new employee, Christy Williamson, and wanted the personnel change reflected in documents created in the Client Information and Project Description forms. Rather than edit each document in which Laura's name appeared, Ben wrote a filter which went through all the Employee fields in the Project Description and Client Information documents, replacing Laura's name with Christy's.

---

## What Filters Do

- **Change** the data in a field to a new value.
- **Add** a new field to a form.
- **Rename** a field.
- **Flag** a field for selection, as for deletion.
- **Scan** documents imported into a database to categorize them by user defined criteria.

---

Filters act on fields in documents and are much more powerful than traditional find-and-replace commands because they can be focused more precisely. Filters can affect the whole database or just selected documents and fields. As a result, they should be tested thoroughly and used cautiously, because mistakes can have disastrous effects.

To substitute the new employee's name, Ben needed to change two fields in the documents. Though the static text identified the fields as Account Rep and Employee(s) Assigned to Project, both fields were named Employee. The client information documents contained the account rep's full name, while the project description documents contained the rep's first initial and last name. Other documents with Laura's name in them—contact reports, action items

—needed no updating because they represented work she had completed, rather than accounts assigned to her.

To write the filter formula Ben selected the Design menu and opened the Design New Filter dialog box (see Figure 7.1). First, he wrote a formula specifying field values to be changed in documents created with the Client Information and Project Description forms. He then wrote a second formula which searched the Employee field in the selected documents and replaced the text strings Laura Smith or L. Smith with Christy Williamson or C. Williamson, respectively. To be sure he had included all the documents, Ben used the Scan choices to indicate that he wanted all the database documents scanned.

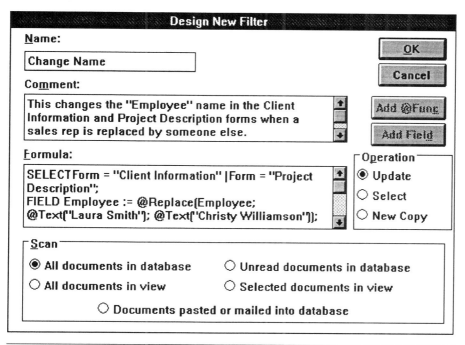

**FIGURE 7.1** Filters use the same syntax as other formulas in Notes. Because a database can include many filters, the Name and Comments boxes should provide information on the filter's purpose.

A filter also automates the process of assigning documents imported into an application to categories in the views: When a filter is marked to scan, Documents pasted or mailed into database, it can categorize them by looking for keywords which match the filter formula's criteria. The matched data is then automatically placed in fields the filter creates in the documents.

A filter also can identify documents for deletion. Suppose Ben Lewis created a support database to record problems and comments from the users of his application. The problem-reporting form could include a field called Status, with the status of each document automatically set to O, for open, when the document is created, and changed to C, for closed, when the issue is resolved. To periodically eliminate the closed documents, Ben could use a filter to identify all the documents with a C in the Status field. The filter's formula would be something like SELECT STATUS = "C".

Although a filter can flag documents to be deleted, it cannot delete them from a database. This important safety precaution prevents possible disasters caused by faulty filters. Ben would use his Select filter by opening a view that included all the documents in the support database, then running the filter. In the view, a checkmark would appear in the left-hand column to flag each selected document. Ben would then delete the marked documents using the Edit, Delete command. A filter can be used in this fashion to help automate any operation that begins with selecting a subset of the database, such as selecting documents for printing.

Filters are a central design element in Notes applications that involve regular movement of data into or out of the database, by importing, exporting, pasting, or mailing documents from other applications. But many application developers find they don't start using filters until after databases have been in service for some time. That's when filters become very important tools for maintaining the application.

# Replication for Maintenance

Replication also provides a way to control document removal and maintenance of the database. It's the easiest way to delete documents by age, because whenever the database replicates it can automatically delete documents saved before a specified date.

Each database has its own replication settings. Most designers set replication schedules with Notes administrators to avoid conflicts in timing and to assure that servers and databases have the right access levels to replicate. The administrator sets LAN connections and routing directions and trades certificates with servers that will replicate their databases with each other (for more on these topics, see Chapter 8). But the developer usually sets some parameters of the replication events through the Replications Settings dialog box. This box is reached through the File Database Information box. In

Chapter 3, we saw Megan McDonnell use Replication Settings to set up her laptop databases for replicating with the server which she planned to dial into.

Ben Lewis set up a database called Daily News, which contained news items about the agency's clients and employees. To keep it uncluttered and current, Ben chose to delete items that had been in the database for more than three weeks. As a result, he set up a regular purge cycle in the Replication Settings box (see Figure 7.2).

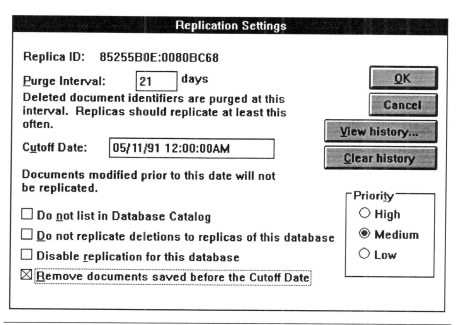

**FIGURE 7.2**  Once the purge interval and cutoff date are set in the Replication Settings box, Notes advances the cutoff date so that no document stays in the database longer than the purge interval.

Purging helps free up disk space by completely erasing the deletion stubs that are left behind in a Notes database after a document is deleted. Deletion stubs are markers that the replication process needs to keep databases in synch—if a user on Server A deleted a document in a database that was replicated on Server B, Notes would use the deletion stub to identify the document and also delete it on server B. After replication, the databases on both servers would match.)

If the Purge Interval were set to zero, Notes would never purge the database and it could conceivably grow very large. But after a deletion has been replicated across all the servers that contain the database, the deletion stub is no longer needed and should be purged.

First, he set the purge interval to 21 days. Because he wants to keep three weeks' worth of documents in the database, he set the cutoff date to three weeks earlier: Because the database was activated on June 1, he set the cutoff date to May 11. Finally, he selected the option, Remove documents saved before the cutoff date.

The cutoff date and the purge interval interact: Notes resets the cutoff date after one third of the purge interval has passed. Documents that have been neither added nor modified after the cutoff date are removed the next time the database is replicated, and deletion stubs that include the date of the removal are left behind. For Ben Lewis's "Daily News" database, this procedure meant that after seven days (one-third of the purge interval), on June 8, the cutoff date was reset to May 18. The next time the database was replicated documents created before May 18 and not modified since then were removed, leaving deletion stubs. The same thing happened on June 15 and June 22. On June 29, the cutoff date was reset to June 8, and for the first time deletion stubs were purged as well—all the stubs of documents removed on June 8.

Replication between two servers is governed by connection documents (see Figure 7.3). A connection document establishes which server will call which server, how frequently it will make the call, and what tasks it will carry out during the connection. If replication is one of the tasks, it also lists which priorities it will replicate. If a connection document schedules a call to another server every hour and replicates only databases marked High priority, databases marked as Medium or Low will not be replicated at that time. They may be replicated at less frequent intervals, and other connection documents will control those intervals (see the box, Replication Settings.)

# Security: Privileges, Encryption, Masks

The structure of the Pegasus Public Relations application is extremely simple on two counts: There is a direct relationship between documents and forms, and there is no internal security within the application. Any user with access to the database could create new documents using any of the forms Ben provided, use any view, and read or edit any document. This simple structure was well suited to Ben Lewis' goal of providing for the easy creation of many

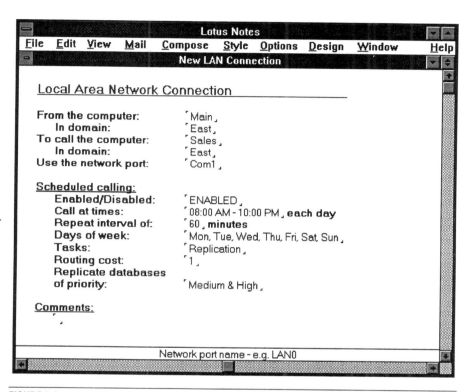

**FIGURE 7.3** A connection document, created in the Name & Address Book, sets up the schedule a Notes server follows to connect to another server to replicate databases shared between the two.

---

# Replication Settings

Options in the Replication Settings box provide the administrator with some management information and controls over replication:

- **Disable replication for this database** is seldom used for active databases. It is useful for databases that are not in active use but have some value as reference material.

- **View History** leads to a dialog box which lists the time and date the replications occurred. It can be helpful if there seems to be a problem with replication.

- **High, Medium, and Low priorities** indicate how frequently the database will replicate. Priority settings work with the Connection documents the Notes administrator sets up in the Name and Address Book to establish how often the servers will replicate.

types of documents, from client data to to-do items. Keeping the database open and easy for Pegasus employees to use helped insure its acceptance.

But such openness doesn't always reflect the way organizations work. Information is frequently shared on a need-to-know basis. Sometimes, the data is sensitive and must be kept private. More often, there is more data than can be managed easily and it must be distributed based on relevance.

Security is part of the design of any Notes application, and control of access to the application is just as important as the security of other corporate data and computing resources. Notes' tools for tailoring the database include:

- **The Access List**. While everyone in a workgroup may have access to a database, that access probably will not extend company-wide. The most basic form of security for a Notes application is a list of its users. Each application has its own user access list, created under the File menu in Database User Access Control. The list can name groups or individuals, and assigns each entry one of seven access levels, ranging from no access to Manager access, which grants the authority to delete the entire application and all its contents (see Chapter 5 for more explanation of the access levels).

- **User Privileges**. Assigning user privileges makes it possible to control access not only to the database as a whole, but also to particular views and forms within it. This restriction is accomplished by assigning privileges to users and groups named in the Access List, and setting the corresponding privilege for the views and forms they will be allowed to use.

- **Encryption**. Encryption provides a system of access control that works in parallel with user privileges. Data is encrypted on a field-by-field basis in documents, and the decrypting key distributed to a selected group of users. The result is that especially sensitive data can be hidden even from legitimate users of the application. Encryption protects the data in sensitive applications even if the physical security of the server has been breached.

- **Masking**. Finally, masking forms can be created to reveal some fields in a document while hiding others. Masks are invoked by form formulas written into the views. This ability to control display of a document in forms other than the one it was created in is a powerful capability, and makes possible a couple of very different approaches to structuring a Notes application as discussed in "One Document, Many Forms," below.

# Controlling Access to the Application

Database security begins with the Name and Address Book. When new users are certified to use the server, their names are added to the Name and Address Book. The Name and Address Book is a Notes database, with forms that allow the creation and deletion of individual entries and groups, and views that display its contents. Generally, only the Notes administrator is assigned the user access level to create new Name and Address Book documents and to edit existing ones. Because of the importance of group lists to the security of applications, the creation and maintenance of a set of group entries that reflect job functions, authority levels, and workgroup organization within the company is one of the cornerstone responsibilities of the Notes Administrator.

For each application that a group will use, the group name is entered in the application's User Access Control List, and assigned the appropriate level of access. For example, a group called Sales was created in the Name and Address Book (see Figure 7.4). It consisted of six authorized users: Bill, Mary, Jon, Sally, Tim, and Diane.

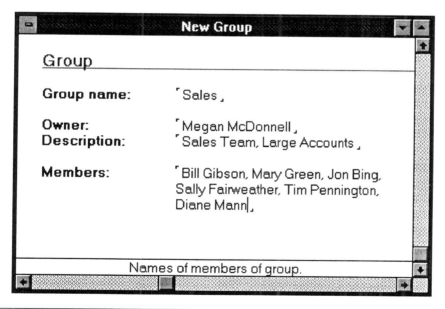

**FIGURE 7.4** Group lists are created by the Notes administrator in the Name & Address Book. A carefully structured set of lists makes it easy to match individuals and responsibilities in Notes.

When the Sales group is added to an application's User Access List with the access level of Editor, any member of the group can create new documents and edit old ones.

If Mary opens the database, she can create a new document or edit an old one. However, if Bob tries to open the database, he can't even get into it. He is not listed in the Sales group, nor is he listed under his own name or in any other group in the application's User Access List (see Figure 7.5; these access levels are explained in Chapter 5).

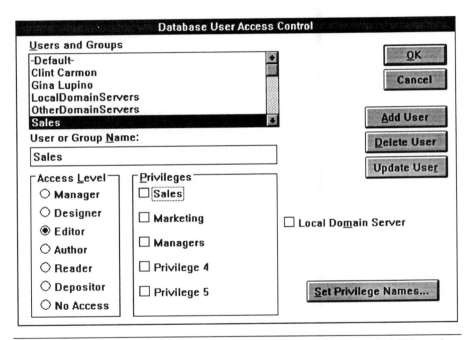

**FIGURE 7.5** Once a list has been created, the designer of an application can assign it an access level. All the members of the group automatically acquire the same access to the database.

If Bob becomes part of the sales team, and his name is then added to that group in the Name and Address Book. he automatically receives rights to all the databases whose User Access lists the sales group. If he leaves the company, he can be deleted from the Name and Address book and will no longer be able to use any Notes application.

The efficiency of a well-maintained set of group lists is clear: If every user of an application had to be added to the User Access List individually, every application would have to be changed with each change of job responsibilities in the company—a time-consuming process. Of course, there are times when it is necessary to put an individual user's name in the User Access list. When a user belongs to a group, but is assigned rights different from the group, for example, those individually assigned rights take precedence over the group rights.

## Using Privileges Within the Database

The User Access levels control the user's ability to create or change data, but they cannot limit what users may do with individual views or forms. How does a developer allow only some of an application's users to see and use the Action Item form? What if he wants users who ordinarily have Editor status to be able to read documents created in a particular form but not create new documents in it? How does he hide a view created for management from those who are not managers? To apply such restrictions, he must assign user privileges. Privileges restrict access to forms and views to those users granted one or more of the five privileges (see Figure 7.6).

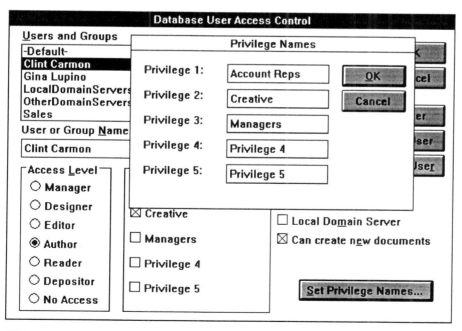

**FIGURE 7.6**  A designer can control use of specific views and forms by setting a privilege as an attribute of the view or form, and through the User Access Control box, assigning that privilege to users.

The privileges have no preset meanings, like the User Access levels. They are merely five keys, or five access codes. Initially Notes lists the privileges as numbers 1 through 5, but the developer can name each privilege to reflect the group which shares it. When a privilege is specified for a form or view, only users who have been granted that privilege can use the form or view. A form's name will not even appear on the Compose menu of a user who does not have the privilege.

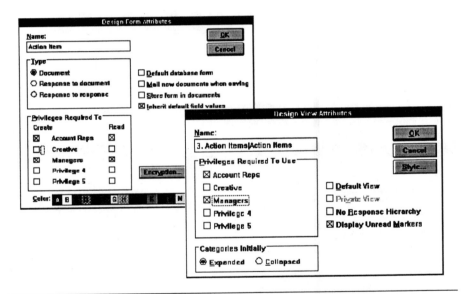

**FIGURE 7.7**  After privileges are created in the User Access box, they can be applied to forms and views' to limit access. The form and view attributes shown above each require users to have manager or account rep privileges to see or use the views, forms and documents named Action Items.

# Encrypting Selected Fields

Notes can encrypt documents, or even individual fields within a document, using an encryption key. The creator of a document can specify a key to encrypt the document before it is saved, or the designer of an application can include a key name in the form attributes, or even put a list of available keys into a field for the user of the form to choose from. The field or form, once encrypted, can be deciphered and read only by someone who holds the same key.

Users share a key which both encrypts and decrypts the data. They can give this key to other users. Possessing the encryption key identifies the user as a member of the group but does not specifically identify who she is. Encryption keys work on a document level, so that different documents can be encrypted with different keys in the same database.

This single-key method is one of two forms of encryption used in Notes (see box, The Keys to Security). For more on dual-key encryption, see Chapter 8.

---

## The Keys to Security

Notes uses two forms of encryption to insure the security and confidentiality of data. Both use digital *keys,* long strings of numbers that work with Notes' software, to encipher and decipher the information.

- **The dual-key system**, with a public key and a private key for each user, is used for electronic mail. Each user has a private key, included in the user's ID, and a public key is included in her entry in the Name & Address Book. When the user *seals* an E-mail message, it is encrypted with her private key. When the recipient opens the message, Notes retrieves the sender's public key from the Name & Address Book

to decrypt it. Successful decryption demonstrates that the message is authentic.

- **The single-key system** is used to encrypt documents and fields in documents that stay in the database where they were created. As a result, the complexities of a two-key system aren't necessary. A key can be created by one user and shared via E-mail with others. When a secret key is received, Notes includes it in the recipient's user ID file. The name of a secret key itself is not a secret, but any user who needs it to decrypt a document must have it in his user ID. These keys are for groups who want to share confidential information.

---

The advantage of using field-level encryption is that, even if the physical security of the Notes server is violated, encrypted fields in documents remain encrypted and inaccessible.

# Example: A Confidential Form

Using privileges and field encryption to create confidential forms is straightforward, but it requires that an application's entire security structure be in place. Ben Lewis discovered this requirement when the management of Pegasus Public Relations asked him to create a confidential version of the Action Item form.

Pegasus' managers had quickly adopted Ben's application, but its lack of internal security had became a stumbling block for them. Sometimes, they found themselves involved in sensitive negotiations with a client. They wanted to record the information and share it among themselves but did not want anyone outside of management to see it. Ben was able to answer their need for confidentiality by using a combination of privileges and encryption. But, first, he had to create a security structure for his application.

He did this by using three groups the Notes administrator had created in the Name and Address Book—Account Reps, Creative, and Managers.

In the File, Database, User Access window, he renamed the first three privileges to be Account Reps, Creative, and Managers (see Figure 7.8). He assigned each of these privileges to the corresponding group in the access list. (And he assigned all three privileges to himself, because he would need them as he tested the application.)

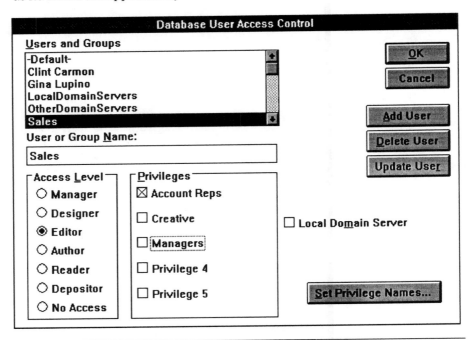

**FIGURE 7.8** By assigning different privileges to different groups, the application designer can limit access to the forms and documents. The Sales group above has Account Reps privileges and can create or read any forms or views restricted to the privileges assigned to Account Reps.

Next, Ben made a copy of the existing Action Item form and named this new form Confidential Action Item. Then he used the Design, Field, Security window to change security for each of the fields to Enable encryption for this field. In Options, User ID, he created a new encryption key named Management and E-mailed a copy of it to everyone on the Managers group list.

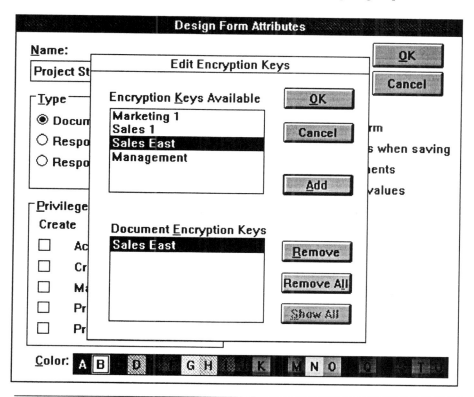

**FIGURE 7.9** Encryption keys are used to limit access to forms or fields. Keys are created and distributed via electronic mail to their users. They become part of the users' ID files.

In Design, Form Attributes, he assigned the Management encryption key to the form. He also assigned the Manager privilege to both Create and Read. This meant the form name, Confidential Action Item, would appear on the Compose menu only for members of the Managers group, and documents created with the form would appear in views only for that same group.

Any information entered in a Confidential Action Item document was doubly protected. It couldn't be called up for reading by anyone who wasn't a member of the Managers group. If that safeguard were circumvented, the information would appear in its encrypted, unreadable form to anyone whose user ID didn't include the key. (This meant, of course, that in order to preserve the security of the confidential action items, every manager had to password-protect his or her USER.ID file containing the encryption key.)

As soon as Ben had tested the new form, he deleted the Management encryption key from his own user ID. Then, even with his manager-level access to the database, he could not see the encrypted documents' contents.

## One Document, Many Forms

The forms in a Notes database govern how the data will be stored, how it will be retrieved, and who will look at it. In the Pegasus application, this relationship between forms and documents is very direct. Each form creates a different functional type of document, and each document is always displayed in the form that created it. This many-documents-many-forms structure means that whenever a document is displayed, every item of data in the document is visible on the screen: Each field in the form becomes a window, revealing the data that was originally entered into it.

An alternative is a one-document-many-forms structure. In this structure, a large document is built in a long form, but it is not displayed in that long form. Instead, subsets of the document's information are displayed in forms that contain only a few of the fields in the original long form. Each field that appears onscreen or is printed is still a window to a data item. Fields which contain data exist in the document but are not displayed in particular forms.

This ability to create a mask, a form that displays the contents of some fields in a document while masking out others, is the starting point for many sophisticated Notes applications. The mask rests on a formula written into a view. This formula governs the selection of the form that will display the document when it is selected from the view.

Ben Lewis could have used such a formula and a masking form in the Pegasus database. The client information documents can be quite long, but they are used often just to check an address, a phone number, or a contact name. Ben could have created a form that concentrated this quick-reference information in a short form. A user might select a client form and then view it in this form (we'll call it ShortForm) by choosing ShortForm from the list of forms on the View menu. By writing a formula in that view's Form Formula window, Ben could have made this form selection process automatic for selected groups of users.

The Creative staff, for example, doesn't create client information documents; they use them only as reference. If they told Ben that they always wanted to see client information in ShortForm, he could write a form formula which checked the current user's privileges (everyone in the Creative group had been assigned the privilege named Creative, remember). When the formula was installed and a user called up a client information document, if the user held the Creative privilege, then ShortForm would appear. If he didn't have the privilege, the Client Information form would appear (see Figure 7.10).

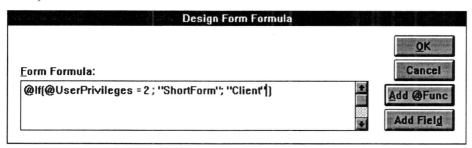

**FIGURE 7.10** This form formula determines which form to use to display a document. A user with the Creative privilege (number 2) will see the form called ShortForm. All others will see the Client form.

The @UserPrivileges function returns a number as a text string for the privileges. That's why the Form Formula checks for "2" to represent the Creative privilege.

If the function of a mask stopped here, it would differ only slightly from using inheritance to selectively move data from one form to another. But inheritance works only in one direction—users cannot write changes made in inherited data back into the original document. Instead, the changes are incorporated into a new document. The mask function overrides this limitation and makes it possible to edit the original document in a new form, but it has to fool Notes a little to get the job done.

Every Notes document includes an invisible field, called Form, that holds the name of the form used when the document was most recently changed. This form name is written into the document as it is saved. Normally when the document is retrieved, Notes uses the form named in the Form field as the frame in which to display the document. A document created in the Client Information form, for example, would be displayed in that form (unless a form formula specified a mask, of course).

Editing and saving a document displayed in a mask would replace the name in the Form field with the name of the masking form. But that can wreak havoc on other uses of the Form field. In the Pegasus application, Ben Lewis used the Form field in the selection formula for the By Client view—the formula limits the view to documents with Client Information in their Form field. But with ShortForm installed in the database, if a Notes user in the Creative department viewed a client information document for Donut Inn, for example, in ShortForm, made a change and saved it then Donut Inn would disappear from the By Client view. The reason: The Form field in the client information document for Donut Inn now holds ShortForm, not Client Information.

Notes gets around this problem by making use of synonyms. We've already seen how Ben used synonyms to order the names of forms on the Compose menu. Saving changes made in masks takes advantage of the way Notes treats synonyms. When a form is called up from the Compose menu, Notes finds the form with the specified name in *first* position in its name list. When a document is saved, Notes writes the *last* name in the form's name list into the document's Form field. To enable changes to client information documents from ShortForm, Ben would edit ShortForm's Name field to read: 7. ShortForm|ShortForm|Client Information, and the rest would be automatic. When a user made a change to the Donut Inn document from within ShortForm, the fields included in the ShortForm mask would be written into the Donut Inn document and its Form field updated with the last name on ShortForm's name list, Client Information. And because its Form field continued to hold the form name Client Information, the document would continue to appear in the By Client view.

## Example: The Personnel Database

Masking forms and privileges can combine to provide complex patterns of access to a set of uniform records. A personnel database for a company of 1,000 employees could have 1,000 documents, each one created using the same personnel form that collects the same information on employee name and address, salary history, and performance evaluation records. Masking forms and associated privileges could be created to give different groups access to different fields within the form. Any employee could check for names and addresses, for example. But only a small group in the Accounting Department could have access to the salary information, and only the department managers could enter and read performance-evaluation information.

The Pegasus application is a many-documents-many-forms database. The personnel example has a one-document-many-forms structure. The best structure for a Notes database depends on the information users will be putting into the database. In some cases, like the personnel example, the database will be homogeneous, consisting of many documents built from the same basic form. The Pegasus database, by contrast, is heterogeneous, taking maximum advantage of Notes' ability to store dissimilar documents in a unified database.

A related consideration is the relationship of the documents' creators to the documents' viewers. In the Pegasus application, these groups are virtually identical: The account reps and Creative staff members who enter information into the database also draw on it as a reference, and the database itself becomes a communications medium not all that different from electronic mail in its immediacy.

The documents in the personnel database, on the other hand, are more likely to be created by one group, the personnel department, and used by other groups—payroll clerks, department heads—with a specific need for one type of personnel information, but no authorization to see other data. For this type of application, the designer has to use masks, privileges, and encryption to provide secure and limited access to sections of the underlying document.

The one-document-many-forms structure has another advantage: It more closely matches the structure of conventional databases, such as dBASE files, which consist of uniform records that each contain every field created for the file. Importing data from these files into Notes, or exporting from Notes to other file formats, is easier when this single large document serves as a unified repository of all the fields in a conventional database record.

# Summary

Advanced application development tools and techniques can help Notes developers and administrators deal with the most nontraditional aspect of Notes —setting up applications for use by groups. These capabilities include using filters, assigning access controls and user privileges, creating encryption keys and encrypted fields and documents, and using masks in a database structure that departs from the simple many-documents-many-forms relationship of previous examples.

An example of a more complex application structure examines a personnel database that gives different groups access to different information contained in one set of documents: The designer uses database-level security features, such as access controls and encryption keys, to provide each group of users with ready access to what they need to know while protecting sensitive information.

Precisely because Notes is so flexible there is no right structure for a Notes application. Developers will doubtless come up with endless variations on both many-documents-many-forms and one-document-many-forms structures —and invent many more as well—in their search for the only really right structure: The one that gets the job at hand done.

# Section 4
# Administering Notes

A Notes administrator's work is never done. Change and growth are constant. There are new users to add, departing users to delete, and replication schedules for new applications to set up. And even in a steady state, Notes needs a guiding hand. E-mail messages may be misaddressed and undeliverable. Databases need pruning. External programs that link to Notes need monitoring. Updates to Notes or external programs, or even the server operating system must be installed. Backups of the Notes files are a necessity.

This section looks at the issues that surround administering a Notes installation. Chapter 8 first examines the need for dedicated personnel and the role those people play. It continues with system installation and management, the extensive security features and requirements of Notes, and issues of network compatibility and utilization. Chapter 9 discusses other network applications that can be integrated with Notes through gateways (such as facsimile servers and other electronic mail systems) and through Notes' application programming interface (such as custom software to provide access to corporate databases from inside Notes).

# 8

........
........
........

# Administering a Notes System

**M**ost Notes users will never have to do the work of administering a Notes installation. But some knowledge of what goes on behind the scenes on the Notes server, and a general understanding of the vital role administration plays in making their Notes applications run smoothly, will help users get the most out of Notes. Application developers will find the issues of security and replication important for the success of their work. The managers of companies that buy Notes will find they need some knowledge of the functions of the administrator to make informed decisions on the levels of support Notes needs in their organizations.

Some appreciation of the role of Notes administrator as it is spelled out in this chapter will help anyone involved with Notes better comprehend its power, recognize its possibilities in their own work, and develop clearer expectations for what Notes can mean to the organization as a whole.

This chapter is not aimed at a technical reader. It does not attempt to cover the network architecture, setting up servers, and resolving the host of related hardware issues that make each Notes installation unique. The focus is on explaining the day-to-day issues that administrators must deal with after Notes is installed—what occurs on a Notes server and how the responsibilities of administering Notes are divided.

The Notes administrator works in four broad areas: Security, server maintenance, server monitoring, and database management. This chapter begins by looking at some of the technological underpinnings of those areas—terms such as *client/server architecture,* and *NetBIOS protocol*—and examines Notes security in some detail. A second section sketches the role and responsibilities of the administrator.

# The Technical Framework of Notes

Notes is built on a technological platform that incorporates many of the recent advances in personal computing, including networks, telecommunication, graphical user interfaces, and client/server architecture. Some of these concepts are difficult to grasp, but a clearer understanding of the program's supporting technologies will help any Notes user make better use of the program. Six concepts are covered in this section:

- Network server versus Notes servers

- Client/server architecture

- NetBIOS

- Replication

- The Public Name and Address Book and Domains

- Security

Notes technology is network technology. It builds on long-established technologies, such as the NetBIOS communications protocol for network operating systems, and on new advances, such as client/server architecture, which divides the processing done by the Notes system between the Notes server and the users' PCs. Notes also breaks new ground by using infrequent connections between servers to replicate changes in a database between copies of that database. And the security for Notes applications discussed in previous chapters is matched by equally stringent security for Notes communication and data-transfer functions.

## Network Servers versus Notes Servers

The distinction between a network file server (sometimes just called a file server) and the Notes server is important. Networks are made up of PCs connected in some fashion—by wires or optical fiber or radio or infrared. This physical net is managed by software, a network operating system that supervises communications traffic on the network and provides access to its resources—services such as shared printers, electronic-mail system, and centralized file servers.

The major network operating systems used by businesses are all server-based: One or more PCs are dedicated to running programs that provide services shared by all the users of the network. The network server maintains the directory of users and administers network security by handling user log-ins and establishing individual sessions. The print server manages a shared printer and the files sent to it, and the E-mail server runs the programs that store and retrieve messages sent across the network. A gateway server provides connections between the network and other computer systems — wide-area networks or mainframes or minicomputers.

Notes itself runs on a server PC, and like all programs that run on computers, it runs under an operating system: software that manages the computer's processor. In the case of the Notes server software, the operating system is OS/2. (Workstations can run under OS/2 or MS-DOS and Windows 3.0.) The major advantage of OS/2 for Notes is that it is a multitasking operating system. OS/2 can manage two or more tasks or jobs concurrently by dividing the time of the processor among them. This means that Notes can manage the databases being modified as users work on them, and can simultaneously perform other tasks such as connecting to another server for replication, or running a filter against a database, or running add-on programs.

The server operating system and the network operating system are separate and not always compatible. When a local-area network also uses OS/2-based operating software, such as 3Com's 3+Open or Microsoft's LAN Manager, Notes and the network software can run on the same server (though it isn't recommended except for very small installations, because it slows both Notes and network operations.)

When a network uses another operating system, such as Novell's Netware, Notes must run on its own dedicated server. Netware and OS/2 cannot work together on the same server. A Notes server speaks to a Novell network through a special program called the OS/2 Requester. Notes can request, for example, that the network send a Notes document to a network printer.

The Notes server works almost independently of the network server since none of its essential functions, including security, are controlled or affected by other programs. If a Notes installation is set up to store Notes data files on the Notes server, and if a user does not need to access the network's printing resources, the network operating system does not even have to be running for Notes to work.

An advantage of Notes' independence  is that Lotus didn't have to create a special version of Notes for every network system on the market. It also means that Notes servers residing on two different kinds of networks can communicate with each other, even if the network operating systems themselves cannot. Notes only has to understand and interpret Notes, not other systems. Two LANs, one running NetWare and the other running LAN Manager, may be unable to communicate with each other, but if a Notes server on one can make a dial-up connection to a Notes server on the other and replicate databases, the users of both networks can communicate with each other and share data—as long as they do it within Notes.

---

## Server Power

The server that handles Notes needs to be powerful. Lotus recommends the following server configuration:

- 80386- or 80486-based PC

- 9MB or more of RAM

- A hard disk of 130MB or larger

- A 9600 baud modem

- A VGA Monitor that is OS/2 compatible

- Asynchronous communications port

- Mouse (optional)

- Network hardware that is LAN Manager NetBIOS compatible

---

The Notes server must be a powerful computer as much because of the demands of OS/2 as of Notes (see box, Server Power). The hardware configuration of a server varies depending on such factors as the number of users accessing the server, whether it will also be used as a FAX server or a gateway, and the volume of traffic on the server. The number of asynchronous ports for dial-up communications, or FAX boards, will depend on traffic, too.

Most large installations will have a number of Notes servers and may even dedicate other machines to act solely as Notes gateways to other E-mail systems or to mainframe computers. In a big system, administration will have a lot of machines to support.

As with any network server, a Notes server intended to support any significant number of users and a lot of traffic is not a place to pinch pennies. A minimum configuration practically guarantees the failure of Notes in the organization—too little disk space and poor response times inevitably result in a Notes system so painfully slow and limited that people won't use it.

# The Client/Server Model

Notes divides its computing functions. The workstations on the LAN, for example, handle text editing, and the management of the desktop and the windowing interface. The Notes server manages the database views, communicates with other servers, and routes E-mail. This division of processing functions between workstations (or clients) and servers that execute tasks the workstations initiate is what defines a client-server system.

Client-server architecture is receiving an ever-increasing amount of attention as networks of PCs push aside minicomputer and mainframe systems. Developers of relational database managers, especially, are working to build systems that use client-server architecture and Structured Query Language (SQL) to bring the processing power of mainframe database managers (and the databases they manage) down to PC networks. Notes is one of the first real client-server applications to make it out of the development labs and into the field.

The Notes server and its clients are peers, with separate but equally important responsibilities: The client creates, and the server disposes; the server organizes, and the client displays. To the user, these processes are transparent. When a user creates a document at his workstation and indicates that he wishes to save it, the server files the document in the database and updates the index. If the document is an E-mail message the server checks the Name and Address Book to find out where to send it. If the message is to be encrypted, the server handles those security services. When a user selects a view from her menu, the server goes into action organizing the view according to its design.

The client-server structure of Notes has advantages. It can give users more processing power without forcing them into expensive PC hardware upgrades. It can work with different kinds of LANs and workstations because the architecture is not dependent on a particular network operating system or microprocessor. However, just as the client-server model is adaptable, it also makes heavier demands on communications between the client and the server. Since each side is just part of a whole process, the interaction between them must be flawless. And while the load on the network may be reduced because large data files no longer must be sent to workstations, the client and server communicate much more frequently than a workstation communicates with a file server. As a result, a server with lots of clients can be very busy. Because of the high volume of requests the server must carry out, Lotus suggests a separate server for Notes, even when it runs over an OS/2-based network. On an active network, the recommendation is one server for each 35 to 40 users.

# Notes and NetBIOS

Notes' client-server architecture requires direct communication between the workstation clients and the Notes server—a communications structure different from the typical network. The network server normally serves as the focal point of all requests from the workstations. Notes, on the other hand, is independent of the network server: Notes users do not need to go through the network log-in process to identify themselves to the LAN, unless they need to gain access to the LAN's file or printer services. However, they do need a way to transport data from their workstations to the Notes server and back.

To manage this communication, Notes uses NetBIOS (Network Basic Input/Output System), a communications protocol developed by IBM. NetBIOS provides a standard set of commands and controls for moving data between nodes on a network that isn't dependent on a particular network topology or operating system. The great advantage of NetBIOS for software developers like Lotus is that it lets them write programs that work on many different kinds of LANs. They don't have to create versions specific to each network environment.

NetBIOS doesn't make Notes independent of all network operating systems. Instead, it provides Notes with a way of treating those operating systems generically. Notes uses NetBIOS to establish a "session" between the server and the workstation. As long as Notes does not need any of the services the network controls, NetBIOS is adequate to manage exchanges over the network without conflicting with the network operating system.

Unfortunately, NetBIOS is not as standard as it might be. Because of differences among networks, each LAN operating-system vendor must create its own version of NetBIOS to work with its products. But because vendors often implement only parts of the NetBIOS command set, not every NetBIOS-compatible LAN will run Notes. Lotus certifies several network operating systems as Notes compatible (see box, Networks for Notes). The marketing of NetBIOS varies from vendor to vendor, as well. It must be purchased separately from Novell, for example, but it is included with Microsoft's or 3-Com's LAN Manager.

# Replicating Databases

Notes' practice of maintaining multiple copies of databases on multiple servers is an unconventional approach to giving large numbers of people access to information. More conventional database managers maintain one copy of the

---

## Networks for Notes

These network operating systems have been tested by Lotus and certified for compatibility with Note:

- Novell Netware with OS/2 Requester
- IBM OS/2 LAN (LAN Requester is included in OS/2 Extended Edition)
- 3Com 3+Open
- Banyan Vines
- Ungermann Bass

---

data and provide access to it via complex wide-area networks. The Notes approach succeeds because of the way its applications are structured, and the way people use the kind of full-text information that its databases contain.

Mostly because of the leisurely pace at which it propagates changes to the data among the multiple copies of the applications, Notes replication is not well suited to some database uses (see What Notes Is Not, in Chapter 2). But replication easily allows workgroups in widely dispersed offices to share information, and it keeps that information on the local LANs, where access is fastest, and off the wide-area networks, where delay and data corruption are most likely.

Replication has other advantages, too. It allows unlimited numbers of people to access the database. If the load seems too heavy for one server, another machine with a replica of the database can be added to the LAN. If there are multiple servers and one goes down, users can switch to a different server and continue to work on the database. People dialing in from remote stand-alone PCs can replicate databases to their hard disks and then work off-line with up-to-date copies of all the necessary documents.

The great advantage of Notes replication is it is an easy, inexpensive way to set up and manage wide-area communications. It uses standard PCs, modems, and phone lines, and it limits the amount of data it transmits in very thrifty fashion.

Replication is a merging of selected documents rather than a copying of whole databases.

Workers in a Los Angeles office, for example, share a database with co-workers in Atlanta. Each group adds and edits documents every day, and Notes, as part of its management of this data, tracks the date and time of each addition or update. When the Los Angeles and Atlanta servers connect to replicate the changes, each server compares the time of their last replication with the time stamp on each document in the database. The Los Angeles server copies to the Atlanta database only those documents that have been created or modified since the last replication. The Atlanta server does the same. The Los Angeles server lists the documents deleted from its copy of the database since the last replication so that the Atlanta server can delete them. And Atlanta lists its deletes for Los Angeles.

When replication between the servers is finished, the copies of the database are congruent—all the documents present in one are present in the other, and all the documents deleted from one are deleted from the other.

The simplest solution doesn't always get the job done, of course, so several factors can combine to make replication sufficiently complicated:

- **Topologies**. As more servers are added to the system, the topology of the wide-area network being created becomes an issue. Which servers should replicate, and when, to most efficiently propagate changes through the system? All the standard topologies are possible, with stars, chains, and rings being most common. For small systems, servers can be daisy-chained so each one replicates with one other. A star topology is a better choice for larger systems in which one server is designated to be the hub that replicates with each of the other servers in turn.

- **One-way replication**. Replication between servers doesn't have to be bidirectional. It can go one way: Server A can replicate changes in its databases to Server B without receiving B's changes in return. This one-way communication can be useful for archiving documents on one server.

- **Server access**. Servers have the same access to applications that users do. It is set in the same way, through the Access Control List, and it has comparable effect: Just as a user with Designer access to a database cannot make changes in its Access List, a server with Designer access cannot replicate changes to the Access List. This is especially useful as a sort of damage-control measure. Most applications set defaults for servers in two groups, "LocalDomainServers" and "OtherDomainServers." The less trustworthy OtherDomainServer, which users normally access less frequently, is limited to Reader or Author status.

## Domains and the Name and Address Book

When a new user is added to Notes, the administrator enters his or her name in the public Name and Address Book. The Name and Address Book is also

---

## A Star for Price Waterhouse

Price Waterhouse uses a star topology for replication and backup. With the Tampa, Florida, technology center as the hub, Notes servers from all Price Waterhouse offices replicate one-way with Tampa. The result is a server in Tampa that contains a master version or a snapshot of all PW's databases. Then the updated databases are replicated back to the servers at all the PW offices.

This plan works well for an installation with a large number of servers. By having all the remote servers replicate one way their changes into Tampa, and then having Tampa replicate databases which contain the changes from all the offices, updates occur more quickly than if the replication were done in a chain mode. As a safety measure the snapshot of all the databases is backed up to tape, and the tape is archived. The star topology provides an ideal centralized back-up as a bonus.

---

the place where administrators can create groups of users and specify the communications paths between Notes installations. The Notes server itself is listed in the Name and Address Book. When more than one server shares the same Name and Address Book, they are all listed, and the Name and Address Book is replicated among them just like any other application.

The grouping of Notes servers that share a common Name and Address Book forms an administrative unit called a domain. A domain can be as small as a single server or as large as all the servers in a company, even though they are widely scattered. Domains make the administration and use of Notes more efficient. Notes checks the Name and Address Book continuously to verify user IDs, address mail, certificates, and encryption keys. For users, the Name and Address Book is a handy source for the names of other users. Because it is such an important application, administrators usually give most users Reader access to it and assign Manager access for themselves.

Administrators manage a domain. Small companies often find one domain to be sufficient for the whole company. However, very large or widely dispersed companies often have more than one domain because it makes it easier to maintain replication schedules, monitor problems, and set up groups. Since group names must be unique within a domain, multiple domains make it possible to reuse easily remembered group names (see Figure 8.1).

It is easy to send mail to another user within the same domain. Users can find the name of the recipient in the Public Name and Address Book. To send mail to a foreign domain (one which does not share the same public Name and Address Book), however, the sender must know the correct spelling of the recipient's name and domain. He does not have to know how to route it to her if the communications path to the foreign domain is already specified in the

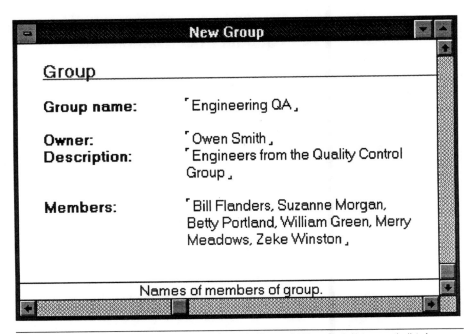

**FIGURE 8.1** The Notes administrator creates group lists in the Name and Address Book. Notes uses the lists for addressing electronic mail and for controlling access to applications.

Name and Address Book. But sending foreign mail, even when the recipient's name is in the Name and Address Book, can get to be complex if the domains aren't adjacent, that is, if they don't trade E-mail directly. In such cases messages must be routed through an intermediary server. Administrators determine the best route and enter it in the Name and Address Book.

## Security and Confidentiality

Notes is the first communications-oriented program to aim at providing a confidential working environment. The security provisions of Notes are intended to insure that its servers cannot be reached by anyone without a valid user ID, that its applications cannot be run by any user who cannot positively identify herself to the server, and that documents and messages actually were created by their putative authors and were transmitted without being intercepted or altered (see box, Three Levels of Security.)

## Three Levels of Security

- **System access.** Notes goes far beyond simpleminded user-name-and-password schemes to challenge users to produce electronic proofs and certificates of their trustworthiness before it grants a user access to a server, or a server access to another server.

  Notes uses RSA dual-key encryption to identify users and servers, to protect transmitted information, and to allow users to electronically sign messages (so that their origin can be verified) and encrypt them (so that only the intended recipient can decrypt and read them).

- **Server access.** Even if users have valid IDs and certificates, their access to the server may be denied or limited. Administrators can create groups in the Public Name and Address Book and limit their rights on the server.

- **Application access.** The User Access Control List for each application explicitly grants or denies users access to that database. Access within the application may be limited through privileges, and encrypting documents or even specific fields within a document. (This kind of encryption using a single key is described in detail in the "Security: Privileges, Encryption, Masks" section of Chapter 7.)

Notes' security functions are independent of any security (or more typically, lack of security) provided by the network itself. The security features reach across LANs, modems, and wide-area networks. Their protection ends only when information moves beyond the borders of Notes. An electronic mail message sent through a gateway to a conventional E-mail system can't be successfully signed or encrypted, because no recipient system supports these functions.

Every user and server within a Notes installation receives not merely a secret password but an electronic identity that includes several components, some of them made public in the Name and Address Book, some kept private in the user ID. To be trusted with access to a server, the user must be able to prove his identity to the system using these pieces of electronic ID.

The key elements in server security are public and private encryption keys generated when a new user ID file is created and a certificate stamped on the ID by a certifier.

# The Certifier

One of the first steps in installing Notes is to create an electronic identity that becomes a character witness for all other identities in the system. There has to be a certifier before servers and users can talk. The certifier is an authority, usually managed by the Notes administrator, and is the only entity in the system who can create his own authorized ID, which contains a certificate. All other new IDs, whether for a server or a user, must be authorized by a certifier. An ID contains the name, the license number of the copy of Notes assigned to that user, and a private encryption key generated at the time of creation. The certifier adds its own certificate to the ID. Unless the certifier puts its certificate into a user's ID, the user will not have access to the servers the certifier controls (see box, The User ID File).

---

## The User ID File

Notes uses the user ID file as a repository for security information. An individual user's file can contain:

- User ID with expiration date
- Notes license number
- User's Password
- Certificates
- Encryption Keys

---

While creating a user ID and stamping it with a certificate is internally complicated for Notes, it is quite simple from the administrator's or user's point of view. New IDs can be generated from the Options, New User menu (see Figure 8.2).

An ID may contain more than one certificate. If a user wants access to two servers, and each server has been certified by a different authority, the user must have certificates from the certifiers of both servers. To obtain a certificate, the user can send a safe copy of his ID through electronic mail to a certifier who will add the needed certificate. A safe copy ID contains enough information to receive a certificate but not enough to access a server. When returned, the user merges the safe copy into his original ID.

All servers in a domain are usually controlled by one certifier because it simplifies communications for users and for servers. If more than one certifier

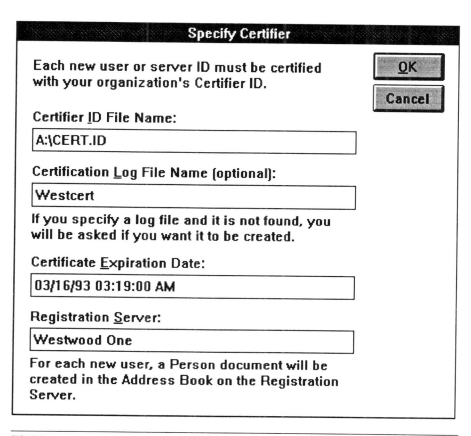

**FIGURE 8.2** This screen is the first of two an administrator uses to create a new user ID. New users must be certified and their names added to the public Name and Address Book.

is involved, the servers' own IDs must contain certificates from all the certifiers in the domain in order that all servers may communicate with each other.

# Certify the Server First

The certifier's first job, naturally, is to create an ID for the Notes server being installed. As part of this ID creation process, the certifier signs a certificate for the server. While certificates are a central piece of Notes security, they are not something anyone would want to frame and hang on a wall. They are strings of bits and characters manipulated according to rigid mathematical rules. This certificate uses the RSA dual-key encryption. It combines the server's public key and the certifier's private key in such a way that any entity wanting to test the server can use the certifier's public key to decrypt the certificate and verify the server's public key. Users or servers with certificates in their user ID files cannot copy them and pass them on to other users or servers. Only the certifier has that power.

The server's name, certificate, and newly computed public key become the first entry in the public Name and Address Book. Other server and user IDs are recorded in similar fashion as they are created. All these IDs have matching certificates from the same certifier, which makes them all members of the same club, and therefore able to communicate.

---

### Who Do You Trust?

Trust has to start somewhere, of course. With Notes, it starts with the certifier ID and the second vital component in security, a dual-key encryption technology licensed by Lotus from RSA Data Security, Inc.

The RSA encryption system's public and private keys are two long alphanumeric strings that are mathematically related, so that material encrypted with one key can be decrypted only with the other. One key is made public in the Name and Address Book. The other is kept private in the user ID. What makes the RSA system so powerful is that one key cannot be derived from the other. If you know User B's public key, you can send encrypted messages, and User B can use her private key to decrypt and read them. But you can't use the public key to figure out User B's private key and then read her electronic mail or masquerade as User B to Notes.

---

## Multiple Access Checkpoints

Notes' security features create several checkpoints the user must pass before Notes grants access to the server and to applications:

- **Server system checks**. When a user tries to access the server, Notes checks the user's ID file and the private part of the RSA key against the public counterpart found in the Name and Address Book. It also checks to see if any certificate there matches one in the server's file. If no match is found, access is refused.

- **Server group checks**. If the user and the server have a certificate in common, then Notes checks the Name and Address Book and the server's NOTES.INI file to see if the user is on any group lists which have been granted or denied access to the server. If the user passes this hurdle, too, then he is given access to the server.

- **Application User Access checks**. To use any of the applications on the server, the user's name, or the name of a group the user is a member of, must appear in the User Access Control List for the application the user selects.

This layered security system works much like the multi-layered security at a high-security research lab. At the main gate, only those people who show a valid ID badge get by the guard. Once inside the building, the badges serve a different purpose, as employees run their magnetically coded edges through a reader to unlock the doors to their individual labs and offices. If the reader rejects the badge, the employee can't enter. If it accepts the badge, the employee can get through the front door, but she may still have to punch a combination into a storage room doorlock or open a safe to get out her labbooks and start her day's work.

These repeated challenges serve their purpose: To keep unauthorized people from wandering around in places where sensitive work is done, where privileged information is available, or where they might do damage. The system tests users to make sure they can be trusted to be who they say they are and they belong where they're trying to go. Fortunately, all these security checks are much less intrusive in Notes than at a high-security defense lab. Once the user specifies where Notes can find his ID file, the rest is automatic. The ID file is the key element in Notes security and needs to be handled with care. It can be stored either on the Notes server, the LAN server or the workstation and password-protected from everyone, including to the Notes administrator.

Even this basic level of protection is often ignored. Administrators can force users to create passwords, but many do not. The passwords can be from 8 to 32 characters in length. Once a new user is registered on the Notes server, he alone has control over his password, not the administration. It is important not to forget that password, because there is no way to recreate it; an entirely new user identity will have to be created.

# Communications Security

The RSA encryption technology used in Notes safeguards server-to-server and user-to-user communication in the same way it polices user-to-server access. It uses the same security elements, first verifying the identity of both parties, and then their right to use the information they seek. In user-to-user communications (that is, electronic mail) messages can be signed and encrypted. Authors can be verified, and both senders and recipients can be certain of the privacy of the communication. In server-to-server communications (E-mail routing and database replication), all transmissions can be reliably encrypted to insure the confidentiality of information whether the transmission medium is a LAN, phone line, microwave link across a corporate campus, or satellite transmission.

The Sign Mail and Encrypt Mail options are two checkboxes that can be set as defaults in the Options Preferences dialog box, or quickly dealt with in the process of sending E-mail (see Figure 8.3). But when selected, they set in motion a great deal of computation.

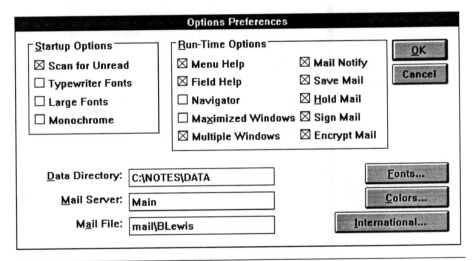

**FIGURE 8.3**  Users can set Sign Mail and Encrypt Mail as defaults in the Options Preferences box shown here, or select these options for individual messages in the Send Mail dialog box.

Signing mail is a two-step process. First, the encryption software reduces the message to a unique 128-bit document fingerprint. The possibility that two documents would generate the same fingerprint seems sufficiently unlikely—less than one in a trillion trillion, according to RSA. Then, this fingerprint is encrypted with the sender's private key and transmitted along with the message. When the recipient opens the message, Notes verifies the signature by decrypting the transmitted document's fingerprint using the sender's public key, and comparing the result to a freshly recomputed document fingerprint. If the two fingerprints are the same, the sender's identity is confirmed and the security of the document itself is also verified. If the text had been altered, or even if a transmission error had occurred, the second fingerprint would be different.

Encryption encodes a document so that it cannot be read by anyone except the person to whom it is addressed. Notes ciphers the document using a special key, then encrypts that key using the recipient's public key and sends the encrypted key along with the message. (This two-step process is actually more efficient than using the public key to encrypt the message: The single key can encrypt and decrypt the message faster than the RSA dual-key system.) At the receiving end, the single key is decrypted by the legitimate recipient's private key, then automatically used to decrypt the message. If someone else intercepts the message and tries to open it, their private key won't work and the message will stay encrypted.

Both signing and encrypting depend on the presence of a public key in a Name and Address Book—the signer's public key in the recipient's book, the recipient's public key in the sender's book. These may be private Name and Address Book applications created by the users from the template supplied with Notes. To find the addressing information it needs, Notes first searches the user's private Name and Address Book installed in her workspace; then it checks the public Name and Address Book. A user who corresponds with users from other domains and exchanges signed or encrypted messages will need a private book, because he usually cannot edit the public book to add a new user or append a key to an ID—that access is reserved for the administrator.

Users can mail their public keys to people in foreign domains by using the Send User ID, Pubic Key dialog box under the Mail menu (see Figure 8.4). The communication path to the foreign domain must be listed in the sender's public Name and Address Book.

## Server-to-Server Encryption

Servers also have IDs and public and private keys, and Notes can use them to guard the privacy of all data flowing between two servers during replication, or between a server and a remote dial-up user.

As part of the replication process, servers verify each others' identities using the same procedures they use to verify users' identities and access rights. The servers must have a certificate in common—each verifies the other's identity through their common acquaintance with and trust of a certifier ID. Once they agree to trust each other, they automatically encrypt all

```
╔══════════════════════════════════════════════════════════════╗
║                    Mail Public Key                            ║
╟──────────────────────────────────────────────────────────────╢
║  To:                                              ┌─────────┐ ║
║  ┌────────────────────────────────────────────┐   │   OK    │ ║
║  │ Gordon Williams                            │   └─────────┘ ║
║  └────────────────────────────────────────────┘   ┌─────────┐ ║
║  CC:                                              │ Cancel  │ ║
║  ┌────────────────────────────────────────────┐   └─────────┘ ║
║  │                                            │              ║
║  └────────────────────────────────────────────┘   ☒ Sign    ║
║  Subject:                                         ☐ Encrypt  ║
║  ┌────────────────────────────────────────────┐              ║
║  │ My public key is included.  You may cut and│              ║
║  │ paste it into a Names database.            │              ║
║  │                                            │              ║
║  └────────────────────────────────────────────┘              ║
╚══════════════════════════════════════════════════════════════╝
```

**FIGURE 8.4**  Users can send their public keys to correspondents in other domains by simply typing in a name. This procedure must be done before encrypted messages can be sent across domain boundaries.

their transmissions when communicating over a telephone line. For the same procedure to occur in LAN communications, the Secure Channel option must be selected in the Network Ports dialog box under Options on the main menu.

To encrypt their transmissions, servers use a single-key procedure much like the one used to seal an E-mail message. One server generates the single key and encrypts it, using the public key of the other server. The receiving server decrypts the single key with its private key, and this single shared key is used for the remainder of the server's communications. When the connection is broken, the shared key is discarded. A new key is generated for every server-to-server session.

## Server Groups

When administrators want to control users' access to the servers, they create groups in the Name and Address Book and use those group names (they can also use an individual's name) to regulate server access. The administrators also determine whether users can create new databases and new replica databases on the server. These commands are set into a file on the server called NOTES.INI. Notes checks this file before it lets users access the server.

Administrators often deny database access to users who have left the company. Even if the employees have taken their user ID files with them, they cannot get back into the server. An employee on extended leave might be denied access while he was away and given back the access when he returned.

The right to create new databases on the server or to create new replicas is not automatic. The administrator must grant it to a group. This can protect the databases and keep their numbers under control, as the number of Notes users grows in a company and applications proliferate.

## User Access and Privileges

Certificates and RSA encryption no longer control access, once a user's identity is accepted by the server. At this point, security procedures oversee whether the user has the necessary rights and privileges to use the applications on the server. Access to each database is specified by its own User Access Control List. The list determines not only which users can work with the database, but exactly what they can do—with options that range from complete control of the database down to no access at all.

In most databases, the User Access Control List contains names of groups created in the Public Name and Address Book rather than long lists of individuals' names. By assigning the same rights to several people in a group, the database manager can type the group name in the User Access List and assign it rights just once.

The Privileges section of the Access List dialog box provides even more closely targeted security. Access to individual forms and views can be restricted to individuals or groups named on the Access Control List.

It is each application's manager, rather than the Notes administrator/certifier, who usually sets up the Access Lists and defines privileges. The manager controls almost every aspect of the database. He can edit and delete any document, and create and change forms and views. He cannot control its replication schedule with other servers, because that needs the cooperation of the Notes administrator. But the manager's most important responsibility is his control over the User Access Control List.

## Encryption Keys

Privileges have some drawbacks. There are only five per database, and a work group could require more. In addition, they are secure only as long as the network and server are secure. If someone enters the server with a program that monitors all network transmissions, he can look at the contents of documents he has no right to see. In a physically secure environment, unauthorized server use is not a problem, but a lot of organizations put their servers in hallways or easily accessible offices. Finally, only someone with Manager rights to the database can assign privileges. While this is really a safeguard, it means that administrators need to grant manager access to a second person, in case the original manager leaves or loses his ID.

To improve the system's flexibility, Version 2.0 of Notes adds encryption of fields within a document. Whereas privileges restrict whole documents or views from users, encryption provides security for the contents of the documents and is applied field by field. It does not affect views unless an encrypted field appears in a view column.

Encryption keys can be created as needed or designed into forms. A user first creates an encryption key under the Options, User ID, Encryption Keys menu (see Figure 8.5). After she types in a name, Notes generates a key that encrypts the contents of any field to which it is assigned. Any user can create an encryption key and send it to another user.

This encryption key works a little differently from the RSA dual encryption keys that protect system security. This key is a single key which both encrypts and decrypts the contents of fields. If a user has the key and wishes to

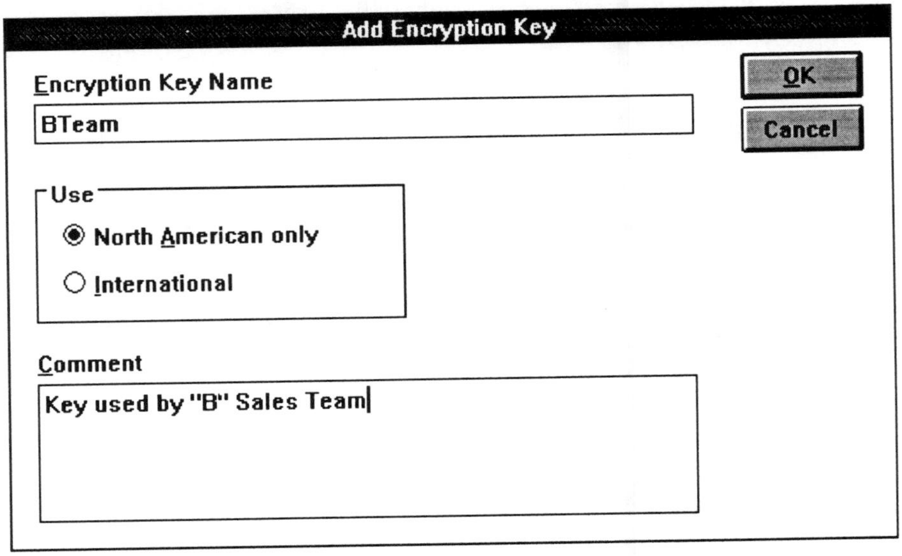

**FIGURE 8.5** Users can create and name their own encryption keys, which can be used to encrypt fields or whole documents. An optional comment field is used to document the purpose of the key.

send an encrypted document to other people, he must send them each a copy of the key before they can read the encrypted data. The Mail menu provides the appropriate forms for sending encryption keys to another user.

Naturally, encryption keys depend on the honesty of users. They need to be shared carefully and given only to people who are trustworthy, because once a user has an encryption key he can send it to anyone he chooses.

Encrypted data is more secure than privileged data. Network diagnostics and analyzers may reveal the existence of data to anyone who is nosy, but it will be in scrambled code and not intelligible.

Encryption provides more flexibility than does privileges. For example, an organization may want all users to have access to documents which contain a couple of fields of confidential information such as someone's private phone number, or a comment about their internal problems that should not be available to most users. In such cases, the document, which might be a form for recording a company profile, could contain a couple of encrypted fields. Those fields will appear blank to someone who does not have the key to unlock them. Those users who have the key will be able to see the contents.

Database designers can assign an encryption key to a whole form. In that case, every field appears encrypted to a user who does not have the key. In such cases, the encrypted documents still show up in a view, even for users who can not open them. Therefore, with such confidential forms, designers often combine privileges with encryption keys to hide the forms and documents as well as give them an extra level of security.

Encryption keys go into the user's ID (see Figure 8.6). If a user loses the ID or the encryption key or deletes it from her ID, she will not be able to read fields originally encrypted with that key, and the administrators will not be able to replicate it. The only way to get it back is to have someone who still possesses the key mail it back.

# Security at the Workstation

The security functions discussed above work mainly at the server level, but some security provisions have been designed to run on the workstation. The two areas where users control their own security most clearly are the signing and encryption of mail (discussed above) and password protection of their ID. Users can set their own passwords and change them whenever they want. Administrators cannot override a password with supervisor rights or decode it by going into a special file. The password stays in the ID file and it is the first line of protection for every user.

```
┌──────────────────────────────────────────────────────────────┐
│                    Mail Encryption Key                         │
│  Encryption Key List                            ┌──────────┐   │
│  ┌────────────────────────────────────────┐     │   Mail   │   │
│  │ BTeam                                   │     └──────────┘   │
│  │ Marketing 1                             │     ┌──────────┐   │
│  │ Sales 1                                 │     │  Cancel  │   │
│  │ Sales East                              │     └──────────┘   │
│  └────────────────────────────────────────┘                    │
│                                                                 │
│  Comment to be included in the body of the mail message         │
│  (changes to this comment will not be stored in your ID file):  │
│  ┌────────────────────────────────────────────────────────┐    │
│  │ For Marketing 1 team                                    │    │
│  │                                                         │    │
│  │                                                         │    │
│  │                                                         │    │
│  └────────────────────────────────────────────────────────┘    │
│                                                                 │
│        Created:  03/13/91 06:58:38                              │
│   Restrictions:  This key is for North American use only.       │
│                  You may send this key to other users.          │
└──────────────────────────────────────────────────────────────┘
```

**FIGURE 8.6**  The Mail Encryption Key dialog box lists the encryption keys in a user's ID file. Any key can be selected for delivery to another user via electronic mail.

# Functions of Notes Administration

The Notes administrator works in four broad areas: Server security, server monitoring, database management, and server maintenance.

In a small Notes installation, one person handles all these areas. In a large installation, these functions may be shared among several people, with each person having different abilities. The larger the installation and the more complex the network and communications, the more imperative it becomes for an organization to dedicate people with specialized skills to Notes. Notes is always integrated into a larger system, and there has to be coordination among the branches. The organization has to coordinate Notes' administration with other kinds of administration, such as network and E-mail. Sometimes, the MIS department handles the Notes' administration, but not always. It is not the purpose of this chapter to discuss how an organization should integrate those areas, but rather to identify the issues Notes administrators need to address.

The four areas of administration are not separate and distinct. There is much overlap:

- **Security** begins at the Notes server and includes the certifier ID, user IDs, certificates, the User Access Control list, and encryption keys. The administrator is the arbiter of these rights people and servers need to communicate with each other and to use the databases. Notes' security functions at several levels, and administrators must know how those levels work individually and collectively to be sure sensitive information is being properly protected.

- **Monitoring**. Notes comes with several applications which automatically record the server's activities. Administrators check these log files to find problems, to make sure replication is proceeding correctly, and to verify mail that is delivered. Monitoring is closely connected to maintenance because the log files help identify where breakdowns have occurred. The person who monitors the Notes server does not necessarily need the technical background or hardware expertise of someone in charge of maintenance.

- **Managing databases** involves two activities. First, the manager monitors log files to see if the database is replicating properly. In addition, the manager maintains the User Access Control list and monitors the size of the databases. Many Notes sites also have procedures the manager must follow for adding new databases to the server and testing it. Developers are often involved with administering databases as they install their projects on the network, but once a database is functioning smoothly, further management usually falls to the Notes administrator.

- **Maintenance** reaches beyond Notes. It requires a broad understanding of the network hardware and software as well as Notes itself to trouble-shoot problems and resolve conflicts between Notes and other systems on the LAN. Planning the Notes architecture, loading the server software and setting up communications are also part of maintaining a Notes installation. Maintenance people should be involved in the installation and configuration of Notes servers.

# Maintaining Security

The top priority for most companies is security—knowing that their sensitive data and communications are being kept confidential. Administrators are guardians of Notes security, and if they fail to provide certain safeguards, the whole system can fall apart. These responsibilities include:

- **Physical security of the servers**. Notes servers should be kept in locked rooms with limited access. Many companies put all their servers in a centralized data center and monitor them from there. Others spread them out among different locations or buildings. Either way, they must be secure from people who could turn them off, pry into the server's databases, or add programs surreptitiously. Because a user running a Notes session on a server has access to that server and its applications that he wouldn't have from a workstation, the physical security of the servers is very important.

- **Safeguarding the certifier ID**. While it makes sense to have at least two copies of the certifier ID, all copies should be protected with passwords, and copies on disk should be kept in a safe place. Certificates have expiration dates, and the administrator needs to schedule the renewal of certificates so that expiring certificates don't leave users unable to access all the servers they hold certificates for.

- **Procedures for adding users**. Security means insuring that legitimate users can get into Notes, as well as keeping illegitimate users out. An important part of security is developing standard procedures for adding new users to Notes and denying access to those who no longer are with the company. Notes administrators usually don't decide which individuals have access to Notes or to certain servers, but if a procedure is in place to efficiently verify that users should be added to the system, they can carry out their work with a minimum of frustration. This system will require that some communications and authorization procedures be put into place between the administrator and the company's managers.

- **Trusted Server relationships**. Administrators set up relationships among servers by exchanging certificates. One of their options when a user is certified reads "Trust other certificates signed by the certifier." This option means that if Server A has a certificate from Server B in its user ID file and the Trust option is selected, Server A will allow access to itself by any user with a certificate from Server B in his user ID. Setting Trusted Server on is an easy way to give a group of users access to a server, but it creates an open door. Administrators must have enough information from users to determine whether the trust relationship is warranted.

Administrators have a great deal of control over the servers and the users' right to access them. This control is good if it keeps the system secure and supports the work of the users. But Notes is a very democratic system. Its value lies in its ability to let workgroups work within Notes the way they work outside of it—to develop their own applications, choose their own patterns of communication, and impose their own access controls. A Notes administrator who is overzealous about limiting access rights or forbidding new applications on servers could wind up administering a system that nobody uses.

The administrators need to understand what their organization wants from them, and the degree of control they should enforce. The mainframe world has provided many examples of conflicts between system administrators and users that grew into outright warfare. This is less likely in Notes, perhaps, because of the program's openness to its users. But nothing in Notes determines its corporate culture. Notes is as democratic or as authoritarian as it is set up and maintained to be. Few companies using Notes have reported complaints from users about administration limiting their rights. But the Notes administrator must be aware of these issues and the need for a balance of power between administration and users, if Notes is to be a vital channel of communication within the organization.

# The Notes Log Files

Notes provides several tools for monitoring the server and its operations. Notes keeps an extensive audit trail of its operation in a group of log files structured as standard Notes applications. Among the applications administrators most often check are:

- **The Router Mailbox** contains mail waiting to be transmitted to other servers. It also contains dead letters, which for a variety of reasons could not be transmitted. Administrators check the dead letters for routing or addressing errors.

- **The Notes Log** records several kinds of information. It tracks when sessions are established with users, when replication events occur and whether any problems occurred, mail routings, the level of activity in each database, telephone calls, and the activity of the users. It is useful for all kinds of troubleshooting.

- **The Database Log** contains a list of all the database files on the server and all the servers which are replicating those databases.

- **The Certification Log** records every certificate a particular certifier has stamped on a user ID.

- **DB Fixup** checks for corrupted files and repairs them if possible or deletes them if not. It can be set to run automatically or it can be invoked by the administrator.

- **Other Log files** can be created for FAX and electronic-mail gateways, newswire gateways, and other applications that involve programs written to run with Notes.

## Keeping Notes Current

No server holds an unlimited number of applications. Sooner or later, applications need to be condensed, archived, or deleted. Procedures for removing data have to be cleared with the workgroup involved or with the database manager. Some of these decisions will likely be implemented in the replication settings for the database, because replication is one way to purge old documents (see Figure 8.7). (The purge process is explained in Chapter 7.)

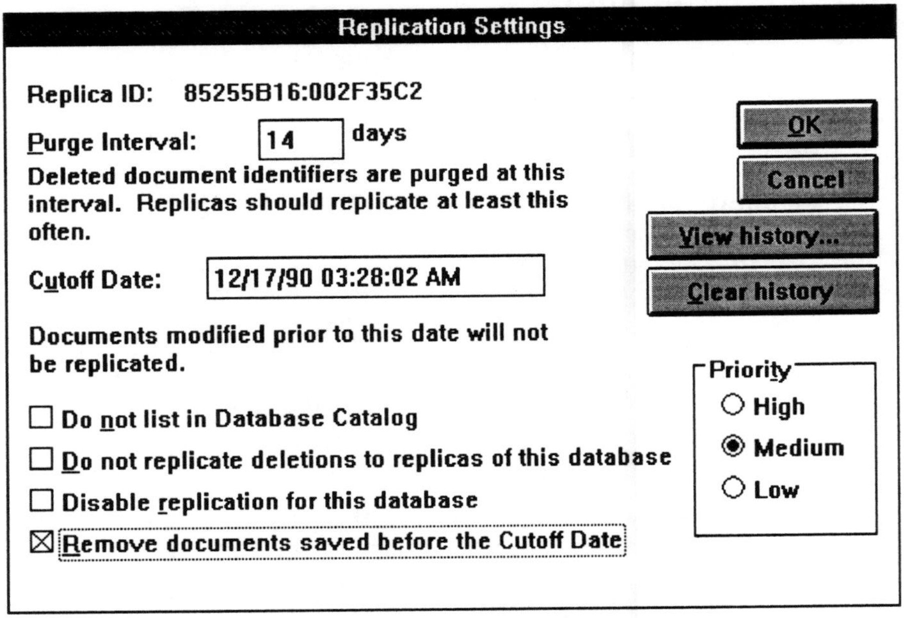

**Replication Settings**

Replica ID:   85255B16:002F35C2

Purge Interval:   | 14 |   days
Deleted document identifiers are purged at this interval. Replicas should replicate at least this often.

Cutoff Date:   | 12/17/90 03:28:02 AM |

Documents modified prior to this date will not be replicated.

☐ Do not list in Database Catalog
☐ Do not replicate deletions to replicas of this database
☐ Disable replication for this database
☒ Remove documents saved before the Cutoff Date

OK
Cancel
View history...
Clear history

Priority
○ High
◉ Medium
○ Low

**FIGURE 8.7** The Purge Interval and Cutoff Date settings work together to control the number of documents in a database in which, for example, users don't need information more than two weeks old.

Handling dead letters is another important function. Notes will alert users who want to know if their mail did not go through, with a delivery failure report. The report tells why the message could not be delivered, but that may not help the user as much as it would the administrator. If, for example, the message could not find a route to the server to which it was to be sent, the administrator must find out why and enter a communications path to that server in the Name and Address Book.

Messages that did not require delivery failure notification may sit in the mailbox file until the administrator handles them. Most organizations consider mail to be important enough that they want to make sure it is always getting from the sender to the recipient.

Installing new applications on the servers has become a well-defined procedure for some organizations. Most Notes installations are configured so that users can create new databases on their own workstations, but they cannot automatically add them to a server. One company has a series of steps for introducing a new database after it has been created on a workstation: First, the database manager must give an administrator Manager access to the application so that it can be moved to a test server. The administrator creates groups for the database in the Name and Address Book and assigns them their access levels and privileges according to whatever the workgroup wants. He also sets up the replication schedule in the database and makes sure the routing is set in the Name and Address Book. Quality assurance people test the database and when they are satisfied that it works well, they archive a copy of the original database, move it to a production server, and notify users through E-mail that the database is ready to use. By following procedures such as these, administrators can prevent problems that users and developers might overlook, not the least of which is the creation of a replication schedule that meshes with other communications loads on the servers that will run the application.

# Summary

The responsibilities of the Notes administrator fall into four areas: Security, server maintenance, server monitoring, and database management.

Some understanding of a set of key technologies and concepts will help clarify the role of the administrator: Network server versus Notes server, client/server architecture, NetBIOS, replication, the Name and Address Book, and domains.

In particular, the administrator is the security officer of the Notes installation, with duties that include the physical security of the servers, safeguarding the certifier ID, establishing and enforcing procedures for adding users, and controlling access to servers by users from outside the domain.

Notes provides a set of tools for monitoring the servers and their operations. It writes an extensive audit trail into a group of log files and databases. Administrators can check what certificates have been created, what applications reside on the server. Log files track replication events and user sessions. Undeliverable mail is saved for the administrator's attention.

# Expanding Notes with Additional Programs

Notes is a system sufficiently complex that getting the most out of it for an organization requires some expert help. This can take several forms, depending on the size of the organization and its needs and goals for Notes. It can range from help with hardware integration, installation and training, to linking Notes electronic mail with other E-mail systems, to creating programs that use Notes' familiar interface yet run outside of it to import data from large databases into Notes. This broad range of services is available from a group of independent consultants and companies fostered by Lotus and called the Alliance Partners.

The first members of the Alliance Partners group were systems integrators and software developers who saw the potential of specialized software systems that would work with Notes' application programming interfaces (APIs) to expand its capabilities. The earliest such programs written to work with the Notes APIs link its electronic-mail services to other e-mail programs. Others provide Notes users access to large databases stored on other computer systems. Still others build databases within Notes using information captured from outside sources such as wire services and commercial online retrieval systems.

When Version 2.0 of Notes was introduced, Lotus authorized some Alliance partners to be value-added resellers of Notes. These VARs can sell copies of Notes in whatever quantity is necessary as they perform systems integration, installation and training, and help clients develop customized Notes applications and systems.

This chapter will focus mainly on those Partners who work with the APIs. (Chapter 10 will cover some of the services other Alliance Partners and Notes VARs offer.) The intent is not to present a "how-to" tutorial on writing programs to the Notes APIs. Few Notes users will have the programming skills required to do that. But the managers of workgroups using Notes should understand the power of programs written to the APIs, what they can do to extend and customize Notes—to provide the kind of selective access to corporate data that turns it into useful information, and to provide connectivity between groups within the organization that had previously been isolated islands of communication.

The first section of this chapter briefly describes, for the non-technical reader, the Notes APIs and how they work. It includes examples of some of the kinds of API-based programs currently in use or under development.

Some of the first and most important API programs have been E-mail gateways, and a second section takes a look at the efforts of two major Alliance Partners in that area: Soft-Switch, Inc. and Touch Communications. Lotus' own FAX gateway for Notes is included here.

The third section covers access to databases, with descriptions of products developed by SandPoint Corporation, Desktop Data, Inc. and Individual Inc. A fourth section explores the voice annotation product of Simpact Associates, Inc. Finally, we briefly discuss Quality Decision Management, whose product does not involve an API program but which offers another kind of service—specialized templates for Notes databases.

# What Is an API?

Many software applications come with their own application programming interfaces. As the word interface suggests, the APIs form a kind of common boundary between those applications and other programs. For example, Notes cannot talk directly to a mainframe computer. It needs an API program to handle the communication and to translate the data from a form the mainframe understands into one Notes understands. An API is an individual function call, and an API program consists of several API function calls.

A program written to use the Notes APIs mimics the functions of Notes within a specific area, such as reading documents or creating E-mail messages in Notes' format. In fact, the Notes developers point out that Notes itself is a collection of over 1,000 APIs with a user interface built on top. However, most of them are not available to programmers. Lotus has released an API toolkit which includes code and documentation for some 130 of the Notes APIs which are the functions that give programmers access to the contents of the databases. Many are mail APIs. None of the functions in the toolkit allow programmers to change the Notes user interface or network protocols.

Programs written using the toolkit run on the Notes server and make a connection between Notes and computer functions that are entirely unrelated and independent. The APIs allow a programmer to write code that serves as a go-between—to act on the Notes databases by linking to a mainframe or an SQL database server, an electronic mail gateway, or even manipulating Notes databases internally.

Writing API programs requires the Notes API toolkit, some expertise in the C language, and an understanding of networking protocols and telecommunications. (The APIs are written in C, and Microsoft C Version 5.1 is the language version supported by the toolkit.) The demand for API expertise within a company depends on its size and its commitment to using Notes as a platform for corporate information management. Some of the larger organizations using Notes have dedicated full-time programmers to the job of creating software systems that use the APIs. But because many API programs are written to meet a specific need and require little or no ongoing maintenance once they are running smoothly, smaller organizations may find it impractical to assign programming resources to Notes. They may prefer to hire an Alliance Partner to write their API programs or to customize programs that the Partner has already written.

It is important to understand that no organization should make a decision to purchase Notes on the basis of the APIs. If Notes does not serve the needs of a group and fit into the particular business environment, then the use of APIs won't change that incompatibility. However, if Notes fills a company's needs, and additionally the company wants to import information into Notes (or export it from Notes), or it wants to add features to it, then the APIs will provide the means to do so.

## What API Programs Can Do

Many of the most basic functions of Notes are treated as API programs. These functions, like routing E-mail, indexing databases, and replication, run under the control of the Notes server. Most API programs of any complexity also run under server control. These so-called "server add-ins," like the basic functions, all manage the databases, each in its own way,and the Notes server controls when and how each is used.

Gateways, agents, and live information feeds are all server add-ins. A gateway allows Notes and an external system to exchange addressed messages. An E-mail gateway, for example, changes the electronic envelope, or format, of a Notes message so it can be read by another mail system. When Notes receives outside mail the gateway reverses the process and changes the envelope to one Notes can read. An agent filters information, acting on it to produce something with added value, usually in order to transfer it into or out of Notes. A live information feed collects information from outside sources, shapes it into Notes documents, and places the documents into databases. Some examples are shown below.

## An E-mail Gateway

In one large department of a company Notes became the favored communications medium, and within that department the users depended on Notes E-mail. But other departments in the company used another E-mail program, cc:Mail, and the Notes users needed to exchange messages with those people, too. The solution was an API mail gateway that put messages created in cc:Mail into the Notes E-mail system, and vice versa. Notes users didn't notice any differences. They continued to compose and address their mail as usual, and mail sent to a Notes user from a cc:Mail user looked like Notes mail. There was one major limitation: Because cc:Mail is character-based it couldn't include graphics or typographical embellishment and thus work with Notes' Rich Text format.

## Getting the News into Notes

A manufacturing company with several large customers subscribed to a news-wire service to track client-related announcements and news. After the company's salespeople began using Notes, the advantages of distributing that news directly to the salespeople assigned to the accounts became obvious. Working with an Alliance Partner, the company built a live information feed that read the categories and company names encoded into the newswire transmissions and sorted them into Notes databases. The feed even sent high-priority stories about certain companies as E-mail messages to their account reps.

## Moving Data from Mainframes to Notes

An organization with Notes installed at several sites discovered that it needed to provide a series of reports created on its mainframe computer in Notes. The solution was an API program which ran on a regular schedule to translate the reports into Notes databases and replicate those databases to all the Notes servers.

## Querying the Database from Notes

A Notes group that wanted to frame queries for an SQL database server from inside Notes posed a more complex problem than simple access to database reports. The solution in this case was the product of a joint effort by a Notes database developer and an API programmer. They developed a Notes application in which the user filled in fields to create a document that was the query. The API program was designed to check the database regularly for queries. When it found one it read the document and, using the APIs for the SQL database server, reformatted the document as an SQL query and passed it to the server. The SQL server would build the table that answered the query and, through its APIs, return it to the API program, which would format the table and place it in Notes.

# Mail Gateways

Among the earliest uses of the Notes APIs were the creation of E-mail gateways. This shouldn't be surprising: Many of the first customers for Notes were large organizations which already had one or more incompatible E-mail systems in place. The organizations didn't want to or couldn't replace those E-mail systems with Notes. As will probably be the case with most companies that already have networks installed, unless Notes is being installed throughout the whole company most organizations will need to maintain more than one E-mail system and to connect them to each other.

Lotus responded to this need with E-mail gateways that bridge Notes to Novell's MHS (Message Handling Services) and DEC's minicomputer-based VMSmail, and others are expected. (Lotus's purchase of cc:Mail, one of the leading stand-alone E-mail systems has prompted speculation that future versions of Notes may integrate connections to cc:Mail, so companies can bring PC users who may not need access to the rest of Notes under the Notes E-mail umbrella.)

Because there are many proprietary mail systems, some organizations have undertaken to write their own gateways. For an organization which uses Notes and one other E-mail system, one bilateral API program between the two systems is all that is needed to connect the two. But for organizations with several E-mail systems on several computer platforms, bilateral gateways aren't the answer. It is common to find companies that have some IBM mainframe users on PROFS, several departments using cc:Mail on PC networks, an art department with lots of Macintoshes running TOPS InBox, and an engineering lab on an E-mail system running on Unix and TCP/IP. Adding Notes to this equation simply elevates the already high level of confusion. At least 10 gateways would have to be set up among the competing systems. Writing a separate gateway for each possible combination of E-mail systems would be very difficult. Running them together successfully would be an administrative nightmare.

The solution is a central clearinghouse which accepts all the mail, translates it, routes it and provides security and transmission functions. Lotus sought this compatibility for Notes very early on, working with Soft-Switch, Inc.and Touch Communications, two Alliance Partner companies specializing in communications technology.

# The Soft-Switch Solution

Soft-Switch, Inc. links incompatible E-mail systems through their software product, Soft-Switch Central. Soft-Switch Central runs on an IBM S/370 under either MVS or VM, or on an 80386-based computer running the Interactive Unix operating system. The software takes care of changing a message's protocol, routing it securely to the appropriate system, verifying transmission, and, optionally, providing directory assistance.

Lotus has developed a Notes gateway to Soft-Switch Central, which works with its own mail router. When a Notes user wants to send a message to someone on a PROFS mail system, for example, the message is routed through the Soft-Switch gateway, running under the control of the Notes server, to Soft-Switch Central where it is converted to a form PROFS recognizes. A message from a PROFS user takes the reverse path: It goes through Soft-Switch Central which converts it and sends it to the Notes Soft-Switch gateway, and it is routed to the Notes user.

Soft-Switch of Wayne, PA, has developed gateways for a variety of operating environments and E-mail systems, including SNADS, cc:Mail, X.400, SMTP, PROFS, DISOSS, TCP/IP, Banyan Mail, 3+Mail, Higgins, The Network Courier, DEC ALL-IN-1, VMSmail, Wang OFFICE, HP Desk, PC/TSO, and Novell MHS. It continues to add to the list. A company running Notes purchases the Notes-to-Soft-Switch gateway and Soft-Switch Central, plus any other gateways it needs. Soft-Switch performs the initial setup, and Notes administrators monitor the gateway log file for transmission or routing problems.

From the user's point of view, perhaps the biggest barrier to using a clearinghouse utility like Soft-Switch Central is that the names and addresses of users on other systems don't appear in their Name and Address Book (or its equivalent in other mail systems), and there is no centralized directory within Soft-Switch Central. A user must know the precise electronic address of his intended recipient. If a sender does not know the receiver's address, he can address the message to "John Doe@SSW" and Soft-Switch Central will look up the receiver's address and route it. However, if the sender misspelled John Doe's name, it will take him some time to find out — he will be notified through a non-delivery report rather than an immediate message. Nor will he have any way of checking for the correct spelling. Soft-Switch, Inc. offers a directory synchronizer, a utility that maintains a list on each platform of all the E-mail users known to Soft-Switch Central.

Soft-Switch can convert many kinds of formatted text to other formats. If a Notes user wanted to send a Notes Rich Text file to a foreign mail recipient as a WordPerfect file she could instruct Soft-Switch Central to make the conversion as it processed the message. Soft-Switch can also convert files attached to a Notes document. The variety of conversions is limited by the capabilities of the receiving E-mail system and the formats it is capable of displaying. The Notes Soft-Switch gateway can be configured to convert incoming messages to Rich Text or ASCII. If a file arrives in a different form — a WordPerfect document, for example — it will be attached to a Notes document.

(Currently no other E-mail system can handle Notes' encrypted documents. If a Notes user sends an encrypted message to a user on a foreign E-mail system it remains encrypted and unintelligible to the recipient. The other system does not understand Notes' encryption method and has neither the key to decrypt the document nor the functionality to use it.)

# Touch's X.400 Gateway

Soft-Switch's server-based clearinghouse is designed for the company that needs to connect different proprietary E-mail systems within the organization. Communication that must reach beyond the boundaries of a single organization poses a different set of problems — and has resulted in a solution that focuses on the creation of a standard protocol for formatting and addressing a message. This standard, the X.400 protocol, is sanctioned by the International Standards Organization (ISO), the international organization which sets data communications standards. The ISO's goal in creating X.400 was a non-proprietary protocol that would allow different kinds of computers, networks and applications to communicate by standardizing the way they format, address, and route mail messages. X.400 works among LAN based, host-based, government, and individual user systems.

Lotus chose Touch Communications of Campbell, CA, to write an X.400 gateway. Touch sells a product called Worldtalk/400 which can run on a 386 PC under Unix. The Worldtalk software allows systems which can support X.400 protocols to send and receive messages. For Notes, the Touch X.400 gateway means the Notes user stays within the familiar Notes environment, and the gateway sends the messages to the Worldtalk/400 Gateway Engine which formats, addresses and routes the message to the X.400 recipient.

There is some overlap of the Soft-Switch and Touch products. Soft-Switch offers an X.400 gateway as well and supports open standard protocols, but its primary focus is on connecting proprietary systems with a proprietary solution. Touch specializes in X.400 products that emphasize standards. A company's needs for one or both depends largely on whether it wants to communicate within the organization or outside it and its plans to grow into X.400 as more telecommunications products strategies become standards-based over the long term.

This emphasis on standards is growing. X.400 seems destined to be very important for enterprise-to-enterprise communications. While organizations will probably continue to use gateways and Soft-Switch and similar systems internally, increasingly they will need a way to communicate with other organizations that may not share a compatible e-mail gateway. This compatibility becomes particularly important when a company wants to communicate internationally as X.400 has gained wide acceptance in Europe.

The issues surrounding X.400 are still evolving. Common carriers like the phone company already offer X.400 services, and they will become more common. Public messaging carriers including SprintMail, MCI Mail, and AT&T Mail also offer X.400 service. These carriers assume the burden of responsibility for security and connectivity. Although two organizations could directly communicate with each other using X.400, they would they have to provide their own security and transmission error checking.

A distributed directory service called X.500 eventually will be offered in conjunction with X.400. It will allow users to look up the address of a recipient —a necessary addition if X.400 is going to become a feasible way to communicate worldwide.

## Fax Gateways

Another type of messaging gateway links Notes to facsimile transmissions. With Version 2.0 of Notes, Lotus introduced a fax gateway that could send outbound faxes, and announced it was working on a method of handling inbound faxes as well. Like the E-mail gateways, a fax gateway increases the reach of Notes—users can fax messages and documents to recipients who don't have Notes or electronic mail.

The fax gateway runs under the control of the Notes server program. It can run on the same machine or a separate one, but it needs a 386 or 486 computer with at least 8 megabytes of memory and an 80 megabyte hard drive. Sending faxes is a memory-intensive process, and a 286 PC is too slow. The Lotus fax gateway is written to run with the GammaFax board made by GammaLink. For a Notes system with a high volume of outgoing fax traffic more than one board can be installed in the server to reduce transmission bottlenecks.

To the Notes user, creating a fax is no different from creating an electronic mail message. A separate mail form for faxes contains the information in the "To" field which routes the message through the gateway to the program that turns the Notes document into a fax image (essentially a bitmapped graphic), and drives the fax board. (A nice touch: For the cover page which is sent with every fax message, Lotus's fax server uses a form which resides in a standard Notes database on the fax server. Users can create their own cover pages and choose which one to send with each message.)

Because fax messages arrive as bitmapped graphics files, large numbers of them could take up a great deal of hard drive storage. Lotus is currently working with another company to develop optical character recognition (OCR) technology which would convert an incoming fax file into a text file so it can come into the Notes database as an editable file.

## Access To Databases

The same gateway structure that defines E-mail gateways can be seen in a class of API applications that aren't usually thought of as gateways—programs that retrieve information from large databases and bring it into Notes. There are a couple of major advantages. The most obvious is simplification: Working with large databases, whatever their type or contents, can be greatly simplified by bringing the process under the Notes graphical user interface.

Forms and views can provide a familiar, natural way to frame a query for a database on a corporate mainframe, or to wade through the articles filed on a wire service.

The other advantage is that through its APIs, Notes can provide this familiar access structure not just to the corporate mainframe DBMS, but also to CD-ROM servers, SQL servers, and the many forms of public databases including on-line information services, specialized government and scientific databases, and newswire feeds. In addition, data retrieved by some of these Alliance Partner products can take such non-traditional forms as graphics, photographs, and even sound.

The Alliance Partners who are creating these innovative uses of Notes bring some unusual skills to their projects. The list grows faster than a book like this one could keep up with, but the following examples indicate the range of the work being done.

## SandPoint Corporation

When the founders of SandPoint Corporation went looking for a way to apply their knowledge of online information services and database retrieval, they decided to make their Cambridge-based company's first product an information manager that worked with Notes. Michael Kinkead and Tom Henry recognized that Notes was a great platform for organizing and disseminating information, so they created an API program that connects Notes to computer databases and online electronic information services such as Lexis, Dialog, and Dow Jones, and to CD-ROM libraries such as Lotus One Source.

They recognized that most PC users want to access information in a way that doesn't require a background in telecommunications or training in how to frame queries in a dozen different online systems. So SandPoint's system, called Hoover, allows a user working within the familiar structure of Notes to make a query and receive results easily and often (in many cases updating the information daily or even hourly). Hoover is an API program that accepts queries created in Notes forms, retrieves data from a variety of sources, and turns it into reports presented as carefully formatted Notes documents.

The two founders describe Hoover as proactive, a software agent that invisibly performs much of the technically complicated work of extracting data from online databases. It operates on the Notes server as a kind of delivery service, gathering requests for data and then delivering the replies. It can batch requests across the user base: If a user doesn't need to have a search run immediately, Hoover can wait a specified period for other requests to be made. It can then run several queries in the same operation, saving connection time and costs. Hoover can also distinguish between new queries and update requests. For updates it keeps track of information that has already been retrieved and adds only information dated since the last search.

Throughout the process Notes acts as a front end and Hoover as the back end. Hoover uses the APIs to collect queries from a Notes database and create response documents within it. Hoover handles the work of retrieving the data from the sources specified in the query and mapping it into the proper Notes form. All of this activity by Hoover is transparent to Notes users because it runs as a separate process under the multitasking capabilities of OS/2 on the server.

Hoover is not a plug-and-play product. Like most Alliance Partners, SandPoint is as much a consulting house as a software seller. Each Hoover installation is different. SandPoint works with a customer to assess information needs, select appropriate information sources, and, most important, design the forms that generate queries and display the responses. Because it builds on all the features of Notes forms, Hoover can encapsulate very complex queries in relatively simple Notes forms. Users are spared the hard work of correctly framing repetitious requests for information. Hoover can transform the data it has acquired to produce presentation-quality documents using Notes' typefont and layout options.

In a typical query Hoover might produce a financial report on a company. The Notes user starts the process by opening a query form and entering the name of the company and the criteria for the search by filling in fields such as keywords, databases to search, beginning and ending dates, authors and titles and maximum number of items to retrieve. The user may also indicate how frequently the search should be executed (once, daily, or weekly, for example) and when they want it to occur (immediately or at off-peak hours). They can also indicate the level of detail they want in the returned data—from just the number of retrievable items to abbreviated citations to full text.

An early example of Hoover at work was a financial analyst who specializes in finding companies for his clients to acquire. He used Hoover to study business trends. In one instance, based on information he uncovered using Hoover, he recommended a southern construction company as a good buy. In a query he asked how many building permits were issued, by region, over a period of time. Hoover queried several online databases, including newspapers and engineering journals. The analyst studied the returned data in different Notes views and saw that in a small geographical area one company had been issued a large number of building permits. Then, through Hoover again, he requested the company's financial statements, news stories, press releases and announcements. Using Hoover he saved time tracking down and selecting the relevant materials, and had been able instead to focus his time analyzing the data.

Hoover is flexible enough that it can access almost any kind of database, from commercial services to a company's own mainframes. Lotus' own Credit Department uses Hoover to bring invoices created on their VAX into Notes. Formerly, the invoices were printed in bulky paper reports. When members of the Credit staff needed to check an organization's status they looked it up in the paper reports. Now, Hoover goes into the VAX each night and fetches a report file on all new invoices for the day. It parses the data, categorizes it by company and writes it into Notes. Using the feature which totals numeric data in views, Notes creates a summary of all the invoices for each company. A Notes user in Credit can quickly call up a customer file and review their credit standing. (Lotus also schedules quarterly Dun & Bradstreet reports. Once a quarter Hoover sends a query to D&B on all the companies Lotus tracks, and brings a credit rating back into Notes.)

## Desktop Data, Inc.

Desktop Data, Inc. of Waltham, MA, offers NewsEDGE as stand-alone product, and became an Alliance Partner in order to develop a version that uses the forms and views of Notes to add value to databases built from the stories transmitted by high-volume wire services. NewsEDGE is intended to meet the needs of investment bankers, traders, media relations and others who must constantly monitor wire services.

The user builds a profile of her interests, specifying industry categories, country, company, or product names, specific words or phrases that will be used to select articles. NewsEDGE, running on its own OS/2 server, receives the datastream of one or more wire services via FM receiver, leased phone line, or packet-switch network, depending on the source. It scans the incoming data, selects those articles that match the profile, and deposits them in a database. In the stand-alone version of the NewsEDGE database users can conduct searches of these articles using boolean operators (and, or, not). Because NewsEDGE Notes is built on Notes forms and views, it doesn't include boolean search capabilities, but it does offer Notes' ease of use and accessibility. The user profile is built or changed in a Notes form, and once in the database articles can be used like any other Notes document. They can be replicated to other parts of the company, copied into other documents, exported to other programs, E-mailed to other Notes users, and tied into a network of references with DocLinks.

Desktop Data and SandPoint, are working together to incorporate some of the newswire-management capabilities of NewsEDGE into Hoover, as well.

# Individual, Inc.

Another Alliance Partner, Individual, Inc. Cambridge, MA, offers a different approach to monitoring the news. Individual describes its product, called First!, as an "information refiner." First! is built on a newswire-management strategy similar to that of NewsEDGE, but the delivery method for the selected information is very different.

First! customers, like those of NewsEDGE, build profiles of their interests, specifying search terms to be applied to the database of news articles. Individual, Inc., runs the profiles on its computers against a database that includes a variety of news sources. It builds the selected stories into a kind of personalized newspaper which contains only the kinds of news and reports the user wants.

Individual distributes these customized collections of articles overnight via fax or electronic mail and they're ready to be read first thing in the morning, just like a newspaper. Customers on Notes can receive their First! reports on Notes' E-mail through an MHS mail gateway. Once received, the information can be edited, cut and pasted, E-mailed and linked in ways that encourage groups to find new uses for it.

# Simpact Associates, Inc.

In San Diego, California, Simpact Associates, Inc. is developing an entirely different kind of API program that stretches the meaning of "data" in a Notes application. Simpact's Remark! adds voice messages to a Notes document. The company describes the product as a "voice processing system architecture" which allows users to annotate Notes documents with digitized voice elements.

Simpact was a Notes customer before it was an Alliance Partner. it felt Notes fit the company's vision of improved internal communications. The company develops products in the area of interactive voice processing, and it became an Alliance Partner when it saw the potential of using its voice-processing technology to enhance Notes.

Digitized *store and forward* voice-mail has become common in businesses. But applications beyond voice-mail have been limited and technologically complex. Remark!'s use of the Notes APIs for voice annotation gives a fascinating look at how Notes' accessible interface can transform seemingly difficult technology into a usable application.

Remark! runs as a Windows application separate from Notes. When it is called it opens a small window on the Notes workspace that looks like a tape recorder's control panel, with buttons for Rewind, Record, Play, Fast Forward, Stop, Pause, and Restart. Creating a voice message is as easy as clicking Record and starting to talk. And Remark! will play back and edit completed messages.

Remark! requires a dedicated PC working as a voice server connected to a PBX, Centrex system or outside phone lines, and to the local area network. Workstations require no additional hardware, just the Remark! software. Users speak into their regular telephones, just as they do with voice mail, to record messages.

A Notes user adds voice messages as comments within Rich Text fields, positioning the cursor in the field, then dictating the message. A Remark! note is indicated by a small marker similar to a DocLink icon. In this way, for example, an editor could add voice comments to a writer's draft, a financial analyst could annotate a graph. Remark! will even record and store telephone calls within documents. Voice messages can be cut and pasted between documents, and encrypted for privacy. Remark! also works with Notes E-mail, and can be tied into a company's voice mail. (Simpact is working on allowing remote Notes users access to voice.)

Simpact stresses the importance of voice as a comfortable communication medium for the same knowledge workers and executives who are Notes' user base. They are used to verbalizing their thoughts in phone calls, meetings, and dictation. Voice messages add emphasis, help clarify meanings, and convey emotion through tone of voice. And importantly, they don't make keyboarding skills a requirement for efficient communication.

Simpact's demonstration of Remark! provides a glimpse of what a multimedia Notes application might look like. It follows the work of an adjustor for an auto insurance company who builds a claim file by combining text, graphic images, and sound. The data from the claim is put into a Notes document. A scanned photograph of the car is added. And a telephone conversation with the claimant is recorded and saved in the file. The document can take advantage of all Notes' categorization and formulas for routing, and review of the file is easy, because all the pieces are kept in one place.

# Quality Decision Management, Inc.

The founders of Quality Decision Management, Inc., of North Andover, Massachusetts, originally planned to write software that would help organizations with strategic planning and quality management. When they saw Notes they realized it provided an environment that would work well with their ideas. They became Alliance Partners for Notes and designed a series of templates that put into action the principles of quality management. One of their beta users enthusiastically described their product, called Quality At Work, as "infiltrating the company with a new way of doing business that is compellingly different."

QDM believes that organizations have to realize that employees are their most valuable resource. They must find ways to tap the wealth of employees' ideas, and, in the process, empower individuals and teams of people to increase productivity, produce quality products or services and gain or retain a competitive advantage. In many organizations there are two approaches to quality, says Andy Jeffrey, QDM's president. Higher level employees consider quality to be a necessity, and lower level employees view it as the latest management fad for prompting workers to do more work with fewer resources. These two groups need to communicate and collaborate if the organization intends to stay competitive. To do that, says Jeffrey, the lines of communication within the organization must be restructured to be both vertical and horizontal, with increasing emphasis placed on horizontal communication as teams of workers replace levels of management.

QDM felt that Notes was the right vehicle for such interaction, and it set out to develop a system in Notes that would foster that communication. The result was Quality At Work, a set of template applications built on the criteria for the Malcolm Baldrige Quality Award.

The prestigious Malcolm Baldrige National Quality Award, administered by the U.S. Department of Commerce and the National Institute of Standards and Technology, was created to recognize the achievements of U.S. companies and to publicize successful strategies for quality management. The award criteria cover the areas of leadership, planning, human resource utilization, quality assurance of products and services, quality results, and customer satisfaction. Only a few companies receive the coveted award each year. Nevertheless, the criteria, judged on a point-total scoring scheme, provide a measure against which any organization can evaluate its employees' commitment to quality management, from the CEO to the entry-level worker.

QDM formulated Quality at Work to help organizations which use the Baldrige criteria but lacked a way to monitor their efforts, or the means to include all levels of the work force. Quality at Work has six modules including a modified mail template. The modules are called Strategic, Malcolm Baldrige Quality Award Criteria, Marketing, Project Management and Quality Function Deployment. Each module can be tailored to specific organizations.

The Strategic and Baldrige Criteria modules help organizations develop and implement strategies. These long-range plans and the data on which they are based need continuous updating and evaluation, says Jeffrey. Too often, he says, reexamination occurs incrementally. When the quarterly business plan is due everyone rushes to devote the time and resources needed to complete it. Then no further action occurs until it is time for the next plan, when the frantic rush begins again. Adding the tools for developing and implementing strategy to Notes lessens the chance of a stop/start approach, says Jeffrey. It makes planning activities integral to the everyday work of the organization. It also encourages team building and greater participation within the organization.

Quality At Work does not ignore the daily management functions that sometimes seems only remotely related to long-range planning. The Project Management and Marketing modules are more tactical. They deal with known ends and known events, but in Notes they can draw upon the collaborative thinking of the organization. The Project module tracks the status of projects, records milestones as they are achieved and assigns tasks through an Action Item form.

Marketing helps users track promotional opportunities, and it coordinates the work of users who may be geographically apart. It, too, contains an Action Item form.

The Quality Function Deployment module is based on a Japanese approach to business that emphasizes meeting customer expectations. This module is both a data-collection and an analyzing tool that helps its users gather information on customer desires and brainstorm about how to meet those expectations and stay competitive.

The mail template has been modified to include an action item form and four views related to it. This came about through Jeffrey's search for a satisfactory way to handle "to do" lists. He found that too often he was handling the same item several times. Writing a note to himself also meant writing one to a colleague in the form of a reminder, request, memo or letter. Updating items required another round of communication. He wanted to handle an item as few times as possible but not lose track of it.

He resolved the dilemma by putting action-item forms in the mail template and other templates. Items meant for individuals which need not be recorded in a database go into the individual's private mail. An action item created within a module, on the other hand, goes into the database in which it was created, and a copy is sent to the mailbox of the user who is responsible for it.

This method allows users to have private to-do lists without having to deal with the same item in two different places. As the user updates or completes tasks, he can delete them from his own mail, but the items duplicated in other Quality At Work modules are preserved in the group's database as public records of the action taken.

Although an organization could use the Quality at Work modules in mix-and-match fashion, QDM bundles all six as a package. This encourages companies to use them all, says Jeffrey, and to address both the strategic and routine tasks of organizations. Everyday users can see that their daily work is leading in the direction of the strategic goals. Strategic planners can get a clearer view of the practical problems the organization faces every day. Each module of Quality At Work deals with an aspect of the theory of quality management, but working in concert, the aim is to provide a practical view of what is happening to the organization. "What we are selling." says Jeffrey, "is a business plan."

# Internal Development of API Programs

There are many Alliance Partners whose services or products are not covered in this chapter. Some, who offer service and training, are mentioned in the following chapter on deploying Notes. Others don't sell products developed with the API, but rather sell templates or highly customized Notes databases.

Likewise, little space in this chapter has been given to developing API programs within a company, yet there are many reasons why an organization would want to invest in the effort of acquiring the API toolkit and learning to use it. Although Notes comes with several import and export filters built in, others can be created through API programs: A company that uses a word processor or database manager not included on the list of import/export format choices could create an API program to do the conversions.

Because the APIs in the toolkit provide a means of acting on the databases, programs can be written to join two Notes databases, to make specific queries of a Notes database or to restructure the documents in a database. The APIs and the toolkit make Notes an open system, much more customizable, and much more compatible with other information-management programs.

# Summary

With its application programming interfaces and an API programming toolkit that documents some 130 functions within Notes, the program can be integrated into a larger communications and computer-services environment. API programs such as electronic-mail gateways, Lotus' own fax gateway, database-access managers and voice-annotation tools let companies use Notes to best advantage.

These sophisticated API programs and others work within the familiar Notes environment to keep powerful computer functions easy to use and free from unneeded complexity. The development of add-in products that use the Notes APIs is in its infancy. As development efforts broaden, both within companies developing their own propriety API programs and among Alliance Partners developing commercial applications and services, new technologies will be propelled by Notes' ease of use to find wider audiences.

# Section 5
# Notes and the
# Organization

Notes' chances for success will be increased if three basic conditions are met. First, the workers and departments affected by what happens in the Notes environment need universal access to Notes. Second, the Notes applications must be built to a critical mass, so most of the information that most people want is easier to find within Notes than outside it. Third, everybody expected to use Notes should have a PC capable of running it. These are all issues of deployment—getting Notes out into the organization, training, and motivating the staff to use it, and providing the resources to make it successful.

But there is an even more basic requirement for success with Notes. The company must evaluate Notes in the light of its organizational goals and decide formally to adopt Notes. It must understand how Notes will meet the company's needs, and then plan carefully and specifically to implement Notes in the organization in a way that addresses those needs and solutions.

The following chapter identifies several factors that must be considered in this deployment plan, from environmental issues within the organization such as anticipating and managing change, to training and support issues, and the ongoing management of Notes' benefits.

# 10

# Deploying Notes in the Organization

The major limit on the adoption of Notes is not technology. It is issues of corporate culture and introducing change into the organization. Most of the early installations of Notes have been in some of the United States' largest corporations. Two decades of experience with computers have conditioned these large organizations to deal with the changes that new information systems can bring. The cyclical introduction of new technology has taught them the importance of careful evaluation and decision-making. The complexities of mainframe hardware and software and the growth of MIS departments early on taught them the cost of maintenance.

Repeated failures have finally taught some organizations that no matter how expensive and dazzling the computer system, the focus must be on the human element, on the people who use the system to do their daily work. The users must be properly prepared and trained, included in the decision-making, given the hardware and software tools, and supported in their use of the system. And they must be led by the example of managers who themselves use the system and reward others who use it, and pushed from behind by programs that diagnose problems of usage and solve them.

As often as companies have adopted—and readopted—new information systems, it seems that deploying a system like Notes would have been reduced to a science. Unfortunately, it hasn't. Too many differences exist between organizations, between management styles and corporate cultures. From interviews with companies that have pioneered with Notes, trainers, consultants, Alliance Partners and Lotus employees who have helped customers implement Notes, there emerge six major categories of concern for the organization deploying Notes:

- **Environment**. Notes means change, and its success in any organization depends on how well that change is managed. Proper introduction and preparation before Notes is online can lessen resistance to Notes related changes.

- **Strategy**. Careful planning for introducing Notes into an organization is important—selecting the right groups to lead the company into Notes, and encouraging its use from the top down.

- **Training**. Notes' ease of use doesn't reduce the need for thorough training programs for users. The training should present Notes to each workgroup in the context of its particular business problems and processes.

- **Quality Assurance**. Once Notes is up and running, it needs quality control to make sure that new applications are useful and unique and that users have enough input into adapting Notes to meet their needs.

- **Support**. Notes runs in a complex environment of computer technologies and group dynamics. The people who support Notes must support this entire environment.

- **Resources**. Organizations that choose Notes must realize that their choice brings with it commitments to invest in hardware, software and personnel.

This chapter briefly discusses how these issues affect the introduction of Notes into the organization. The intent here is to provide a summary of the best ideas of people who have worked in organizations implementing Notes.

# Manage The Environmental Change

Introducing Notes into an organization inevitably causes complex change that affects the culture of the company. Managing this change requires much planning and preparation, even before the decision to buy Notes is made.

The issues presented here don't represent a neat, step-by-step solution. They are all elements in the process an organization will go through as it decides what changes it wants to make in its own structure and goals, and how Notes will help effect that change.

## Why Notes?

Peter Rothstein, a principal with The Human Interface Group and a group technology consultant specializing in management strategy and technology to support business processes, has had extensive experience with Notes. He says the first question to ask is, "Why is the organization buying Notes, and what does it hope to accomplish because of this purchase?"

Companies that have had the most success in incorporating Notes into their work environments have initially focused not on Notes, but on the areas of their operations where they see a need for change. Once they have identified the areas of concern, they are then in a position to decide whether Notes is appropriate. In the case studies detailed in Chapter 1, for example, all the companies had spent considerable time determining their needs and the kinds of change they wanted to make before they adopted Notes.

## Clarify the Vision

Once a company's management has targeted the areas it wants to change and decided on Notes, it must then clarify its vision and spell out its primary goals. The initial vision will be that of the decision makers. Even small, entrepreneurial companies with a flattened management structure need leaders to help the others envision what Notes can do.

One company did this by introducing new users to Notes through a "Company Vision" discussion application. The database contained documents, written by managers, on Notes' abilities to help the company. The new users read the documents and were encouraged to respond to them by adding new ideas or asking questions. This process provided early reinforcement of Notes as a team or group technology tool.

Clarifying the vision also helps the Notes application designers create databases appropriate to the business's needs and processes. Notes receives a weak start if new users have to use applications that have only limited relevance to their real work. If the way the work is to be done in the future is to be effectively changed from the way it was done in the past, the Notes designers will need to understand the goals and incorporate the new processes into their work.

## Enlist Top Management

While the support of top management might seem obvious—they probably authorized the purchase of Notes—it is not a given. Managers have been known to purchase products in which they have no personal interest. But Notes is different. It is not another software package the CEO buys because the MIS department asks for it. If Notes is to make a difference and be accepted by all those who must use it, it has to have the support from the top down. Managers should plan to use Notes every day, even if that means they must learn to type before they can learn to use Notes.

Managers should use Notes to set a good example, of course, but for an even more important reason. As they use Notes they will develop their expectations for the program and how it can help their business. In addition, they should hold informal and formal discussion and concern sessions with all those who will use it, from the secretaries to the division heads.

One vice-president of a financial organization implementing Notes pointed out that many users resist change and want to relearn as little as possible. He cites the example of the PC user who is perfectly happy with a word processor package he knows well and is not at all interested in changing to a newer one recommended by his MIS department. He already knows it, why should he learn another? This reticence, said the vice-president, is what Notes must overcome. Introducing a new system to the user community and the company culture means trying to reskill people who often feel threatened. To get users to embrace the new technology management must keep the users' needs and feelings in mind.

Some of the companies that are adopting Notes through their MIS departments may overlook this need for sensitivity to the non-technical user. MIS staff members are used to trying out new products as part of their job. They naturally like what's new and more powerful. "We all just loved Notes from the start and found it very easy to use," reported one MIS manager of the people in his own department. When they began to introduce Notes beyond their own department, though, they ran into some resistance. They had not prepared users for the change. The users came to their first training session having no idea what Notes was about. Some felt confused and intimidated. The MIS manager's view of the situation was that "there will always be resisters." But one wonders if better introduction and preparation might have lessened the new users' resistance.

## Prepare for Changes

Kate Merritt, a principal of Executive Learning Partners, has worked with companies introducing new technologies and building the analytical and interpersonal skills workers need to use them. She says that Notes is a great conceptual leap for people to make. It is not automating how people work, but changing the way they work. Whereas spreadsheets or word processors speeded up and automated jobs we had done manually, Notes is not about automation. In fact, she says, one of the problems with automation has been that companies have not questioned the way they have done their work or even the work itself. They only automated the work they were already doing. If a business process was slow and awkward before PCs, it became fast and awkward after the computer took over.

Ms. Merritt adds another note of caution. She says the lack of computer models for the kind of many-to-many communications that Notes offers makes the concept difficult to grasp. The idea of a word processor replacing a typewriter is much easier to understand than Notes' ability to enhance the human interaction that keeps businesses running. This, of course, is another reason why everyone who will use Notes should be involved in its introduction. Secretaries should contribute ideas about the ways their work might change, not merely be expected to unquestioningly conform to the ideas of someone who has never done their kinds of work. The same applies to all levels of work-groups—each person will develop a greater interest, enthusiasm and sense of ownership if she is involved in planning for Notes.

# Strategic Planning—From the Top Down

With its goals clearly stated, the organization can plan for Notes' introduction and its ongoing support. Here again careful planning pays off. Many of the strategic issues are closely tied to the environmental ones. The key is that the introduction of Notes is too complex and involves too many people to be handed off to an individual, an MIS department or outside consultants. Its success, requires clear direction and ongoing support at all levels of the organization.

## Make an Implementation Plan

One of the most basic decisions is how Notes will be deployed. Will it be implemented enterprise-wide, pilot-tested in selected departments, or put into individual departments with no immediate plans to widen its base?

As we saw in Chapter 1, Price Waterhouse is implementing Notes across the entire organization. It will take some time, but from the beginning this large accounting firm intended for every knowledge worker to be connected to Notes. Price Waterhouse is a good candidate for enterprise-wide implementation. It has a relatively flat organizational structure and most of its employees naturally work in teams without pyramidal layers of management.

Other companies have chosen to be more cautious and introduce Notes with pilot installations in one or two departments. Most of the companies interviewed for this book were not introducing Notes in true pilot programs, with formal periods of use and evaluation (although most of the companies involved in the beta test of Version 1 of Notes did). One vice-president for technology involved in implementing Notes believes that Notes should not be introduced as a pilot. A pilot too often suggests the software is experimental, that a tentative commitment has been made to it, and the organization might change its mind. He says all of those factors can lead to a lack of commitment by users.

Companies offer several reasons for introducing Notes only in selected departments. They may not be sure it is appropriate for all aspects of their business, or they do not have the funds to put it in all departments. They may also lack a plan for enterprise-wide implementation. Or they may want to learn how to support it and encourage its use before making it widely available. It takes a while to develop the infrastructure to support enterprise-wide Notes use, and to ensure that appropriate applications are in place. Other companies have purchased Notes for very specific purposes. They know it will never be deployed enterprise-wide, yet it is what selected workgroups within the larger organization need.

The best-laid plans for limited implementation can go awry, and even enthusiastic acceptance doesn't obviate the need for careful planning. Several companies reported in interviews that they bought Notes to meet a clear and immediate need in one department but quickly recognized other areas in which it would improve the business process. Several companies have reported that Notes is spreading by word of mouth. Enthusiastic users tell others about it, and soon new groups are requesting it. Some managers have purposely held groups back from using Notes until they have time to evaluate the current Notes group and develop plans for wider implementation. "We never expected this kind of interest," a bank vice-president reported. "We're now working on a plan to introduce Notes in all areas where it would help team efforts."

An organization needs to guard against putting Notes on every computer just because several work groups rave about it. Its success depends on the kind of work a group does and how they do it, not on an enthusiastic report from on outsider. A vice-president at one financial institution that was an early adopter of Notes cautioned against installing Notes too quickly. Groups starting with Notes need enough training and support to be successful, she said, and in a large company that training and support must be offered in stages.

# Watch for Critical Mass

When Notes is planned for more than one department, there must be a schedule for introducing it, department by department, and for keeping users active in it until there is a critical mass. One of the problems workgroups face is that they must maintain their interest in Notes until enough people are on it to make it worth using. Most workgroups are not neatly self-contained, but overlap with other groups. Members who act as liaisons to other groups find it especially annoying to wait for other workgroups to come on line. There is no easy formula for planning the order in which groups are added. Sometimes other factors control the situation. For example, a group that has new, more powerful PCs and is on a network may get Notes before a group with old XT PCs because the company doesn't have to make as big an investment in hardware.

# Make Notes Necessary

The surest strategy for building Notes to critical mass is to make Notes use necessary in the organization, to force essential work onto Notes, and to make knowledge of what is on Notes a requirement. The best way to accomplish these goals isn't by issuing official mandates, but using the natural cultural forces of the organization—by indirection.

One company reported that when Notes was introduced users were encouraged but not required to use it. The first workgroup on Notes was a small team using it to track and organize all their development work. As the department grew, new members had to use Notes to follow the progress of the development project. As a result, the Notes system has become the complete record of the status and history of all the department's projects.

A high-level manager in a financial consulting company has forced the use of Notes by requiring his staff use it to keep track of their peers' work. His objective is to cut the length of meetings and to make them more productive. Everyone felt too much time was devoted to reporting on events, yet everyone needed to be kept informed of them, and some required action on the part of the group. The manager required his people to record in Notes all the activity reports that had taken up so much meeting time. He expected his managers to show up at meetings already prepped on their peers' work. Anyone who failed to file a report in Notes would waste meeting time. And anyone who didn't read others' reports wouldn't be able to keep up with what was happening in the company.

In both these cases, the team leaders drove the implementation in its initial phases, but the pressure to use Notes was a natural business pressure with clear benefits for everyone concerned. Requiring Notes' use through such means helps users appreciate its effectiveness and gives them a valid reason to use it—so they do not get left out.

## Start with High-Profile Workgroups

Price Waterhouse made sure the first workgroups on Notes were important and highly visible teams within the company. A large energy firm found that by first introducing new technology to a team of top managers and their secretaries, it made the point that it was serious about it. At Lotus, president Jim Manzi was an early and regular Notes user. Similar stories are told at many Notes sites as companies have carefully seeded Notes in high-profile workgroups.

Peter Rothstein says the leaders of the seeded groups must be committed to using Notes themselves and to improving the ways the group works. He advises against playing it safe and introducing Notes in a low-profile, low-prestige department first. People will take their cue from where Notes is introduced. To make sure everyone knows the commitment to Notes is strong, introduce it in high-profile groups.

## Make Notes Part of a Suite of Programs

Notes was never meant to run alone. Organizations still need specialized programs such as spreadsheets, word processors, graphics packages and more. Notes will be just one of several programs most users run. Companies would do well to standardize that platform both to make working easier for the users and to limit the number of problems that could occur using Notes, especially with translating to and from obscure file formats.

A couple of large organizations in New York have standardized on a platform of Windows 3.0 programs. They use combinations of Notes, Microsoft Word, Lotus Ami Pro, Word for Windows, Microsoft Project, and Microsoft PowerPoint. As other Windows products appear the staff will evaluate them and recommend some as part of the platform. The most frequently heard argument for standardizing on Windows is the ease of use and the standard graphical interface.

Windows isn't required by any means, and other operating systems have advantages. One company using a relational database and Notes with an API program has preferred to set up all its Notes users in OS/2. Another company has standardized on two DOS-based programs, WordPerfect and Lotus 1-2-3. However, as both of those products have Windows-compatible versions, this organization, too, may eventually migrate to a Windows platform.

# Don't Skimp on Training

The ease of use of Windows and Notes can mask the need for thorough user training. It is true that if you can use a mouse, in an hour you can be using Notes. But that kind of introduction to Notes doesn't deliver the depth of understanding that means you and your department will still be using Notes in a month or a year. The best training procedures present Notes to prospective users in the context of the work they already do. Training that includes basic application design, even though most Notes users may never develop applications, will acquaint users with the possibilities of Notes and yield further ideas about using it in the organization.

The temptation to skimp on training is pandemic in the PC world. It is compounded by such factors as the persistent myth that PCs are easier to use than other computer systems; and the penny-pinching conviction that we're already spending more than we should on these machines. In addition there is the notion that the prospective Notes users, because they tend to be the most visibly productive employees in the organization—salespeople and analysts and managers—"don't have time for detailed training," or are "bright enough that they can figure it out on their own."

No company would expect the same of mainframe terminal operators. Order-entry clerks, CAD draftsmen, and cost accountants are much more likely to receive adequate computer training on the applications they use than the typical PC user. The reason seems to be that in most companies big enough to use mainframes these are sizable groups of people doing work critical to the function of the business. But PC users, even in large businesses, have not been perceived as sizable, homogenous groups, and PCs haven't been seen as doing work critical to the business.

Perhaps the lesson here is that companies can best maintain the necessary focus on training new Notes users by forgetting that Notes runs on already installed PCs, and instead treating it as if it were a major new computer system being installed for the first time—as, indeed, it is.

## Introduce Notes Before Doing Training

Before Notes users begin their formal training sessions they should receive pretraining. Some of the pretraining issues have already been mentioned as environmental issues. Involving users in comment and concern sessions and other types of brainstorming, for instance, is essential to creating a receptive atmosphere for Notes. Pretraining can also take the form of software demonstrations. The goal is to get users to buy into Notes. The sessions should offer enough information so users arrive for their first training class, they are familiar with Notes and they understand some of the tasks it can accomplish.

## Who Should Do the Training?

The logistics of training become more critical the larger the number of Notes users an organization plans to have—and the shorter the time period it allots for deploying Notes. Selecting the trainers becomes a tactical issue. Some companies have taught their own staff to train users. Some have purchased training from Lotus. Others have hired consultants familiar with Notes and the dynamics of introducing new technologies to workgroups.

Interviews reveal no clear-cut trend: Many companies are hiring outside consultants, but almost equal numbers are assigning in-house trainers. Each approach has advantages. Using staff members dedicated as Notes trainers can be expensive, but it insures on-site support after the training is over. As with any kind of training, consultants can offer a range of experience and skills broader than a company can maintain in-house.

## Train with Relevant Materials

The most successful training seems to be contextual, that is, not just button-pushing and mouse-pointing instructions, but training that shows users how to solve their business problems. Peter Rothstein and Kate Merritt both emphasize how important it is to keep the business issues in the forefront. In her own training Merritt follows the principle that when training people in analytical skills, the technology (in this case Notes) is not only a tool the managers will use, but it is also a good teaching methodology. For example, it is easier and much faster to use a spreadsheet program to train users in the concepts of a P&L statement than it is to try to describe it to a class.

It takes much preparation and study of a company's business processes to develop the appropriate training tools within Notes, but there is a big payoff for the effort, says Ms. Merritt. Training secretaries is different from training project managers. They probably will not use the same kinds of applications. Contextual training can build knowledge of the program on the users' knowledge of their work, rather than the generally much narrower base of their computer skills.

Notes administrators and developers need specialized training. Administrator's training will always have to be highly individualized because each Notes system will be different. It also requires a much higher level of technical understanding than end-user training. Most administrators agree they have to be familiar with networking and communications as well as Notes. For these reasons many companies have hired consultants to handle this aspect of training.

While administrators need a high level of hardware knowledge, database developers need a different combination of skills. Their interpersonal skills must be well developed since they will be consulting with users frequently. Several developers reported that previous database programming experience helped them understand Notes more quickly.

# Build Team Use with Training

An important aspect of contextual training is developing training exercises that emphasize the benefits of Notes for workgroups by forcing them to work in Notes. Kate Merritt and Peter Rothstein worked together on a training project which focused on teams. They developed a project ideas database, and students entered actual projects they felt needed doing. Teams formed as each member signed up for a project he wanted to work on. The teams completed the projects working within Notes. After the training class ended, the students were able to continue the work they had begun.

# Train on Application Development

Every Notes user should have some basic application development training, even if they aren't expected to design a Notes database. A review of the design basics will help them understand the complexity, the possibilities, and the limits of Notes. If users know what Notes can do their expectations will be more realistic.

# Ongoing Quality Assurance

When Notes is online and applications are being added to the system, the need for some quality assurance will become apparent. The system doesn't need a Notes czar, however, because rigid control runs counter to the democratic spirit of Notes and could quickly choke development of new applications and use of the system. Too much democracy, on the other hand, can turn into an anarchy of nearly identical applications and a decline in the value of the system to its users. The goal is to make sure Notes is used, and that it remains a vital system for communicating information over time. The best balance of control and freedom is a few well publicized standards for application development and a little gentle diplomacy.

## Develop Design Standards

Applications need a consistency throughout an organization. Some standards develop largely from user input. For example, a utility company designed all their response documents on light blue backgrounds to make them instantly recognizable. Another group wanted all static text to appear in the Helvetica font.

Standards also solve the problems that arise if two or more people or groups both want to launch similar applications that overlap functionally across the organization. There should be a system in place, for example, to determine which application most closely adheres to group standards.

## Give the Databases a Guardian

Using Notes raises many issues of control and consensus. Group technology consultant Susanna Opper points out that people often forget that products like Notes require consensus from a group if they are to work well. Even when a group has agreed on standards, it still needs someone to take responsibility for enforcing them or negotiating deviations from them. One solution is to have each group using Notes appoint a moderator. The moderator does not need to be the Notes administrator, although they should work closely together. The role tends to fall naturally on the group member most interested in developing Notes applications. She must be a part of the business team as well as a liaison to the technology side. Moderators will deal with a variety of issue (see box, The Moderator's Job).

---

### The Moderator's Job

Each Workgroup must take responsibility for its use of Notes, and the easiest way to do this is to designate a group member to be the contact point for the Notes administrator. This moderator role is most often filled by the group member with the most expertise — the person sought out by other group members with questions. The moderator has a role in helping the group manage its Notes tools:

- **Database proliferation** must be controlled. Notes doesn't work unless applications are shared. And applications won't be shared if each person develops his own applications and refuses to use others. Someone has to prevent too many of the same kinds of databases from proliferating. The moderator should be able to negotiate agreement without bruising egos.

- **Design guidelines** should be in place for users who want to add more fields, forms and views. One company using Notes initially granted Designer access to all the users. As a result the users felt free to alter forms, and especially to add new views. "It was overload," a designer reported. "We had more views than anybody could possibly need. It was confusing." The organization now administers User Access controls more carefully.

- **Database size** must be monitored, and the databases condensed them when they become unwieldy. Users should understand the ground rules and not be surprised when documents disappear from large applications.

---

# Include Users in Development

It should hardly need repeating, but users of Notes applications should be involved in the development effort. The people who will use an application should be encouraged to make suggestions about it. Their ideas will almost certainly improve it, and even if they don't, their participation in the design process means they will feel a larger sense of ownership in the finished database, use it more willingly, and therefore help it toward success.

## Show Off Notes' Possibilities

Every Notes installation needs its own P.T. Barnum to relentlessly promote the possibilities of Notes. The promotion should begin in demonstrations and training. As users begin to become accustomed to Notes, they should be introduced to more complex examples. New applications should be talked up in E-mail and made available for users to try.

Users should be encouraged to explore Notes, even if this means the moderator or system administrator occasionally has to fend off an earnest but harebrained idea. It is very easy for people to settle into a rut and use just the applications they started with, or, as they move to new groups to use the same old applications. If something else is more appropriate they must be made aware of it.

# Support For Both PCs and People

A computer system that, once set in motion, needed no ongoing support, no retuning, no user retraining, would defy the laws of entropy. Notes is a complex product that runs on complex hardware, and no two installations present exactly the same problems—integrating several types of networks, combining Notes E-mail with another system, getting information off a mainframe and into Notes, or attaching to an online data feed. Server size, user base, replication schedule, and communications traffic over modems are different at each location and require different installations. Each setup is different. Even if consultants help with the installation, long after they've departed Notes will need support and maintenance, and a company will still need internal support staff prepared to deal with the daily complexity of Notes at the administration, communication and networking levels.

## Use Notes to Support Notes

Provide online Notes support in a Notes database as well as persons who can assist users with their problems. Several companies have implemented support databases, and the Help database that comes with Notes offers excellent aid too, although its purpose is to explain the Notes commands and environment and it offers almost no help with network or other software related problems.

## Don't Make Notes the Scapegoat

Technical people who work in areas related to Notes—networking, communications—should be trained to distinguish between Notes problems and other hardware and software problems. A Lotus engineer who worked with many early Notes users recalls troubleshooting a Notes installation that was blamed for all the network's problems. When he examined the system he found the network's haphazard design didn't meet its manufacturer's specifications. As soon as the network hardware and software were brought up to spec, Notes worked fine. Being able to differentiate Notes problems from other systemic problems will save much downtime and frustration.

## Problems of Shared Applications

Notes applications are fundamentally different from stand-alone PC programs like spreadsheets and word processors, and the support staff must be sensitive to these differences and the interpersonal issues they raise. In 1-2-3, for example, if a user chose to do complicated financial work without using macros to speed up the work, he could get away with it as long as the final work was correct. A Notes application, on the other hand, requires an implicit agreement among its users that they will participate in it and use it as it was intended. Most organizations report that so far this has not been a big problem. But issues have arisen in the area of security and privilege. People may not want to participate in a database in which everyone else has access to what they write. They may worry that their private E-mail is being read by someone else. Or they may complain the available forms and views are not what they want. Support people need to be attuned to such complaints so teams can resolve such problems before they become serious.

# Notes Requires Major Resource Commitments

Perhaps this should be first on the list of issues in deploying Notes because it affects so many others. However, it has been identified in a few organizations as a serious problem, and a failure to make the initial and ongoing commitment of resources can limit Notes' effectiveness.

# The Consultants' Role

A company must make some strategic decisions about when and if it will use consultants or value-added resellers in its deployment of Notes. The use of outside help depends on factors such as the company's own resources, the expertise of in-house personnel, and the extent and complexity of the Notes system being planned.

One LAN manager who helped set up Notes in his company with an Alliance Partner recommends getting assistance with the initial installation and setup. He says Notes is a very sophisticated program, particularly at the administration level, and a company needs expert help to set it up correctly.

With each Notes sale Lotus includes installation assistance in the purchase price. Several Alliance Partners specialize in setting up Notes on networks and doing initial administrative tasks, either as consultants or as value-added resellers of Notes. The Lante Corporation in Chicago is an example. According to its president, Mark Tebbe, Lante helps companies analyze their business practices and communications, and helps them develop better ways to utilize technology. Lante uses this assessment process to design Notes applications for customers. The company's knowledge of how Notes works with networks, replication schedules and security means it can design complex applications and Notes configurations that address specific business problems new Notes customers wouldn't have the expertise to tackle, says Tebbe.

# Assemble a Technical Team

Implementing Notes requires a team of people with different technical skills. No one will know everything about a Notes installation. Pacific Gas and Electric, for example, assigned four technical people to work on Notes. Each had experience and important knowledge in special areas such as working with new software, networks, and Notes application design. This team blazed the trail for Notes in the organization, preparing the network, testing the software, and developing databases before the end users become involved.

# Identify a Senior Technical Resource

Just as an organization needs a top manager to support and push Notes implementation, it also needs a senior technical resource, a person who is familiar with software, hardware and network issues that affect Notes. Such a person needs to coordinate the technical and business sides of Notes deployment. She also needs to work with other technical staff, outside consultants, and developers. Just as a high level officer gives Notes importance, a high level technical person gives its installation and operation importance.

## Involve Support People from the Start

Even when using a consultant to help with the installation of Notes the in-house technical team should be involved. Sometimes minor adjustments need to be made after installers have left, and if the technical staff has been involved they are better able to handle problems over the phone.

# Summary

Deploying Notes successfully requires planning and preparation. In the earliest stages planners must identify the nature of the work and the business process which they want to change—an important exercise that requires visionary thinking and a clear understanding of how Notes can be a useful tool in the work.

When these goals and processes are defined, managers and leaders must publicly support Notes and make sure others understand it well enough to feel a sense of ownership in its implementation and use. They must also deal with other issues such as natural resistance to change. Doing all this before Notes is on line is very important to its success.

Resistance to the changes Notes will bring about can be lessened by careful introduction—a process that should begin even before Notes is online with introduction-and-discussion sessions for prospective users.

The strategy for placing Notes in the work groups needs to be clear. How wide is the implementation? Which groups will use it first? What will the total platform be, of which Notes is a part? How can management make it impossible to do one's work without using Notes?

Training needs to be done in the context of the actual work experience of the users. It should be customized for each group of users according to their own work. Everyone should be introduced to basic application design even if they never plan to design a database. Familiarity with the components of application development helps users see Notes' possibilities.

When Notes is online and applications are being added to the system responsibility for some quality assurance must be assigned. Some well-publicized standards and a little gentle diplomacy will go far in dealing with problems that may arise with the databases. And prevention remains the best cure: The user of applications should have input into the design process make sure they feel a sense of ownership in the result.

Notes needs a level of support appropriate to its technological complexity. The support staff—not just for Notes but for the network and communications as well—should be trained to distinguish between Notes problems and other hardware and software problems. And Notes support personnel must be able to resolve the kinds of problems that arise when users share applications.

Finally a company needs to commit resources—hardware, software and people—to setting up and maintaining Notes. They may decide to use outside help, but it is still a good idea to have qualified employees who are involved in Notes and available to help.

# Epilogue
# The Value of Notes

There is considerable experience with Notes. Some of the companies with the most experience, those that began at the beta-test stage, were profiled in Chapter 1. More organizations made the commitment when Version 1.0 was released in December of 1989. Still more worked with Version 2.0 as it came to market in the winter and spring of 1991. These companies have found success with Notes in very different—and sometimes unexpected—directions. But the common thread that runs through the experience of these organizations is the change Notes has made in their communications.

For these companies Notes hasn't replaced anything. They still use the telephone, fax, express, even electronic mail. But Notes has added something. It's a new form of communication that connects staff members across time and distance. It isn't just a way to request a phone call, or assign a task, or leave a reminder. It is a way of conducting a dialog among people who no longer have to be in the same place at the same time to communicate this effectively.

What is the value of Notes? Most often, companies answer this question by talking about Notes' impact on shared work. Three companies provide examples. All three use Notes in the business of software development: Nantucket Corp., of Los Angeles, Simpact Associates, of San Diego and Reston, Virginia, and CCH Computax, in Torrance, California. These companies believe Notes has improved their workflow and helped them do a better job. Although each has a wish list of features for future versions of Notes, they all see more uses for it in their organizations.

## Simpact Associates, Inc.

Simpact was introduced in Chapter 9 as an Alliance Partner which developed Remark!, the voice annotation product for Notes. But Simpact was a Notes customer before it became an Alliance Partner. The company bought Notes as a way to improve internal communications.

Simpact develops products in three areas: communications connectivity, network security, and voice processing. Its employees are mainly knowledge workers who often work independently yet must constantly coordinate their projects. Simpact describes itself as a relatively open company where decision-making is widely shared. But this decision-making must involve employees in offices in both San Diego and Reston. And it must rest on shared information. As a communications technology company, Simpact provided a solid foundation for Notes: Both locations were equipped with local area networks that communicated across a T1 link that carried both voice and data.

Simpact put Notes to work in product documentation, in strategic planning, informal group discussions, and project management. As might be expected, the staff uses its voice annotation technology frequently. The documentation effort benefited greatly from Notes' ability to keep track of specifications and drafts and graphics and revision notes. (Although Simpact has noticed one problem with Notes: People sometimes hesitate to put documents they regard as work-in-progress into Notes. They feel it is too public a repository for anything that isn't polished.) Other applications followed: A Version Releases database tracks all the versions of software Simpact develops. A Market Plan application keeps a historical record of Simpact's marketing strategy as well as its future plans. It works as a reference for employees and has been especially helpful to people who miss meetings but need to know what happened.

Simpact's staff uses Notes for informal group discussion and for planning. They travel frequently, and even when they're in their offices those offices are widely separated. Simpact found that within its relatively flat organizational structure, strategic planning discussions, for example, produced added value as Notes encouraged not just minutes-of-the-last-meeting, but responses, suggestions, and permutations of ideas.

## CCH Computax

CCH Computax develops microcomputer-based tax software for accounts and sells tax processing services on its mainframe computers at more than 30 sites around the country.

In Torrance, California, Harold Vatcher, Vice President for Product Technology, heads up the software development part of the company. Vatcher and Fred Hauer, the inhouse Notes developer, brought Notes into the Product Development Division to develop a problem-tracking database. It didn't work well. The project needed a relational database with stronger query and reporting capabilities than those in Notes. But Notes filled a need they hadn't foreseen in their Production Support Facility.

Computax's software is in a constant state of flux until the government publishes its final revisions to the tax code early each calendar year. Computax needed to log technical and operational problems, to share the data, and to allow developers to discuss problems and resolve them. Customers with problems wanted quick responses. Vatcher observes that "We'll get back to you in a few days" isn't good enough. Customers with tax problems want their answers yesterday.

Before Notes, customer complaints came in to the Customer Support staff, were directed to the developers, answers were sent back to support and finally communicated to the customer. Notes streamlined the process. Developers at different sites could work together to track down problems. The Support database itself became an analysis tool. It provided an overview of problems that surfaced common elements. The discussions on how to resolve difficulties went on at a much higher level. Recording solutions in the database reduced the duplication of effort—the DocLink symbol became a frequent feature of the developers' work.

"I don't know how we would have put the product out and kept it up and running without Notes," says Vatcher. "The sharing of information is phenomenal. Users who never used to share information now do it through Notes."

## Nantucket Corp.

The development division of Nantucket Corp. software of Santa Monica, California, was looking for a good E-mail system when they found Notes. Nantucket, whose main product is a dBASE compiler called Clipper, is a classic technology-driven company. To compete it must keep its products at the leading edge of technology. It understands that to do that it must use the best technology in its own operations. Nantucket liked what it saw in Notes' many-to-many communications, and its ability to control users' access to information.

Perhaps because it is in the business of supporting developers, Nantucket has done a particularly thorough job of implementing Notes in the organization. The biggest users of Notes are the technical marketing and software development and testing departments. Each Nantucket product is assigned its own database where the developers and marketing staff exchange information. In addition there are databases for bug reports and activity reports and trade show schedules and even a database of Notes help called Say What? that is maintained by Nantucket's Notes administrators and support staff.

Each time a database is created, Nantucket gives it a birth certificate which tells who has access to the database and logs activity. When a database is discontinued it gets a death certificate which explains why it is no longer in use.

The development staff is widely dispersed. Some people work primarily from home, some overseas (Nantucket has offices in the UK, Germany, Brazil, Russia, Japan, and Canada), and some in offices in other U.S. locations. Security is very important because developers need to keep their work confidential. Sometimes they want to restrict entire Notes applications to a select group of users. In other cases they want to share some of the information with everyone who had access to the database and restrict the remaining data to a select few. They make full use of Notes' controls over user access, privileges, and encryption.

Nantucket maintains a corporate policy database in Notes that shares information about the company. Employees enter questions and ideas and company officials respond. The database is a good idea in a company with as many high-level knowledge workers as Nantucket, though hardly earth-shaking. But Notes' ability to transcend time and distance gives it added importance within the organization. The discussion is open even for remote employees while ideas are still being formulated. For the first time, say employees from the UK office, they can have an impact on corporate policy, rather than merely keeping up with the changes after the fact.

In all three of these companies—Simpact, Computax, Nantucket—Notes is living up to its promise. All three report that Notes improved internal communications and the sharing of information. All three have found uses for Notes they didn't envision when they made the decision to use it. And for all three Notes has become an essential piece of the machinery that runs their business:

- **Easy communication**. These organizations have widely scattered offices. They have found that Notes' electronic mail and the replication of data across local and wide area networks make possible a form of discussion that isn't bound by location or time zone. Simpact's example, in particular, shows this "time-shifted" communication being used as an enabling technology for the company's flattened organizational structure.

- **Structured communication**. Raw communication is not the value of Notes. Its application development functions build communication tools that add structure and intelligence to the sharing of information. All three companies mentioned the importance of having information stored in an accessible centralized repository. Simpact has found that combining all the parts into a finished product is easy when all the pieces are in the same Notes database. Computax has learned the value of this structure with its Support database: The focusing of the discussion and the overview of the data Notes provides have improved the company's problem-solving performance.

- **Secure communication**. For all three companies, intelligent sharing of information means extensive use of Notes' security features. They use encryption keys, user access lists and privileges to make the security tight yet flexible. They do this for all the usual reasons associated with exclusivity—to insure the confidentiality of information, to limit access. But in Notes, security has a more positive, inclusive side. It is the platform on which workgroups are built. Nantucket's developers have used Notes to create communications structures that reflect the way they work, sometimes sharing information widely, sometimes holding an idea close.

Notes encourages collaboration, so the best ideas can be suggested and the best minds can work together on a problem in a way no other software provides. The result of such collaboration is a wider spectrum of discussion, a better understanding of projects, policies, and issues, and faster response to problems. That is the revolutionary change Notes brings: It changes communications in the organizations which use it.

# Index

# About the Authors

Sally Blanning DeJean began her professional life as an Assistant Professor of English at Jefferson College in Louisville, Kentucky, where she took her first class in computers. Her career changed course in California when she purchased an Apple IIe personal computer for her children and soon realized how many things she could do with it herself. She started a small business teaching other PC owners applications like Wordstar and dBASE II. She has worked as a trainer and sales representative for computer stores, and in PC support and network management in a corporate MIS environment. Mrs. DeJean writes for computer publications and consults to businesses.

David DeJean was a newspaper reporter and editor with the Louisville, Kentucky, *Courier-Journal* and *The Louisville Times*. He was editorial director for the *The Los Angeles Times'* Gateway videotex service, an experiment in developing and delivering an electronic newspaper. He has worked and consulted in other leading-edge technologies for business, as well, including services delivered via cable TV, satellite videoconferencing, and home banking. He has combined his interests in journalism and computers by working for an industry news weekly, *PC Week*, writing for *PC Magazine*, and, since it was launched in 1988, serving as a Senior Editor of *PC/Computing*.